THE EVERYTHING

Spells & Charms Book,
2nd Edition

Dear Reader,

Do you believe in magic? Whether or not you realize it, you've undoubtedly done magic spells in the past. Blowing out candles on a birthday cake, for instance, is a good luck spell. Hanging an evergreen wreath on your front door is a form of protection magic. Prayers, chants, oaths, and many everyday practices are types of magic. Simply put, magic is the art of using thoughts, words, and deeds to cause certain changes to occur—and to produce outcomes through means that conventional science can't explain.

Initially, you might be a bit skeptical about delving into magic. Hollywood tends to focus on the sensational aspects of magic, which can make the whole idea of magic seem scary or even ridiculous. In reality, most magicians don't put hexes on people; they don't turn frogs into princes or fly through the air on broomsticks. Instead, they use magic to help them get better jobs, attract the right romantic partner, safeguard their homes and families, and improve their health.

Maybe you're curious. Maybe you've dabbled with magic a bit and want to learn more. Maybe you're ready to take charge of your own destiny. If so, this book is for you.

With best wishes,

Skye Alexander

Welcome to the EVERYTHING® Series!

These handy, accessible books give you all you need to tackle a difficult project, gain a new hobby, comprehend a fascinating topic, prepare for an exam, or even brush up on something you learned back in school but have since forgotten.

You can read an *Everything*® book from cover to cover or just pick out the information you want from our four useful boxes: e-questions, e-facts, e-alerts, e-ssentials. We give you everything you need to know on the subject, but throw in a lot of fun stuff along the way, too.

We now have more than 400 *Everything*® books in print, spanning such wide-ranging categories as weddings, pregnancy, cooking, music instruction, foreign language, crafts, pets, New Age, and so much more. When you're done reading them all, you can finally say you know *Everything*®!

Words of wisdom from experts in the field

Important snippets of information

Urgent warnings

Quick handy tips

Editorial

Director of Innovation: Paula Munier

Editorial Director: Laura M. Daly

Executive Editor, Series Books: Brielle K. Matson

Associate Copy Chief: Sheila Zwiebel

Acquisitions Editor: Lisa Laing

Development Editor: Brett Palana-Shanahan

Production Editor: Casey Ebert

Production

Director of Manufacturing: Susan Beale

Production Project Manager: Michelle Roy Kelly

Prepress: Erick DaCosta, Matt LeBlanc

Design Manager: Heather Blank

Senior Book Designer: Colleen Cunningham

Interior Layout: Heather Barrett, Brewster Brownville

Interior Illustrations: Brewster Brownville

Visit the entire Everything® *series at* www.everything.com

THE
EVERYTHING®
SPELLS & CHARMS BOOK

2ND EDITION

Cast incantations that will bring you
love, success, and good health

Skye Alexander

Avon, Massachusetts

To my familiar, Domino

An Everything® Series Book.
Everything® and everything.com® are registered trademarks of F+W Publications, Inc.

Published by Adams Media, an F+W Publications Company
57 Littlefield Street, Avon, MA 02322 U.S.A.
www.adamsmedia.com

ISBN 10: 1-59869-386-7
ISBN 13: 978-1-59869-386-7

Printed in the United States of America.

J   I   H   G   F   E   D   C   B   A

Library of Congress Cataloging-in-Publication Data

Alexander, Skye.
The everything spells & charms book / Skye Alexander. – 2nd ed.
p. cm. – (An everything series book)
Includes index.
ISBN-13: 978-1-59869-386-7 (pbk.)
ISBN-10: 1-59869-386-7 (pbk.)
1. Magic. 2. Charms. I. Title. II. Title: Everything spells and charms book.

BF1611.M27 2008
133.4'4–dc22
2007015892

This book is available at quantity discounts for bulk purchases.
For information, please call 1-800-289-0963.

Contents

Top Ten Ways Magic Spells Can Help You

1. Increase your personal power

2. Attract wealth and abundance

3. Enhance your love life

4. Give your career a boost

5. Protect yourself and your loved ones

6. Safeguard your home and property

7. Improve relationships with friends and family

8. See into the future

9. Improve your health

10. Take charge of your life

Introduction

▶ WHEN YOU HEAR the word *magician*, do you imagine a bearded old man wearing a pointed hat and waving a jeweled wand, or a gypsy woman in a turban hunched over a crystal ball? In reality, most magicians look pretty much like you. They work at regular jobs, live in typical homes, raise families, and lead normal lives. The mechanic who repairs your car or the waitress at the corner café might be a magician. What's different about them is they seem to be a little luckier than other people. That's because magicians know a secret: Luck doesn't just happen, you create it for yourself.

Magician comes from the Latin word *magi* (the plural of *magus*), meaning wise men or women. The best-known magi are the Three Wise Men referred to in the Bible, who came from the East to offer gifts to the baby Jesus. Magi can be healers, shamans, priests or priestesses, astrologers, dowsers, seers—anyone who has learned to access the cosmic web of energy and information that animates the universe and to direct it for his or her purposes. If you choose to seek out this knowledge for yourself, you, too, will enter that rank by the time you finish this book.

But the real secret is that you're already a magician. Everyone is. Magical power is your birthright, a natural ability you were born with. You may not realize it, but you perform magical acts on a regular basis. You can't *help* doing magic, because you—along with all other human beings—are a creative being who constantly participates in the evolution of earthly events. As quantum physics has demonstrated, when you focus your attention on something, your energy influences the behavior of the molecules that you are watching. You quite literally change whatever you observe. That's magic.

The goal—and the challenge—is to use magic with conscious awareness and intent. Spells are one way to do this. When you cast a spell, you shape your desire into a ritualized formula and galvanize the full force of your intentions, your emotion, and your will to bring about a predetermined outcome. You shift energy. You feel the power in your blood, your bones, your cells. Maybe, in the deepest recesses of your mind, you reawaken memories of an ancient time when you lived in constant contact with the Earth, the cosmos, and your own instinctual nature. To cast a spell is to enter into an intimate relationship with ancient archetypes and your own personal mythology. Spell-casting creates an immediate and direct connection between your conscious and unconscious minds, and it awakens the innate wisdom that has lain dormant in the recesses of your being.

There are many ways to tap your magical power and many ways to focus the creative energy of the universe. This book introduces a number of philosophies, paths, and practices. Some will appeal to you, and some won't. Take what you like and leave the rest.

Regardless of which course you choose to follow, when you do magic, you enter into an agreement with the universe that if you do your part, the rest will unfold. In casting a spell, in performing a ritual, you take what Carlos Castaneda called a leap into the void, trusting that you will land on both feet.

Chapter 1

A Magical Universe

You live in a magical universe. Children often understand this quite clearly, even if adults don't. To a child, the world is alive with possibilities. Most people miss this wondrous fact because they've been trained to look only at the physical realm and to focus on the mundane aspects of daily life. Magic, however, teaches that physical existence is only the tip of the iceberg. As you develop your magical abilities, you'll also rediscover the truly awesome power that abides in the universe—and in you.

The Cosmic Web

From the perspective of science, everything is energy. From the perspective of magic, the world is surrounded by an energetic matrix that connects everything to everything else. This matrix, or cosmic web, not only envelops Earth like an aura, it permeates all things that exist here and extends throughout the solar system and beyond. The web pulses with subtle vibrations that magicians and other sensitive individuals can feel. Regardless of whether you are consciously aware of these vibrations, you are affected by them—and your own energetic vibrations continually affect the matrix.

Like the World Wide Web, the cosmic web teems with information. Every idea, word, action, and emotion, all going back to the beginning of time, are stored in this energetic matrix. Anyone who knows the password can access this vast storehouse. That's why Edgar Cayce, the "Sleeping Prophet," who had little formal education or medical training, could go into a trance and discover cures for the thousands of sick people who sought his aid. He psychically "downloaded" wisdom that great minds before him had placed in the cosmic web.

ALERT!

Magic isn't dangerous, if done correctly. It isn't difficult; anyone can do it. Magic isn't evil—it's a natural part of life. Remember, magic isn't a parlor game. Practice it with sincerity and clarity.

How many times have you gotten a phone call from someone you were just thinking about? It's not an accident. Your thoughts and the other person's connected in the cosmic web before you spoke to one another in the physical realm. When you do magic, you purposefully tap into this infinite web. You intentionally send and receive thoughts and feelings via the web's vibrational network—it's almost like corresponding with a friend via e-mail. As you become skilled at using magic, you'll learn to navigate the cosmic web just as easily as you surf the Internet. The first step is to sensitize yourself to these vibrations and become aware of the energetic field around you.

The Natural World

Generations ago, our forebears lived in close contact with the natural world. Their very existence depended on their ability to be in tune with weather patterns, planting and harvesting cycles, celestial movements, the changing tides, the animal, plant, and insect kingdoms, and much more. Most people today, on the other hand, are alienated from the natural world much of the time. It seems normal to live in temperature-controlled homes, work in offices sealed off from nature, and drive on freeways with the windows rolled up.

In order to do magic, however, you need to reawaken your awareness of the natural world so you can begin tapping the Earth's vital energy. You need to experience your connectedness to everything around you. You need to enliven your senses. Once you've honed your five physical senses, you can begin developing your sixth sense.

Take a half hour away from your usual schedule to sharpen your senses. Go to a favorite place in nature. Breathe deeply and notice the scents you inhale. Take regular sense-stimulating breaks to bring yourself into harmony with the natural world.

The natural world is just as natural as it ever was, except that there's less of it than there was a century ago, and most people don't devote as much time as they should to enjoying it. As your magical consciousness increases, so will your appreciation of the world you live in. Many of the spells in this book use natural ingredients such as herbs, flowers, and stones. In Chapter 10, you'll learn to harness nature's energy to enhance the power of your spells and rituals.

Power Places

The place where you choose to do your magic is as individual as the kind of magic you do. Some people prefer a special spot that they set aside for the purpose of performing magic spells and rituals. Other people choose different locales, depending on the magic they're doing, the time of the year, or for other personal reasons. You may wish to designate an interior and an exterior place for your magical work. Once you select a space, consider it sacred.

Find a spot that feels comfortable for you. This could be a place that holds special meaning for you or one that seems to resonate with the right vibes. Privacy is a key factor, too, especially if you live with other people or pets. Cats are notoriously curious about anything new going on where they live. They've often served as witches' familiars, and if you have a cat, it may want to participate in your practice. It's also a good idea to choose a spot that won't be visible to your neighbors or the general public.

Interior Places

Your goal is to create an atmosphere that helps you feel centered, calm, and powerful. Remove anything that might disturb your peace or distract you from your purpose. The walls, furnishings, and floor should also be colors you find appealing. Some people enjoy soothing blues and greens, while others respond to the intensity of purple, fuchsia, or even black.

Some people prefer power spots that have an almost Zen-like spareness; others like surrounding themselves with objects that remind them of magic and enchantment. It's up to you. Make sure your space includes something comfy to sit on and a surface of some kind where you can put candles, incense, and other tools of the trade. This surface might be as simple as a wooden box or a board supported by bricks, or as ornate as a formal altar. Again, this is a matter of personal preference.

If the surface is used for other purposes, smudge it before you use it. The smudging process entails burning sage and allowing the smoke to waft over the surface. Many people opt to smudge the space in which they do magic before performing each spell or ritual, in order to clear any unwanted vibrations that might interfere with their work.

Even if you don't have a perfect spot, you can transform any ordinary place into a sacred space with your intent, passion, and belief. The more you work magic in a certain spot, the more it will take on the essence of your intention and the magical power you raise. If you have a favorite object—

such as a statue, stone, crystal, or painting—keep it in the area where you cast your spells. A *power object* such as these helps maintain the magical atmosphere even when you're not there. A small object can be moved around or taken along when you travel. Power objects help to focus your mind while you work and remind you of your objectives.

Outdoor Power Spots

Many magicians prefer to work outdoors. Druids, for instance, have long performed their magic in oak groves. To find a power spot in nature requires some time and intuition. Even if you decide to cast spells in your own backyard, you'll want to find a spot that feels right.

You can do this by slowly walking the area you've chosen, remaining alert for any unusual or intense body sensations: a sense of peace, an elevated awareness, a slight chill on the back of your neck, a cozy warmth in the pit of your stomach. You'll know which spot is ideal for you.

If you wish, you can dowse to find the right spot. You've probably heard of dowsing as a way to locate water. Some dowsers use forked sticks or metal rods that are sensitive to whatever they're looking for. The dowsing tool dips down when it comes to the best location. A forked branch of a willow, if you can find one, is an ideal dowsing device, but you can make a simple dowsing rod from wire hangers. For any dowsing tool to work, though, it must be infused with your intent and purpose. Request aloud that the dowsing rod locate the right spot for your spell-casting.

The Seven Directions

Whether your power spot is indoors or outside, it's important to determine the four cardinal points of your area. A fundamental reason for being aware of north, south, east, and west is that these compass points anchor you in the natural world and orient your position relative to the sun, moon, stars, planets, and Earth.

In magic, the four compass directions are more than mere geographical designations. They possess special meanings and associations. The four directions are depicted in Hindu mandalas, Native American medicine wheels, Celtic stone circles, and many other outer expressions of mystical and magical belief. Some magicians choose to cast a circle around the sacred space where they perform spells and rituals. You'll learn more about this in Chapter 10, but in a nutshell a circle is cast to protect the people involved in the spell, safeguard the magic they're doing, and prevent outside energies or entities from interfering with the work. When casting a circle, a magician begins at the easternmost point and symbolically draws a protective circle around a designated area, moving in a clockwise direction from east to south to west to north and finally coming back to the east.

Some schools of thought teach that guardians or archangels stand as sentries at the thresholds of these four directions. The archangel Raphael is often associated with the east; Michael is said to preside over the south; Gabriel guards the west; and Uriel resides in the north. You can petition these guardians and ask them to lend their assistance to your magical rituals and rites. Each of these guardians and directions also corresponds to one of the four elements: air, fire, water, and earth respectively. Connecting with them and drawing upon their powers can greatly enhance the effectiveness of your magical work.

In addition to the four compass points, there are three other directions you'll need to consider. The first of these, *Above,* refers to the heavenly realm and all entities and forces residing on that plane: God, Goddess, angels, spirit guides, ancestors, and so on. The second, *Below,* corresponds to the heart of Mother Earth, the foundation of physical existence. *Within* means your own inner dimension, the Self. It's important to align yourself with all seven of these directions and to balance their energies when you're doing magic. They are all sources of power, and they all influence outcomes.

The Four Elements

When magicians refer to the *elements*, they don't mean the table of elements you learned about in high school chemistry. Rather, these four—earth, air, fire, and water—are fundamental energies that operate in the physical world. You could think of them as the building blocks of life. Their physical aspects are readily apparent—rocks and soil, wind, the sun, lakes and streams. In magic, however, the vibrational qualities of these four elements are equally important.

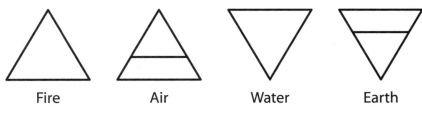

Fire   Air   Water   Earth

Alchemical Symbols for the Four Elements

The elements play a key role not only in magic but in many metaphysical practices as well. In astrology, each of the twelve zodiac signs falls into one of these four elements. (Aries, Leo, and Sagittarius are fire signs; Taurus, Virgo, and Capricorn comprise the earth signs; Gemini, Libra, and Aquarius make up the air signs; and Cancer, Scorpio, and Pisces are water signs.) The four suits of the tarot correspond to the four elements: wands relate to fire, pentacles to earth, swords to air, and cups to water. Each of the four compass directions discussed earlier is also associated with one of the four elements: north is linked with earth, east with air, south with fire, and west with water. Colors, shapes, sounds, smells, textures, food—just about everything—can be grouped into one or another of the elemental categories.

Part of your development as a magician involves understanding and learning to draw upon these elements in order to produce the results you desire. In some instances, you may wish to emphasize one of the elements; in other situations, you might find it advantageous to combine the elements to create balance. Each element has its own properties, and it's up to you to decide how to use them. In later chapters, you'll learn more about the elements and their applications in magic spells.

The following table serves as a simple guide to the elements and their correspondences.

The Elements

Element	Qualities	Direction	Color	Magic Tool
Fire	Action, vitality, passion	South	Red	Wand
Earth	Stability, sensation	North	Green	Pentacle
Air	Communication, thought	East	Yellow	Athame
Water	Emotion, intuition, creativity	West	Blue	Chalice

Fire

Fire's fundamental vibration is masculine or yang. Its energy is active, assertive, stimulating, hot, dry, outer-oriented, energizing, individualized, and self-directed. Metaphysicians also connect the fire element with Spirit and will, for its creative force animates matter. In alchemy, an upward-pointing triangle serves as a symbol for the fire element.

To understand the nature of the fire element, consider the sun. The centerpiece of the solar system, the sun's warmth, light, and vitality are essential to life on Earth. The color red, sports, physical combat, vigorous activity, spicy foods, rock music, cactus, and Corvettes all partake of the fire element. Can you ascertain the common denominator that underlies all these seemingly disparate things?

ALERT!

Fire magic brings the energy of the fire element into your spell. Candle magic is perhaps the most popular form of fire magic. The process of charging a crystal in the sun is an example of another simple fire spell.

Magicians draw upon the fire element when they wish to initiate new projects, break up stagnant situations, or add zest to any endeavor. If you lack initiative, fire magic can help you get started. If you're doing a spell to launch a business venture or stimulate passion in a lackluster relationship, you'll want to include a hefty dose of the fire element.

Earth

Earth's vibration is feminine or yin. Fire may serve as the activating force, but earth provides the substance that gives form to your desires. Stable, receptive, fruitful, passive, nurturing, quiet, slow-moving, inner-directed, and enduring, earth energy is depicted best by Mother Earth herself. In alchemy, a downward-pointing triangle with a horizontal line through it symbolizes the earth element.

The color green, agriculture, oak trees, rocks, massage therapy, bread, cashmere, leather furniture, and government bonds all correspond to the earth element—can you see why? Magicians tap earth's energy when they want to encourage growth and/or abundance, to make a dream a reality, or to produce a long-lasting result. If your goal is to attract wealth or protect your home, you'll want to incorporate the earth element into your spell.

Earth magic often involves drawing upon the fertility of Mother Earth. Some prosperity spells, for instance, recommend planting seeds to represent your objectives. As you water and care for the seeds, you symbolically nurture your dreams. As the plant grows and flourishes, your intentions will bear fruit.

Air

Air's energy is masculine or yang. Its alchemical symbol is an upward-pointing triangle with a horizontal line through it. Usually this element is associated with ideas, the mental realm, communication and language, instability, flexibility, rapid movement, and social interaction. If you want to get a good sense of the air element, think of the wind. The wind is never still and can quickly change from a balmy breeze to a gusty gale. The wind also carries pollen to fertilize crops, just as ideas move between people to enrich cultures.

Air magic involves communication. Words of power, such as the fabled word "ABRACADABRA," invoke air magic. Magicians frequently use chants, affirmations, and incantations in spells and rituals. Whether you speak these words aloud or write them down, specially chosen words and phrases can help activate your intentions.

Here are some familiar things that fall under the domain of air: the color yellow, computers, books, birds, flute music, telephones, fans, voile, and incense. Can you see the underlying similarities between these objects that link them to the air element? If you wish to stimulate new ideas, to enhance communication or cooperation between people, or to help someone ace a test, consider drawing on the energies of air to empower your spell.

Water

Water's vibration is feminine or yin. Alchemists use a downward-pointing triangle to symbolize this element. Receptive, passive, cool, quiet, inner-directed, adaptable, fluid, intuitive, undifferentiated, and creative, the water element is usually linked with the emotions. To understand the characteristics of this element, observe its many natural forms. The ocean's tides, the rain that nourishes crops, and the stream that erodes soil and even rocks over time all depict various aspects of water.

Water's essence is present in the color blue, sailboats, alcoholic beverages, poetry, painting, dreams, and perfume—can you see why? Spells designed to encourage romantic feelings between two people, to inspire imagination, or to defuse antagonistic situations can benefit from a splash of the water element.

Water spells often involve liquid of some type, such as water, wine, or fruit juice. Pour the liquid you've chosen into a special goblet or chalice. Focus on your objective, mentally projecting your intentions into the liquid. Then drink the beverage to make your wish come true. If your spell involves a relationship with another person, invite him to share the magical drink with you.

Elementals

Many beings that ordinarily remain unseen by most people live side-by-side with humans in the physical world. Folklore and fairy tales frequently refer to these entities. Seafaring legends, for instance, often mention mermaids, and leprechauns appear with regularity in Irish lore.

Most people discount these creatures as pure fantasy, but magicians recognize them as elementals. You could think of these nonphysical beings as ambassadors for the four elements. Each is a citizen of his or her particular realm, and each possesses unique qualities that are characteristic of the element that the creature harkens from. If you befriend them, elementals will serve as devoted helpers and eagerly assist you in performing magic spells.

Salamanders are fire spirits. They are naturally drawn to people who exhibit courage, creativity, and initiative. When you do spells that involve action, inspiration, vitality, or passion, salamanders can serve as liaisons, marshalling the forces of the fire realm to assist you.

Gnomes are earth spirits. Sometimes called trolls or leprechauns, these elementals are practical, no-nonsense creatures that may appear a bit gruff. However, they possess a wonderful appreciation for material things and can be valuable aides when you're doing prosperity spells.

Sylphs are air spirits. They naturally gravitate to intelligent, literary, and analytical people. In matters concerning communication, these elementals can be great allies—call on them when you're doing spells that involve contracts or legal issues.

Ondines are water spirits. Mermaids and sirens fall into this category. These beautiful, but sometimes capricious, beings are drawn to emotional situations and relate best to sensitive, intuitive, and artistic people. Invite these elementals to assist you when you're doing love spells.

Always remember to thank the elementals that assist you in your spell-working. If you behave disrespectfully toward them, they may retaliate by playing nasty tricks on you. These beings enjoy small gifts that express your appreciation. Be generous, and your elemental friends will continue to serve you faithfully:

- Salamanders like candles and incense. Burn these to honor your elemental helpers.
- Gnomes adore jewelry and crystals. Bury a token in the ground as a way of saying "Thanks."
- Sylphs enjoy flowers. Place fresh blossoms on your altar or lay them in a sacred spot outdoors as an offering.
- Ondines are fond of perfume. Pour some in a stream, lake, or other body of water.

Solar and Lunar Cycles

From the beginning of time, the sun and moon, and their ever-changing relationships to our planet, have fascinated human beings. Early civilizations honored these heavenly bodies as deities. Our distant ancestors noticed that the sun's apparent movement brought about the seasons and that the moon's phases altered the tides and affected fertility in humans and animals. Even in today's sophisticated, modern society, it's easy to see how solar and lunar forces operate in everyday life.

The sun, moon, and planets play important roles in magic, too. Choosing the right time to do magic, when solar and lunar vibrations are most auspicious, can greatly enhance the power and effectiveness of a spell. In Chapters 11 through 18, you'll learn the best times to perform different types of spells.

Moon Phases

It's easy to see the moon's shifting faces as it traverses the night sky. Every month, the moon goes through eight distinct phases. Four of these are particularly important in spell-working. Because the moon changes so rapidly, you don't have to wait long for the type of lunar energy you seek to become available.

For two weeks, from new moon to full moon, the moon is waxing, or increasing in size. This is a good time to cast spells that involve increase or expansion. For the two weeks from the full moon to the next new moon, the moon wanes, or diminishes in size. This is a good time for spells dealing with decrease or letting go.

If, for instance, you wish to earn more money or get a promotion at work, do a spell during the waxing moon. As the moon's light grows, so will your fortune. Conversely, if you seek to reduce your responsibilities at work or at home, cast a spell during the waning moon. Maybe you want to decrease your debt, end a relationship that no longer satisfies you, or lose weight. Spells designed to address these objectives are best done during the waning phase. As the moon shrinks, so will the conditions you've targeted with your magic.

The new moon is the best time to plant symbolic seeds that represent whatever you're trying to create in your life. At this time of the month, cast spells to launch a new business, begin a relationship, or start a family. As the moon moves toward its full phase, you can watch your endeavor develop. The new moon is a good time to do divination, too. Some months contain two new moons. The second one is called the black moon. It is considered more powerful than a regular new moon, so any seeding spells you do under a black moon may manifest more quickly.

The full moon represents the time of harvest. Under its bright light, you observe the fruits of the seeds that you planted during the new moon. Concentrate now on the culmination of these spells. In some cases, you may see the results of your new moon spells by the subsequent full moon, but it can take several full moons for some spells to manifest. Spells for healing and empowerment are best performed during a full moon (unless the desired result involves loss or decrease, such as shrinking a tumor or lowering blood pressure). Some months contain a second full moon, known as the blue moon. This is a particularly powerful time for manifesting what you initiated at the new moon.

Once you begin casting spells according to the moon's movement, you may notice subtle differences in yourself—your emotions, your body rhythms, fluctuations in your menstrual periods, your libido levels, your hormones, your dreams, the intensity of your intuition. The moon, after all, is our closest celestial neighbor. It is intimately connected to the ancient worship of the Goddess, to the feminine principle, and the collective unconscious. Developing an awareness of lunar rhythms will help strengthen your link to the Divine.

Keeping a Lunar Journal

You may find it useful to keep track of the moon's phases for a few months. In a notebook or computer file, write a paragraph or two about how you feel during each lunar phase—describe your emotions, experiences, thoughts, and anything unusual or especially meaningful that happens. You might also wish to record your dreams and examine them in connection with the moon's position. This practice will enable you to track your own energetic shifts, so you can work successfully with lunar power.

The Wheel of the Year

For centuries, Earth-honoring cultures have followed the sun's passage through the sky. Our ancestors divided the Wheel of the Year, as the sun's annual cycle is known, into eight periods of approximately six weeks, with each spoke corresponding to a particular degree in the zodiac wheel.

In Wicca and other Pagan belief systems, these eight holidays (or holy days) are called *sabbats*. It's no coincidence that many modern-day holidays fall close to these ancient solar dates and are still celebrated in similar ways. Each of these special days affords unique opportunities for performing magic spells and rituals.

Samhain

The most holy and solemn of the sabbats, Samhain (pronounced *SOW-een*) is observed on the night of October 31. It is a time to remember and honor loved ones who have passed over to the other side, hence Halloween's association with the dead. Also known as the witches' New Year, Samhain begins the Wheel of the Year. Wearing costumes on Halloween stems from the early practice of making wishes on this date (similar to New Year's resolutions). The colorful custom of dressing up as the person you'd like to be in the coming year serves as a powerful magic spell and visual affirmation.

Magicians believe the veil that separates the seen and unseen worlds is thinnest on Samhain. Therefore, this is an ideal time to try to connect with nonphysical entities such as ancestors, angels, or spirit guides. Many people also do divination on Samhain, when insights and information flow easily.

Winter Solstice or Yule

The Winter Solstice occurs when the sun reaches 0 degrees of Capricorn, the shortest day of the year in the Northern Hemisphere, usually around December 21. In pre-Christian Europe and Britain, the joyful holiday celebrated the birth of the Sun King, who brought light into the world during the darkest time of all. It's easy to see parallels between this ancient view and the Christmas story.

Putting up an evergreen tree symbolizes the triumph of life over death, for these plants retain their needles even during the cold winter months.

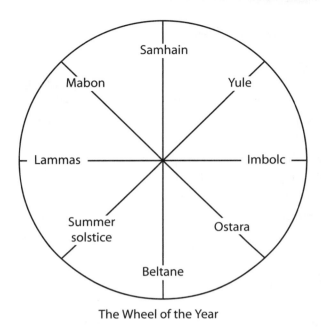

The Wheel of the Year

Traditionally, a Yule log is burned on the eve of the Winter Solstice. Ashes from the Yule fire are collected and used in magic charms to bring blessings in the months ahead.

Imbolc, Brigid's Day, or Candlemas

This holiday honors Brigid, the beloved Celtic goddess of healing, smithcraft, and poetry. The sabbat is celebrated either on February 1 or around February 5, when the sun reaches 15 degrees of Aquarius.

Imbolc means "in the belly," and the holiday honors creativity in its many diverse forms. Brigid is known as the lady of the flame or hearth, so fire plays a prominent role in the festivities that mark her special day. Sometimes she is depicted with a cauldron, which represents the womb and the receptive, fertile quality of feminine energy. At Brigid's Day rituals, participants may build a fire in a cauldron and drop requests written on slips of paper into the flames. Often candles are lit in her honor, each representing a wish or intention a celebrant hopes that Brigid will bring to fruition.

Spring Equinox or Ostara

Usually celebrated around March 21, the Spring Equinox occurs when the sun enters 0 degrees of Aries. This sabbat recognizes one of two dates each year when daylight and night are of equal length. Thus the holiday celebrates a time of balance, equality, and harmony.

The first day of spring, Ostara is a fertility holiday, a time for planting seeds—literally or figuratively—that you want to bear fruit in the coming months. This is an ideal time to launch new ventures or begin a new relationship. The word *Easter* derives from Ostara, and the custom of painting eggs (symbols of fertility and promise) has its roots in this sabbat.

Beltane

Beltane is usually celebrated on May 1, although some people prefer to mark it around May 5, when the sun reaches 15 degrees of Taurus. The second fertility holiday, Beltane coincides with a period of fruitfulness, when flowers blossom and new life emerges. The Maypole, around which young women dance, is an obvious phallic symbol.

In early agrarian cultures, celebrants built fires on Beltane and led livestock between them to symbolically bless them and increase their fertility. Human couples, too, saw Beltane as an auspicious time to express creativity, sensuality, and fertility. Beltane rituals often included sexual activity, and children conceived on this date were said to belong to the Goddess. Whether you wish to spark creativity of the mind or body, Beltane is an ideal time to cast spells for growth and abundance.

Summer Solstice or Midsummer

The longest day of the year in the Northern Hemisphere, the Summer Solstice generally occurs around June 21, when the sun enters the zodiac sign Cancer. To agrarian cultures, this was a time of plenty, when crops were ripening and winter's barrenness seemed far away. They celebrated this joyful holiday with feasting and revelry.

The symbolic seeds you planted earlier in the year now begin to bear fruit, too. This is a good time to collect herbs and flowers to make good-luck charms, especially those designed to attract abundance. Remember to give thanks on this holiday for the riches you've already received.

Lughnassadh or Lammas

Named for the Celtic god Lugh, this holiday is marked on August 1 or around August 5, when the sun reaches 15 degrees of Leo. Lughnassadh (pronounced *LOO-na-saad*) is the first of the harvest celebrations. Farmers cut grain at this time for baking bread and brewing beer. The old English song, "John Barleycorn Must Die," describes this holiday's preparations and festivities.

"To everything there is a season, and a time for every purpose under the heaven."—Ecclesiastes 3:1.

Pagans today still enjoy sharing bread and beer with friends on this sabbat. While you're kneading the bread, add a dried bean to the dough. The person who gets the bean in his or her piece of bread will be granted a wish before the next turn of the wheel. Remember to share your bounty with the nature spirits who helped produce the harvest—leave some food out for them as a gesture of thanks.

Autumn Equinox or Mabon

The second harvest festival, the Autumn Equinox usually falls around September 22, when the sun moves to 0 degrees of Libra. Day and night are now equal in length, so this sabbat represents a time of balance and harmony.

Early Pagans fashioned a doll from corn, wheat, or straw to represent the Sun King, whose powers are waning, and tossed it into a fire as an offering to Mother Earth. You might also choose to braid three stalks of grain together, each stalk symbolizing a wish that you want to come true. Hang the braid in your home to remind you of your intentions.

Chapter 2

It's All in Your Mind

You've heard the expression, "I'll believe it when I see it." In fact, the opposite is true: You'll see it when you believe it. Objective reality, as Werner Heisenberg demonstrated in the 1920s, doesn't exist. According to the Heisenberg Uncertainty Principle, the observer influences the circumstances being observed, a discovery that's being expanded upon by today's quantum physicists. By focusing your mind on something, you actually affect it and even bring it into being. That's the basis of all magic.

Fairy Tales, Myths, and Movies

Most people first discovered spells and potions, wizards and witches, and the endless struggle between good and evil through stories like *Snow White, Cinderella, Alice in Wonderland, Beauty and the Beast, The Wizard of Oz,* and *Peter Pan.* Fairy tales show that the world is filled with magic. Mirrors, stones, and gems have certain powers. Animals talk, plants think, and with a sprinkling of dust, kids can fly.

By adulthood, most people have forgotten about magic. As a result, life becomes a little less rich; imagination starts to shrivel. The details of daily life take over. Revisiting some of that early magic through books and movies, such as *Lord of the Rings,* the *Harry Potter* series, *E.T., The Fisher King,* and *Star Wars,* can reawaken curiosity and wonder at any age. Magic is alive, and belief is the key that opens the door to all sorts of possibilities.

"There is no use trying," said Alice, "one can't believe impossible things." I dare say you haven't had much practice," said the Queen. "When I was your age, I always did it for half an hour a day. Why, sometimes I've believed as many as six impossible things before breakfast."—Lewis Carroll, *Alice in Wonderland*

Belief, in fact, lies at the core of any spell. Without it, all you have are words and gestures, light and dust, nothing but bluster. But what, exactly, is meant by *belief*? Go back to Oz. The lion sought courage. He *believed* that he was cowardly. That belief ruled his life until the wizard pointed out how courageous he actually was. The lion then underwent a radical shift and realized that he always had possessed what he desired most—it was his belief that he *didn't* have courage that crippled him.

That's true for most people. Maybe, for instance, you want abundance. To you, that means financial abundance in the form of money in the bank, along with the freedom from worrying whether the next check you write is going to bounce. But to other people, your life might appear to be incredibly abundant: They see that you have a loving family, wonderful friends, and a job you enjoy.

Sometimes, a shift in your deepest beliefs happens because someone whose opinion you respect points out that the thing you desire is something you already have. Other times, you reach the same conclusion on your own. In either case, the end result is the same. Your beliefs shift, and ultimately, your reality changes.

Your Beliefs Influence Your Reality

In *Star Wars,* Luke Skywalker's training to be a Jedi knight involved learning to use the light saber that Darth Vader brandished with such finesse. But it wasn't enough to merely learn the mechanics. Skywalker had to believe in his own intuitive perceptions so that he could feel the Force. He had to believe he was capable of achieving his quest.

A belief is an acceptance of something as true. A thousand years ago, people believed the world was flat—until Columbus proved otherwise. Until the sixteenth century, when Copernicus's studies showed that the Earth orbited the sun, most people believed the Earth was the center of the solar system. Individuals conducted their lives according to their beliefs, regardless of whether the facts matched their ideas.

Your experiences, the people around you, your personal and professional environments—every facet of your existence is a faithful reflection of a *belief* you hold. Do you believe all the good men are already taken? Do you believe you can't make money as an artist? Do you believe you'll catch a cold as soon as winter weather rolls in? If so, chances are good that your beliefs will produce exactly the results you expect.

Many people have self-limiting beliefs that were laid down in childhood by parents, teachers, and other authority figures. Beliefs also are gleaned from the cultures and societies in which you live. An American woman living in Manhattan, for example, won't have the same core beliefs about being female as a Muslim woman in Iran. An Italian man won't have the same beliefs about being male as an Aborigine man.

Changing Your Beliefs

If you don't like what's happening in your life, you first need to identify the beliefs that are interfering with your happiness. Make a list of the things you aren't satisfied with and that you'd like to change. Then examine the ideas you associate with those things, the underlying beliefs that are holding you back. Where did these ideas come from? Be brutally honest with yourself. Until you change your beliefs, your outer-world reality won't improve.

"When you change the way you look at things, the things you look at change."—Dr. Wayne Dyer

You can begin to change your beliefs and the circumstances they create by reprogramming your thoughts. For example, say you'd like to travel, but you believe the world is a dangerous place. And say you've identified your mother's fear of unfamiliar places as the root of your self-limiting belief. Write a positive statement, called an affirmation, that reverses your old ideas. For example, you could write, "I live in a safe universe" or, "I am protected at all times and in all places." Say this affirmation aloud at least a dozen times a day. Post your written affirmation in a spot where you'll see it often throughout the day. Over time, you'll influence your subconscious to accept the new belief. Once your subconscious believes the affirmation, instead of the old idea, you'll begin to see the process of transformation operating in your experiences.

You might also adopt physical practices to reinforce your new belief. Stop watching nightly newscasts that focus on the violence in the world. Take short trips to places you haven't been before. Consider leaving your car or apartment door unlocked.

Begin to question why you do certain things. It's the best way to start uncovering your invisible beliefs about yourself and about how life works. If you determine that your beliefs are preventing you from realizing your full potential, consider reading *The Power of Intention,* by Dr. Wayne Dyer, *You*

Can Heal Your Life, by Louise Hay, and *Anatomy of the Spirit,* by Caroline Myss.

You'll know that your beliefs are changing when the quality of your experiences and relationships change. Are strangers reacting to you differently? Have you stopped locking your doors or *forgotten* to lock them? Is your life opening up in unexpected ways?

Intent, Desire, and Magic

The purpose of a spell is to manifest something that you need or desire. That need or desire (or both) comprises your intent. When you cast a spell, your intent is as vital to your success as your beliefs. What are you trying to accomplish? What's your goal? What outcome are you seeking? How badly do you want what you're trying to achieve or accomplish?

"Every intentional act is a magical act."—Aleister Crowley

Many of us have had the experience of getting something we desired, even without the ritual of casting a spell. The magic ingredient that makes your wish come true is *intent.*

Here's an example. Vicki had to stop at her local supermarket to drop off a roll of film. The film section was at the front of the store. Although she was hungry, she was in a hurry and didn't have time to run all the way to the back of the store to the produce section. As she approached the supermarket door, she thought about how much she would love to eat a sweet, juicy peach. The closer she got to the door, the more vividly she imagined that peach. She could see its rich color, could smell it, could almost feel it in her hands. When Vicki reached the front door, she spotted a display of fresh peaches. In the many years she'd been shopping at this store, she had never seen a display of fruit at the front. She bought peaches, of course, and they tasted every bit as good as she'd imagined.

What's fascinating about this story is that it aptly illustrates how intent constantly creates magic in life. Yet despite our astonishment and delight when magic like this happens, people usually write it off as a coincidence and eventually forget about it altogether. If you pay attention, however, you'll soon begin to notice that "coincidences" occur all the time. The more you believe in the power of intent, the more often you'll see your desires manifest.

Consciously Creating Circumstances

If you can create circumstances without consciously intending to do so, think how much more successful you'll be if you really put your mind to it. With enough willpower and passion, you can achieve almost anything you can imagine.

Everything in the world started out as a thought in someone's mind. Before a building can take form, an architect must envision it. The same is true in magic. Before you can get the job you want or the relationship you desire, you must be able to imagine having it. It's not necessary to envision every step along the way or decide exactly how all the events leading up to the outcome will unfold, but you must clearly see the end result.

In fact, *seeing from the end* is essential. Don't get discouraged if, in the course of moving toward your goal, you appear to hit a snag or matters don't seem to be progressing the way you'd expected. Hold firmly to your vision of the outcome you desire, and trust that it will manifest.

ALERT!

Doubt is to magic like water is to fire. If you doubt you'll accomplish your objectives, you'll derail the train of thought that was carrying you toward your destination.

As a magician, one of the first tasks you need to master is disciplining your mind. Instead of letting your mind run amuck, start paying attention to your thoughts. Eliminate the ones that run contrary to your desires or that undermine your confidence. *A magician never puts her mind on something she doesn't want to happen.* As soon as you notice yourself thinking something negative or self-limiting, stop yourself and mentally X-out the thought. Then immediately replace it with a positive one.

Defining and Asking for What You Want

This sounds easy, but for many people it's not. They may know what they want *right this instant*, but they don't have a clue about the bigger picture. They're focused on the trees and can't see the forest.

As an example, let's say you've had several bad relationships. Before you start looking for a new romance, make a list of the qualities you seek in a partner. The act of writing the list prompts you to really think about what you want, to put *energy* and *intent* behind your objective. In a sense, the list becomes your spell. You direct your mind to consciously create the circumstances you desire: to find a partner who's right for you.

Take your time, be honest, and make sure to include everything that's important to you. Be very clear and specific when asking for what you want. Remember the old saying, "Be careful what you wish for." Ambiguous statements tend to yield confusing and sometimes unwanted results.

Letting Go

Once you've determined what you seek and can clearly visualize the desired outcome, let it go. Don't second-guess yourself or wonder if you'll be successful. And don't keep changing your mind. If you went to a restaurant for dinner and gave the waiter your order, then a minute later called him back and changed your order, then a minute later changed your mind again, you'd never get anything to eat.

The same is true with magic. One of the biggest problems many people have is that they get in their own way. Do it right the first time, and then give the universe a chance to manifest your intention.

Affirmations and Incantations

Words have the power to influence outcomes. Many magic spells and rituals include special words, phrases, statements, poems, chants, or prayers.

Whether you write your intentions or speak them aloud, putting your goals into words helps focus your mind and empower your spells.

Affirmations are positive statements that you create to produce a result. Here are the important things to remember when writing an affirmation:

- Keep it short.
- Be clear and precise.
- Only include images and situations that you desire.
- Always use the present tense.

Here are some examples of the right and wrong ways to write affirmations:

- *Right:* I am healthy in body, mind, and spirit.
- *Wrong:* I don't have any illnesses or injuries.
- *Right:* I now have a job that's perfect for me.
- *Wrong:* I want to get a better job.

If you aren't exactly sure of all the details, it's okay to leave some things up to the universe to work out. In the example above, "I now have a job that's perfect for me" covers the bases without being specific.

Incantations differ from affirmations in that they are usually written as rhymes. The catchy phrasing makes it easy to remember. You don't have to be a Wordsworth or Dickinson to create an effective incantation; the important thing is to follow the same rules when writing an incantation as when writing an affirmation.

Here's an example of a simple love incantation:

As the day fades into night
I draw a love that's good and right.
As the night turns into day
We are blessed in every way.

The uses for affirmations and incantations are limited only by your imagination. Write an affirmation or incantation on a slip of paper and insert it into a magic talisman or amulet. Put it under your pillow at night. Repeat it regularly throughout the day, such as while you're in the shower or driving to work, and especially just before you go to sleep. Write it on a sheet of colored paper, decorate it with images that resonate with you, and post it in a place where you'll see it often. Be creative!

Black, White, and Gray Magic

Most people think that magic comes in two distinct varieties—stage magic, like that which magician David Copperfield performs, and ancient magic, like that associated with Merlin. Stage magic, or illusion, involves trickery and deception. The type of magic this book discusses has been passed down through the centuries by wise men and women and is done to produce beneficial results for yourself or someone else, not for mere amusement.

FACT

To distinguish "real magic" from stage illusion, some practitioners choose to use a different spelling: *magick.*

In Chapter 6, you'll see that there are many schools and expressions of magic. Although their outer forms may differ, all magic involves focusing the power of intention to produce results. Your intention not only provides the fuel that energizes spells, it also colors the spell. Your motive for doing a spell determines whether it's white or black magic or something in between. Magic spells can be grouped into three basic categories:

- **Black magic** is any spell done to harm someone else.
- **White magic** includes all spells and rituals performed for the purpose of connecting with the Divine or to obtain higher knowledge.
- Everything else falls into the **gray** area.

That's not to imply that there's anything wrong with doing gray spells. Most spells, in fact, qualify as gray, including spells to increase abundance, land a better job, or find a parking space on a crowded city street. So long as you don't injure anyone else or interfere with his or her free will in order to get what you want, you're in the clear. Doing a spell to attract a romantic partner who is right for you is an acceptable use of magic. But if you're in love with a married man, and your intention is to break up the marriage so you and your lover can be together, you're dabbling in black magic.

Black magic doesn't always involve the ritual of casting a spell. Remember, your intent is what matters. Many people perform black magic without even realizing it. If, in the heat of the moment, you wish something bad to happen to someone or envision getting back at someone who's hurt you, you're doing black magic. Angry thoughts produce angry results.

ALERT!

Science shows that every action generates a reaction. In magic, whatever energy you put into the universe returns to you threefold. Be sure your spells are designed to produce the greatest good for everyone.

A good way to make certain your spells are on the up-and-up is to close with a statement such as, "This spell is done in harmony with Divine Will and for the good of all concerned." That way, the universe gets the final say. Higher Mind will direct you and the energies you've raised so that your spell unfolds in the proper way, harming none. "The Wiccan Rede," a guide for practitioners of Wicca, sums this up nicely.

The Wiccan Rede
Bide the Wiccan law ye must
In perfect love, in perfect trust,
Eight words the Wiccan Rede fulfill:
An' ye harm none, do what ye will.
What ye send forth comes back to thee,
So ever mind the Rule of Three.
Follow this with mind and heart,
And merry ye meet, and merry ye part.

Chapter 3

Synchronicity, Signs, and Symbols

There are no coincidences. From the perspective of magic, nothing happens accidentally. This is not to say that everything is fated or predetermined; rather, what occurs in your life was initiated at some previous time by your own conceptions or someone else's, or both. Past, present, and future form an integrated continuum. With each thought, word, and deed you lay the groundwork for your future. Furthermore, your thoughts, words, and deeds don't exist in a vacuum—they interact with everyone else's to create our collective experience.

Synchronicity

For many years the noted Swiss psychotherapist Carl G. Jung observed that many events and situations, in his own life as well as in the lives of his patients, seemed strangely connected, but not by a causal link. In 1952, Jung published an essay in which he discussed an idea he called "synchronicity." His theory suggested that meaningful events that defy the usually accepted laws of cause and effect occur so often, and in such amazing ways, that they cannot be discounted as mere coincidences.

"The exact contrary of what is generally believed is often the truth."— Jean de la Bruyere

Over the years, for example, you might have noticed that whenever you find coins in unexpected places, you subsequently receive a significant sum of money. That's an example of synchronicity. Everyone experiences meaningful occurrences of this sort from time to time, but most people don't pay attention to them. Science may not be able to prove why such things happen. Magic, though, offers a very good explanation: the cosmic web discussed in Chapter 1. If you accept that everything in the universe is linked via this web, synchronicity makes perfect sense.

Symbols

The world is replete with symbols. From the beginning of time, human beings have used symbols to convey ideas. More than a convenient form of shorthand, however, symbols are images that encapsulate the essence of whatever they represent. When you see one, you instantly understand something fundamental and profound about what's behind the symbol. A good logo, for instance, reveals important information about a company— not just what the firm makes or does, but the company's mission and how its principals want the business to be perceived by the world. Rolex's crown bespeaks royalty; Nike's signature checkmark connotes speed. You could think of these symbols as visual metaphors.

Numbers, letters, and geometric shapes are common symbols you see around you every day, usually without giving them a second thought. The average person only recognizes the obvious meanings of these familiar images, but to someone versed in occult knowledge they reveal something deeper. (Chapter 5 details the secret meanings of numbers and letters.) Astrological glyphs, the *I Ching*'s hexagrams, rune marks, and the suits on tarot cards are other examples of symbols that wise men and women have used for centuries. Even colors contain symbolic associations—the chakras, for instance, are usually linked with certain colors. The following table lists qualities associated with a variety of colors.

Color Symbolism

Red	Passion, anger, heat, energy, daring
Orange	Confidence, activity, warmth, enthusiasm
Yellow	Happiness, creativity, optimism
Green	Health, fertility, growth, wealth
Light blue	Peace, clarity, hope, innocence
Royal blue	Independence, insight, imagination, truth
Indigo	Intuition, serenity, mental power
Purple	Wisdom, emotional depth, spirituality
Pink	Love, friendship, sociability
White	Purity, clarity, protection
Black	Power, wisdom
Brown	Stability, practicality, grounding in the physical world

Because the subconscious responds better to images than words, symbols provide a way to directly communicate with your inner self. Artists frequently include symbols in their work in order to present ideas. For example, the medieval artisans who fabricated stained glass windows for

Europe's great cathedrals chose images that portrayed religious concepts to the masses, who at that time were largely illiterate.

FACT

Your subconscious instantly comprehends a symbol's inherent meaning, even if your rational mind doesn't.

Magicians often use symbols to embody ideas. The tools that magicians employ in rituals—the wand, chalice, athame, and pentagram—symbolize the four elements. Symbols can also be placed in charms as a way of emphasizing specific energies and intentions. You might wish to add a rose quartz heart to a love charm or slip a silver coin into a prosperity talisman. Some magical practitioners like to wear clothing adorned with meaningful symbols or to decorate their sacred spaces with poignant imagery. Symbols can even be acted out physically. *Mudras,* for instance, are symbolic gestures that express concepts or intentions.

Universal and Personal Symbols

Some symbols transcend time and place; they mean basically the same thing to all people around the world. Archaeologists have found these symbols inscribed on stones in Mexico and in temples in India. The cross, for example, isn't unique to Christian belief; it existed in ancient Celtic, Egyptian, and Native American cultures, too. This simple yet powerful image represents the union of the archetypal male energy or heaven (the vertical line) with female energy or earth (the horizontal line).

The star is a common symbol of hope, while the circle is a well-known symbol of wholeness. Spirals represent life energy in many cultures. Triangles signify trinities, whether Father-Son-Holy Ghost, maiden-mother-crone, past-present-future, or some other threefold concept. The tree is another universal symbol, usually seen as a conduit for knowledge. The Buddha received enlightenment while sitting beneath a bodhi tree. The Celtic World Tree unites the different realms of experience. The Norse god Wodin brought the wisdom of the runes to humanity after hanging on the tree Yggdrasil for nine days.

Other symbols are personal; they connote something distinctive to you that may not concur with the usual meaning. Lilies might represent purity to you and death to someone else. Initials and family crests are examples of personal symbols. For example, if you are of Irish descent, Celtic knots may hold special significance for you.

If an image resonates strongly with you, you may choose to view it as your personal symbol. Arrows, crescent moons, sailboats, conch shells, or apples might signify something profound to you. You might feel an affinity with wolves, so you could display photos and figurines of wolves in your physical surroundings. Personal symbols, like totem animals and power objects, can help you focus your own power and draw upon energies outside yourself. Notice incidents of synchronicity that involve your symbol, too. Any time your symbol appears unexpectedly, it's a wake-up call. Pay attention!

Creating Sigils

A sigil is a uniquely personal symbol you create in order to produce a specific result. In a sense, a sigil is a way of communicating with yourself via secret code because no one else can interpret the symbol. Although there are various techniques for designing sigils, the easiest one involves fashioning an image from letters.

Sigil for "Love"

Start by writing a word or a short affirmation that states your intention. Delete any letters that are repeated. Entwine the remaining letters to form a design. You can use upper- and/or lower-case letters, block or script. Position them right-side up, upside down, forward or backward. The finished image depicts your objective in a graphic manner that your subconscious understands, although it won't make sense to anyone else.

Both creating the sigil and applying it are magical acts. You can draw a sigil on a piece of paper and slip it into a magic charm. Display a sigil on your wall or altar to constantly remind you of your intention. Carve one on a candle, and then burn the candle to activate your objective.

Have a jeweler fabricate your sigil as a pendant or pin and wear it as a talisman. Some people have even had sigils tattooed on their bodies. Give your imagination free rein. There's no limit to how many sigils you can draw or how many ways you can use them.

Dream Symbols

No one knows exactly where dreams come from or why people dream. Yet researchers and psychotherapists believe your dreams are conveyances of messages that can help you in your waking life. Because the unconscious and subconscious parts of the mind use the language of symbols to communicate, dream messages are usually presented in symbolic rather than literal form.

Some symbols appear in many people's dreams; others are unique to the individual dreamer. Over time, general meanings have become accepted for the most common dream symbols. Personal symbols, though, usually hold special meaning for you and you alone.

Common Dream Symbols and What They Mean

House	You and your life: The basement represents your unconscious, the main floor shows your daily living situation, the attic or upper floors describe your mental or spiritual side.
Car	Your body and your passage through life: The driver represents who's controlling your life; the car's condition reveals health and physical matters.
Water	Emotions: The type of water (deep, murky, cold, turbulent, etc.) indicates the quality of your feelings.
Sex	The act represents the merging of your masculine and feminine sides, or incorporating another person's qualities into yourself.
Death	Represents a transition or change
Birth	Represents a new direction, perspective, or endeavor; creativity; a symbol of opportunity.
School	Learning lessons: Taking an exam represents being tested in an area of life.
Monsters	Represent things you fear or parts of yourself you haven't integrated.

Images that turn up repeatedly in your dreams are especially important. If you experience recurring dreams, your subconscious may be trying hard to convey something to you that you need to know. Pay attention. For example, if you frequently dream that you're driving along a freeway and see a huge exit sign with flashing lights, it could be a sign that you need to change your direction in life, perhaps by leaving the fast lane and moving at a slower pace.

You may discover that you can communicate with other people via dreams. When your waking consciousness is temporarily stilled, it's often easier to access the energy matrix that links you with everyone else. Like telepathy, dream communication knows no boundaries. Your thoughts and another person's can connect instantly, even if you're at opposite ends of the world. It's even possible to intentionally send messages to someone while you're sleeping or to arrange to meet in the dream world. Some people, such as the Aborigine, believe that they actually journey to another realm of existence when they dream and that what transpires there is every bit as real as what goes on in the waking world.

Sometimes dreams reveal the future. When your perception is loosened from its ordinary, physical confines, it can range far and wide, even beyond the limitations of time. A dream that lets you see in advance what's coming may help you to prepare yourself or avoid a problem altogether.

Learning to interpret your dreams opens a door to greater understanding in all areas of your life. Quite likely, you'll gain insights and information that you can use in your magical work. While in a dream state, you might find that you can tap into the reservoir of knowledge contained in the cosmic web, which some people refer to as the Akashic Records. You might even be able to revisit past lifetimes or travel to other realms of existence.

The Power of Visualization

Author Shakti Gawain brought the concept of creative visualization into widespread public awareness. But magicians have long known that visualization fuels magic and precedes manifestation. In magic, a picture truly is worth a thousand words.

Creative visualization involves forming a mental picture of the result you intend to manifest. Don't think about the problem or condition you wish to change. For instance, if your goal is to heal a broken leg, don't think about the injury; instead, envision the leg strong and healthy. Clear, vivid images tend to generate faster and more satisfactory results. See yourself rolling in a pile of $100 bills or happily performing the job you desire.

"We are what we think. All that we are arises with our thoughts. With our thoughts, we make the world."—The Buddha

Practice forming images in your mind. The more personal and active you can make these scenarios, the better. Hold the vision in your mind as you fall asleep and bring it into your consciousness as soon as you wake up in the morning. Sometimes cutting pictures from magazines, using photos, or creating your own artwork can strengthen your visualization process. Display the images in a place where you'll see them often throughout the day, to continually remind you of your objective.

Developing Intuition

Whether you call it ESP, a hunch, a gut reaction, an inner knowing, or psychic power, everyone has intuition. It may raise hairs on the back of your neck, cause a twinge in your solar plexus, or make you feel light-headed. It may speak to you in moments of crisis or utter calm, in the middle of a city traffic jam or while you're taking a shower. Regardless of how your intuition communicates with you, it's important to remember that your so-called sixth sense is just as normal and just as important as the other five senses.

Think how much you'd miss out on if you lacked the sense of sight, hearing, taste, smell, or touch. The world would be a much duller place. Now try to imagine how much more you could get out of life if you had another sense on top of those five. The good news is that you do! The bad news is, most people ignore it.

In her book, *Awakening Intuition*, Mona Lisa Schultz, M.D., Ph.D., explains, "Intuition occurs when we directly perceive facts outside the range of the usual five senses and independently of any reasoning process." Because intuition doesn't "make sense" (that is, doesn't rely on our five physical senses), people tend to discount its validity. Yet many noted scientists have acknowledged that intuition played a significant part in their discoveries.

FACT

In his later years, Nobel laureate Jonas Salk, who found a vaccine for polio, wrote a book about intuition titled *Anatomy of Reality*. In it he proposed that creativity resulted from the union of intuition and reasoning.

From the perspective of magic, intuition could be considered the connection between your conscious mind and the cosmic web. Magic encourages you to strengthen your intuition and to value what it can offer you. Sometimes intuition is the most important factor in spell-working. You can memorize tables of information, like the properties of different herbs, gemstones, or colors. You can follow all the prescribed steps in a ritual, and you can implement the instructions for a spell to the letter. But if you don't trust your intuition to guide you, you'll never develop your full potential.

Listening to the Voice Within

The hubbub of modern society and the busyness of daily life tend to drown out the still, small voice within. Your attention is turned outward, toward the demands of your job, your family, your social obligations, and the everyday tasks that consume so much of your time and energy. Underneath all that noise and activity, however, resides the voice of intuition, your inner wisdom, your link to the big picture. Most likely, you've heard that inner voice speak to you from time to time.

ALERT!

Write down insights, hunches, and epiphanies you receive, even if they don't make sense at first. Notice, too, when your rational mind balks at these intuitive messages. In order to succeed as a magician, you may need to overcome your early training and to suspend disbelief.

Part of your magical training involves learning to listen to the voice within. The outer world produces a lot of static that can interfere with your intuition's signal. Meditation is one way to silence that static and tune into your inner wisdom. If you prefer, you can take a walk, enjoy a bubble bath, look at the stars, or spend time petting an animal companion. Notice the thoughts, feelings, and impressions that arise during these quiet moments. Invite your intuition to talk to you openly, as a friend and guide, and respect its wisdom. Pay attention to your physical and emotional reactions, too, especially those that seem to contradict what your rational brain tells you. Chills, tickles, or a sensation of light bulbs going off in your head can be signals that your intuition is sending you a psychic e-mail.

Strengthening Your Sending and Receiving Ability

Like other forms of communication, intuition involves both sending and receiving. Some people are better senders, while others are better receivers. You might also discover that you can communicate telepathically with some people better than others. Generally speaking, family members have closer intuitive ties than strangers, and identical twins tend to be able to read each other's minds with great facility.

You can hone your telepathic skills by practicing with a partner. A popular exercise requires one person to choose a card from a regular poker deck and mentally focus on it, without showing it to her partner. The second person tries to read the identity of the card from the first person's mind. The reader may pick up a color (black or red), a number, a shape, or the complete card. After several sessions, the two people swap places so that the sender becomes the receiver. If you try this exercise, be sure to keep track of your correct hits. Over time, your success rate should improve.

FACT

Go with your first impression—it's usually illuminating, even if it isn't 100 percent accurate. For instance, the sender might be thinking about a swan, and you as the receiver might get an impression of a feather comforter. These near-hits show you're on the same wavelength.

Another method involves mentally sending a visual message to your partner, from a distance, at a prearranged time of the day. The sender chooses an image and focuses on it, visually transmitting the picture to the receiver, who attempts to remain open and receptive so the image can come through. Do this once a day for two weeks, then change roles so that the sender becomes the receiver. Keep a record of your experiences.

Meditation and Prayer

Meditation in one form or another has been a part of every major religion throughout the world. During meditation, you stop thinking about mundane things like work, relationships, finances, and daily chores and instead become fully present in the moment. Mental chatter ceases temporarily, and you experience a profound state of relaxation in both mind and body.

According to Dr. Martin Hart, president of the American Society of Alternative Therapists, meditation "provides a direct access route into the unconscious, without using artificial means." Because the unconscious stores everything you've ever experienced, he says, "a greater level of information is available to us and this allows us to make better choices in the conscious state."

Many magical practitioners engage in regular meditation because it builds mental muscles. Daily meditation is to the mind as daily exercise is to the body. Meditation enables you to clear the clutter from your mind and focus your thinking. It also opens the channels of communication between you and the higher realms. Because the mind is the force behind magic, it stands to reason that the more mastery you gain over your thoughts, the more effective your spells will be.

Prayer, too, plays a key role in magic, especially for the purpose of healing. The religious community has never doubted the power of prayer to heal body, mind, and spirit. According to Larry Dossey, M.D., author of *Healing Words* and *Prayer Is Good Medicine,* in cases of intercessory prayer (praying for someone else at a distance), the consciousness of the person who is doing the praying actually influences the body of the person who is being prayed for. While this may sound strange to some, many healers realize that their own energies can interact with the energies of their patients. Shamans have utilized this phenomenon for centuries to aid the healing process.

FACT

A survey by the National Institutes of Health found more than 250 studies that supported the beneficial effect of prayer on a range of illnesses, including cancer, heart disease, colitis, and hypertension.

Like affirmations, prayers contain positive images that stimulate results. Prayer, of course, is more than mere words. It's a complete, unified attitude that brings body, mind, emotions, and spirit together. It is a state of receptivity, awareness, trust, forgiveness, and thanksgiving. Prayers may invoke the assistance of God, the Goddess, a Divine Spirit, the All-Knowing Power of the Universe, your guardian angels, the ancestors, or whatever other presence you feel is guiding your life.

Dossey says it's not necessary to follow any particular format or method when praying. In fact, he recommends doing away with any preconceptions you may have about the "right way" to pray. You can pray first thing in the morning, before meals, or you can pray before you go to sleep, when you're stuck in traffic, during down times at your computer, or while exercising at the gym. You can pray silently or aloud, alone or with others.

Followers of the Sufi way pray while dancing. Buddhists chant, and medieval Christian pilgrims crawled through labyrinths as they prayed. A few years ago, thousands of Native Americans and others walked across the country, praying as they walked. In the last decade or so, global prayer circles have become popular. In these, millions of people around the world pray at the same time for peace and other matters of international concern. You can even join an online prayer circle.

The following prayer, known as the Loving Kindness Prayer, comes from Buddhist tradition. However, you don't have to be a Buddhist to appreciate its gentle, uplifting message or to share it with others.

May I be free from fear. May I be free from suffering.
May I be happy. May I be filled with loving kindness.
May you be free from fear. May you be free from suffering.
May you be happy. May you be filled with loving kindness.
May all beings everywhere be free of fear and suffering.
May all beings everywhere be happy and filled with loving kindness.

Recognizing Signs in Everyday Life

When you see dark clouds roll across the sky and hear thunder roar, you know a storm is coming. Because you recognize these signs, you can predict what's going to happen next. Our ancestors were well versed in reading weather patterns, the ocean's tides, animal behavior, and so on; their lives depended on interpreting signs accurately.

Today, most people have lost the ability to understand nature's patterns, yet many of the judgments and decisions they make each day are still based on reading signs. Savvy investors watch the stock market's ups and downs. A mechanic listens to noises in a car's engine to determine what's wrong. When you meet someone for the first time, things like a handshake or other forms of body language tell you a great deal about the person.

If you pay attention, you'll also notice that the universe regularly sends you signs to help guide you along your path in life. It's a bit like relying on road signs along the highway. Signs tend to be personal and unique, which means that your sign will probably be different than your mother's or your husband's or your best friend's. You may hear a voice, feel a tingle in your left foot, smell a familiar scent, or see a meaningful object, such as the coins mentioned at the beginning of this chapter. A sign might show up in a dream, during meditation, or while you're washing dishes. What's important is that you recognize the sign and understand its meaning.

Ask to receive signs. You may choose to receive one sign each day, preferably in a way you wouldn't ordinarily expect, that will show you that your plans or goals are materializing according to your intentions. You can also ask to be given a sign when you get off track. Over time, you might develop a special "sign language." Acknowledging the value and validity of signs encourages your intuition to keep communicating with you.

Hunches and Premonitions

Everyone gets hunches now and again. Perhaps you felt a strong urge to stop in a store, and to your delight you found an item you'd been searching for. Or you entered a contest on a whim and won a prize. Hunches are another method your intuition uses to send messages to you. Start following your hunches, and see where they lead you.

Premonitions are like hunches, only stronger and more rare. Many people have experienced premonitions that prevented them from taking a plane that crashed or a boat that sank. But premonitions do more than simply presage danger; they can just as easily guide you toward good fortune. You might receive a premonition in a dream, as a waking vision, through an intense emotion or sensation, or even via another person.

A good way to validate your hunches and premonitions is to keep a journal. Whenever you get a strong feeling that you should or shouldn't do something, make a note of it. Date each entry. Describe the sign that alerted you. Explain what action you took and what happened as a result. (Some results may not be immediately apparent and could take time to unfold.) After a while, you'll learn what certain signs mean and which hunches you should follow.

Paying Attention to Meaningful Events and Patterns

The old saying, "Things happen in threes" may have some truth to it. Start noticing things that happen repeatedly. Also notice when things out of the ordinary occur or when they occur in a way that's unusual. The universe may be trying to get your attention.

Here's an example. For several months, Katie noticed the numbers 11:11 kept appearing in her life quite frequently and in unexpected places. Often she glanced at the clock at exactly 11:11. Once, when stuck in traffic, she noticed the license plate on the car in front of her was 11:11. Another time she found an envelope containing $11.11. When she investigated the significance of this number, she learned that 11:11 represents a gateway into a higher level of awareness. Her intuition was sending her a sign that the changes she was experiencing would open doors for her and expand her knowledge. Today, whenever this sign turns up, she realizes that an opportunity for growth is being presented.

Animal Appearances

Seeing a robin is a familiar sign that spring is coming. The appearance of an animal, bird, or insect—especially one you don't ordinarily see—can also be a special sign from the universe to you. In his book *Animal-Speak*, Ted Andrews explains how to interpret these signs according to the characteristics and/or behavior of the animal. "In understanding the language of animals," he writes, "we must develop the mindset that *everything has significance.*"

Start paying attention to the creatures (other than family pets) that you come across. Did a butterfly flit past your windshield on your way to work the other day? Did a snake get into your garage? Is a particular kind of bird nesting in a tree in your yard?

If you spot a swan, it could be a reminder to appreciate beauty, to awaken your creativity, or to handle a situation with grace. Seeing a beaver might be a sign that it's time to make repairs in your home or to work hard to bring your dreams to fruition.

Native American traditions recognize that spirit guides can take the form of animals. Individuals align themselves with certain creatures to which they feel a close association. These totem animals can help people learn about themselves and receive guidance from the invisible world. If you feel a strong affinity with a particular animal, bird, reptile, or insect, it could be your totem. When that animal appears to you, either physically or in a dream, its presence usually augurs something significant.

Smells, Sounds, and Visions

In the physical world, you receive information through your five senses. Smells, sounds, and sights draw you toward things you need or desire, and they warn you away from things that are potentially harmful. Your intuition might communicate with you through olfactory or auditory signs, too, although the stimulus you're being alerted to may not be physical.

Let's say, for example, that for several days you keep smelling an unfamiliar perfume, but you can't ascertain where it's coming from—the fragrance doesn't seem to emanate from any obvious source. Then, at the end of the week, out of the blue you meet the woman of your dreams, and she's wearing the very same perfume. You received an aromatic premonition that something wonderful was coming into your life.

"There are more things in heaven and earth than are dreamt of in your philosophy."—Shakespeare, *Hamlet*

Clairvoyance means being able to see things that don't exist within the physical field of vision. Clairaudience means hearing things that don't have a physical correlation. When my sister went into a coma suddenly, I awoke to the sound of tiny bells tinkling, although there were no bells in my bedroom. If you experience a sensory awareness that you can't link to a physical source, it could be a sign. Look into it more deeply to discover what it means.

Chapter 4

Oracles and Divination

Human beings, it seems, have always wanted to know what tomorrow will bring. Since ancient times, people in cultures throughout the world have looked to oracles to shine light into the darkness. Whether the oracle is a diviner—a seer or psychic who can gaze into the future—or a device such as tarot cards, oracles serve as conduits between heaven and earth. Divination, the art of predicting the future, literally means letting the divine realm manifest.

4

Ancient Diviners

At the foot of the southern slope of Mount Parnassus, in the temple of Apollo, a woman known as the pythoness (a priestess) sat on a gold three-legged chair, called a tripod, perched above a chasm in the rocks. She chewed laurel leaves, which were sacred to Apollo, and inhaled the fumes that drifted upward from the chasm. Entranced by the leaves and the fumes, she muttered unintelligibly while a priest stood nearby and interpreted her mutterings. This was the famed oracle of Apollo at Delphi, from whom ancient Greece's wealthy and powerful sought advice. Commoners went to the oracle at Dedona, dedicated to Zeus, to get answers to their questions. Petitioners wrote yes-or-no questions on strips of lead and put them in a jar. The priestess then picked out questions and answered them.

Three thousand years ago, the Chinese court astrologers of the Chou dynasty read not only the stars but the clouds, rain, and wind as well. These seers interpreted the relationships between heaven and earth in order to foretell what lay ahead.

The rulers of ancient Sumeria and Babylonia employed an elite group of priests to read the future and provide guidance. Often a *mas-su-gid* (a Babylonian diviner) interpreted patterns in the entrails of sacrificial animals. The predictions reported by these priests were considered to be divinely inspired.

In the Scottish Highlands, Celtic oracles known as *frithirs* served as prognosticators for their people. Four times a year, on the first Monday of each quarter, the *frithir* would fast, then step outside blindfolded just before sunrise. Upon removing her blindfold, the *frithir* opened her eyes and interpreted the significance of the first thing she saw.

Oracles serve as a direct link between your conscious self, your subconscious, and Divine Wisdom. When you shuffle tarot cards, cast runes, or use any other oracle, you open your consciousness to perceive what your higher mind already knows and wants to communicate to you.

Today, despite the modern world's movement toward the rational and away from the mystical, countless people still turn to psychics, astrologers, and other readers for many of the same reasons their ancestors did. The same questions and concerns continue to cause consternation: Should I marry this person? Is this job right for me? What will happen if I take this trip? How can this illness be healed?

You don't have to consult another person to get answers to the pressing questions in your own life, however. Instead, you can use a different type of oracle, a divination device such as those discussed in the following sections of this chapter. These tools enable you to access your own inner knowing. By showing you what's going on beneath the surface of a situation, they help you find ways to solve your own problems.

The I Ching

Believed to have been created in China by Confucius about a thousand years before the birth of Christ, the *I Ching*, or Book of Changes, consists of sixty-four hexagrams (patterns made up of six lines), each with a different meaning. Three millennia later, Richard Wilhelm and Cary F. Baynes collaborated on a translation that introduced Westerners to this ancient oracle. The Wilhelm-Baynes edition (published in 1950 by the Princeton University Press) is still considered the standard for *I Ching* enthusiasts. It has sold more than a million copies since its initial publication.

FACT

According to some researchers, the *I Ching* evolved from an even older Chinese divination method. This technique, which dates back 5,000 years to the time of the Emperor Fu Hsi, is based on interpreting cracks in the shells of tortoises.

Traditionally, seekers used yarrow sticks to determine which hexagrams answered their questions. Today, most people toss three coins six times to form a meaningful pattern. Each toss corresponds to a line in the hexagram. When more heads than tails turn up, it signifies a solid or yang line. When more tails than heads appear, the result is a broken or yin line. When you get three heads or three tails in a toss, you have what's called a *changing line*. Changing lines are particularly meaningful and show the development of the matter at hand.

I Ching hexagrams are formed from the bottom up. Your first coin toss corresponds to the bottom line of the pattern, and the top line represents your sixth coin toss. Once you've drawn your hexagram, look it up in the *I Ching* to learn what it means with regard to your question or concern.

Some of the new *I Ching* kits use cards, marbles, or other methods to produce an answer. A boxed set of six red-and-black plastic sticks, made by a Dutch company called Blozo Products and distributed in the United States by Music Design, is a convenient and accurate tool for *I Ching* readings. You can even do readings online.

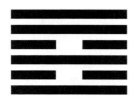

I Ching Hexagram

"The hexagrams reflect the path we follow and where it leads. If our attitudes are out of harmony with the great harmony of the cosmos, they reflect this. If we are in harmony, the counsel given will help us keep our inner balance. If forthcoming events may threaten our inner equilibrium, the hexagrams give us warning."—Carol K. Anthony, *A Guide to the I Ching*

Because the *I Ching* is linked with ancient Chinese laws and customs, some Westerners feel it's too rigid and patriarchal. Scores of modern writers have updated the original text to make it less hierarchical and more accessible to today's users.

Sample Reading

Patricia wanted to know if she'd find a publisher for her next book. She took a few moments to reflect on her question and then tossed three pennies six times. The hexagram that resulted corresponded to the *I Ching*'s hexagram number 12, "Standstill." Initially, Patricia felt discouraged. Hexagram 12 definitely described Patricia's situation. Her editor had received her proposal more than a month ago, but he hadn't replied.

But the fifth line in the hexagram was a changing line, and it gave her hope. Patricia turned to the Wilhelm-Baynes translation of the *I Ching* and read the meaning of the hexagram she'd thrown. The fifth line gave the following counsel:

> *Standstill is giving way.*
> *Good fortune for the great man.*
> *"What if it should fail, what if it should fail?"*
> *In this way he ties it to a cluster of mulberry shoots.*

The words "What if it should fail?" intrigued Patricia because that's precisely what she'd been asking herself. The part about the mulberry shoots seemed so opaque to her Western mind that she nearly slammed the book shut. Instead, she read a bit further: "When a mulberry bush is cut down," explained the text, "a number of unusually strong shoots sprout from the roots. Hence the image of tying something to a cluster of mulberry shoots is used to symbolize the way of making success certain."

ALERT!

It's tempting to ask a question again if you don't like the answer you received. But this demonstrates your lack of faith, not only in the oracle but also in yourself. Instead, request additional information about the subject. And remember, the oracle can only describe what's likely to occur given the circumstances that exist right now. If something changes, the situation you're inquiring about could change, too.

As it turned out, the editor to whom Patricia had sent her manuscript rejected it. But shortly afterward, several other publishers expressed interest in the book, and she ended up selling it to one of them. As the *I Ching* predicted, her project, symbolized by the mulberry bush, was cut down initially, but other possibilities arose, and Patricia was ultimately successful.

The I Ching and Feng Shui

The current popularity of feng shui has stimulated interest in the *I Ching* among people who might not otherwise turn to an oracle for advice. Feng shui (pronounced *fung-shway*) is an ancient system designed to help you create harmony and balance in your environment. (You'll learn more about this magical practice in Chapter 6.)

Feng shui practitioners utilize a tool called a ba-gua to evaluate living and work spaces. The eight sectors, or gua, of this octagonal device correspond to the *I Ching*'s eight original trigrams (three-lined patterns that can be combined to form the hexagrams in the *I Ching*). Together, they represent the interaction between heaven and earth.

I Ching Trigram	Feng Shui Gua
Ch'ien, The Creative	Helpful people, friends
Chen, The Arousing	Knowledge, spirituality
K'an, The Abysmal	Self, identity, career
Ken, Keeping Still	Family, community, heritage
K'un, The Receptive	Marriage, primary relationship
Sun, The Gentle	Wealth
Li, The Clinging	Fame, future, public image
Tui, The Joyous	Creativity, children

Although these pairings may seem peculiar or meaningless to many Westerners, the underlying qualities represented by the *I Ching*'s patterns and the ba-gua's sectors are similar, at least from the perspective of the ancient Chinese. For example, receptivity and adaptability, as symbolized by the trigram K'un, are qualities necessary to a harmonious marriage. Creative expression of all kinds brings joy, as shown by the connection between Tui and the feng shui gua that corresponds to children and creativity.

Many good books are available on both subjects. Understanding these basic principles will help you to interpret the guidance offered by the *I Ching* and apply feng shui's magic in your home.

Using the I Ching in Spells

By combining feng shui and the *I Ching*, you can generate some very effective magic spells. Decide what you'd like to attract into your life. Is it love, money, or fame? Then draw the *I Ching* hexagram "Ta Yu: Possession in Great Measure" (number 14) on a piece of paper. If your intention involves love, use pink or red paper. If you want to increase your wealth, choose green or gold paper. (See Chapter 3 for more information about colors.)

Next, use a ba-gua to determine which part of your home or office correlates to which feng shui gua. Then display the hexagram in the sector that corresponds to your intention. For instance, if your goal is to improve your public image or reputation, place the hexagram in the future/fame gua of your home or workplace. If you're looking for love, put the hexagram in the relationship gua.

To fine-tune situations, look through the *I Ching* and select a hexagram that most accurately describes the condition you desire. Draw that hexagram on a piece of paper and position it in the appropriate gua. If, for example, your marriage is tumultuous and you seek peace, choose the *I Ching* hexagram "T'ai: Peace" (number 11) and put it in the relationship gua of your home to calm those stormy seas.

The Tarot

The tarot's origins are shrouded in mystery. No one knows exactly when or where the oracle came into being. Evidence suggests that tarot decks much like the ones used today, such as the beautiful fifteenth-century Visconti-Sforza deck, may have existed in Italy and France during the Renaissance. Some researchers believe that gypsies brought the cards to Europe from the Middle East, where they may have been hidden during the medieval period to protect them and their owners from persecution.

Most contemporary tarot decks contain seventy-eight cards. Twenty-two of these make up what's known as the major arcana, which researchers believe comprised the original tarot. The other fifty-six cards are called the minor arcana. These were probably added at a later date and may have been inspired by an early Italian card game called *tarrochi*. As you examine a tarot deck, you'll undoubtedly notice that the minor arcana cards look much like today's poker decks, with four suits of ten numbered cards each. The main difference is the tarot's minor arcana features four court cards per suit—king, queen, knight, and page—whereas a poker deck only has three. One card from the major arcana, The Fool, also appears in modern playing card decks, renamed the Joker.

You can tell fortunes with a regular deck of playing cards. When doing so, it's usually best to confine your questions to everyday matters and mundane concerns. Because poker decks lack the major arcana, the spiritual dimension won't be covered in your readings.

Tarot readers generally consider the major arcana to represent divine wisdom, spiritual forces, or fate. These are the most powerful cards in the deck; they indicate situations and events that affect your life in dynamic ways. Taken together, the twenty-two "majors" also describe the steps in a course in spiritual development.

The minor arcana cards depict everyday events, mundane activities, and areas in life over which you have control. The court cards often describe the people around you. For instance, kings may refer to mature men, while pages represent children or young people. The numbers on the cards have special meanings, too. Fours, for instance, signify stability, and sixes represent give and take.

When you consult the tarot, you usually start by shuffling the cards while contemplating a question or situation you want to know more about. Then you lay out a certain number of cards in a prescribed pattern known as a spread. The meanings of the individual cards in conjunction with the meanings of their positions in the spread provide an answer and/or guidance.

All oracles operate on the principle that symbols and imagery enable you to connect with your own higher knowledge and receive guidance from it. The idea is that you already know the answer to your problem; you just need to be able to see it from a different perspective. Oracles provide that perspective.

The most popular tarot deck today is known as the Rider-Waite deck, created in 1909 by Pamela Colman Smith in collaboration with Arthur Edward Waite and published by William Rider and Son. Recently, innovative artists and tarot enthusiasts have begun interpreting the cards in myriad and exciting ways. Some decks incorporate cultural, philosophical, or spiritual themes into their designs. Others base their images on a specific motif, such as angels, dragons, or crystals. A number of decks combine tarot with other divination systems: astrology, the *I Ching*, or runes. U.S. Games Systems, the largest distributor of tarot decks, publishes a series of tarot encyclopedias that catalog more than 1,500 different decks dating back to the Renaissance. With so many options available, the hardest decision for many people is which deck to choose.

Tarot and the Four Elements

The four suits of the tarot symbolize the four elements discussed in Chapter 1: fire, earth, air, and water. If you look at a regular deck of playing cards, you'll see that its four suits resemble those of the tarot and correspond to the four elements as well. Chapter 9 discusses the relationship between the elements and the four principal tools used by magicians—the wand, pentacle, athame, and chalice—which appear as the four suits in tarot cards.

Tarot Suit	Poker Deck Suit	Element	Magic Tool
Wands	Clubs	Fire	Wand
Pentacles	Diamonds	Earth	Pentagram
Swords	Spades	Air	Athame
Cups	Hearts	Water	Chalice

These connections are intentional, not coincidental. The four elements comprise the energetic building blocks from which the world is structured. The tarot, therefore, is designed to take these energies into account when responding to a question or concern. The suits that appear in a reading are an important factor. They reveal the qualities or dynamics inherent in the question and suggest the modus operandi necessary to bring about a resolution.

A reading that includes many pentacles, for instance, indicates a situation that involves money, material concerns, and/or practical matters. It also may advise you to address the issue in a slow, steady, organized, or pragmatic way. If many cups appear in a reading, it's likely that you want to know about a relationship or an emotional situation. The tarot may suggest that you follow your bliss or listen to your heart.

Sample Reading

The following five-card spread can be used to gain insight into virtually any concern or situation.

1 The present or general theme of the reading

2 Past influences still having effect

3 The potential within the situation

4 The reason behind the question

5 The future

Five-card Spread

Here's an example. Maria sought advice about a potentially stressful family gathering. After shuffling and cutting the cards, she first drew the three of cups. This card represented a celebration, which clearly described the upcoming holiday get-together that Maria was worried about. The second card Maria selected was the two of swords, which showed that her relatives didn't always communicate clearly and honestly with one another. The five of wands, Maria's third card, indicated that Maria feared ego battles between family members would mar the occasion. The fourth card in Maria's spread was the Magician. This meant she should take control, using her personal power to govern the situation. It also suggested she could do a magic spell to keep peace in the family. Maria's fifth and final card, the ten of cups, told her everything would go smoothly.

Using Tarot Cards in Spells

The vivid imagery on tarot cards makes them ideal for doing magic spells. Although most people only consider the tarot as a tool for divination, you can choose individual cards from the deck to enhance spells. The prevalence of magical symbols on the cards suggests that the tarot's creators intended the oracle to be used for magic purposes, too.

You may want to select a card that represents something you desire and place it on your altar to help you focus on your intention. Say, for example, you wish to attract prosperity. Display the nine or ten of pentacles, both of which signify wealth, on your altar or in a place where you'll see the card often. If you know feng shui, put the card in your wealth gua to boost your finances.

You can also combine candles with tarot cards to work magic. Choose a card that symbolizes your intention and place it in front of a candle. Then light the candle and gaze at the card to impress the card's meaning on your subconscious. To streamline the process, some candle manufacturers produce candles with tarot card images already printed on them. Tarot cards can be incorporated into magic charms, too. Select a card from a deck you don't ordinarily use for readings and slip it into a talisman pouch, along with other magical ingredients. If you're making a love charm, for instance, choose the Lovers or the two of cups.

Some of the spells in Chapters 11 through 19 use tarot cards. These are just suggestions, however. The possibilities are virtually infinite, limited only by your imagination. Once you become familiar with the tarot, feel free to design your own spells.

The Runes

According to Norse mythology, the god Odin (or Wodin) brought the runes to human beings. For 2,000 years, this oracle was used throughout Northern Europe and Scandinavia, until 1639 when the Christian church banned it. Viking and Saxon invaders brought the runes to the British Isles. In the United States, J. R. R. Tolkien's trilogy *The Lord of the Rings* introduced many readers to the runes and Ralph Blum's bestseller, *The Book of Runes*, taught them how to use the oracle.

Early runes were carved on stones, wood, and bone. The most popular version of the runes comes from an old Teutonic alphabet, the Elder Futhark, which contains twenty-four letters. Each rune is a letter. Unlike the letters in modern alphabets, however, these ancient glyphs aren't intended simply to form words. Instead, they individually convey complex meanings.

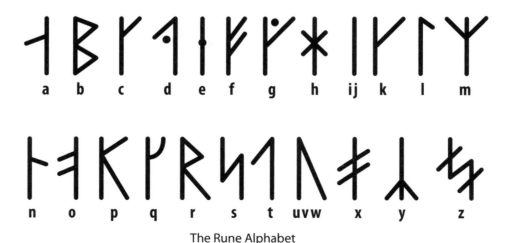

The Rune Alphabet

Each rune is named for an animal, object, condition, or deity. For instance, the rune "Uruz" correlates to the wild ox and represents the quality of strength. Although most people today don't have contact with wild oxen, the rune's inherent meaning—strength—is still relevant.

FACT

The word *rune* means a secret or mystery. It also refers to things that are whispered, to knowledge that's revealed to us during moments of stillness and contemplation. To understand the meaning of the runes, it's necessary to quiet the restless, analytical mind and allow the truth to gently penetrate into your consciousness.

The easiest way to do a reading with runes is to spread out all the rune stones in your set, then close your eyes and mix up the runes while you contemplate your question or situation. Select one. Its meaning provides the answer to your question. More complex rune readings involve casting several runes onto a cloth and interpreting their positions. Or you can lay out runes in patterns or spreads just as you might lay out cards in a tarot reading. In these instances, the positions of the runes as well as their individual meanings become significant.

Runes, like most oracles, aren't particularly good at timing events and outcomes. You probably won't be able to pinpoint when a job offer will come through or when you'll meet the love of your life. It's usually not a good idea to ask about something in the distant future, either. For best results, focus on current issues that are foremost in your mind.

Sample Reading

Brad wanted to know if he should accept a job offer he'd received. He spread out his rune stones and drew the rune Jera. This rune advised him that he could harvest rewards if he accepted the offer, but not immediately. To gain additional information, he closed his eyes, mixed up the runes, and selected three more to represent the past, the present, and the future.

Brad chose a rune called Nauthiz to symbolize his past. This rune represents limitations, and indeed, for quite a while he had been feeling stifled in his current job. Next, he drew Kano to signify the present. This rune, which means opening, suggested he was ready to receive new opportunities and responsibilities. The final rune he selected, Dagaz, in the future position showed that the new job he was considering offered a breakthrough that would lead to greater achievement.

Using Runes in Spells

Runes can be used for magical purposes as well as predictive ones. In early times, runes were carved on swords, amulets, jewelry, and household objects to encourage blessings—such as love, fertility, health, prosperity, or victory in battle—as well as to ward off harm. A runemaster was believed to possess the ability to communicate with divine forces and to command supernatural powers to do his bidding.

FACT

Usually, when people speak of the runes, they are referring to the letters in one of the old Norse alphabets. However, letters from other alphabets, such as the Irish language Ogham (which links each letter with a tree), can be used for divination, too.

You can use rune symbols in your own spells, just as the ancients did. If you're making a love charm, for example, you might want to paint the rune Gifu, which looks like an X, on a small stone and slip it into the pouch, along with other love-drawing ingredients. Carve runes that represent your intentions on a candle, and then burn it to make your wishes come true. You could also paint or inscribe runes on your magic tools to enhance their power. Leslie Wind, a jeweler in Rockport, Massachusetts, engraves runes onto pendants, rings, and earrings. Her customers wear them as handsome talismans to attract health, wealth, and happiness.

The Pendulum

A pendulum is great for obtaining information quickly, and it can be used to answer virtually any yes-or-no question. Typically, a pendulum consists of a small weight—a crystal or some other stone, for instance—hung from a chain or a piece of string. You hold the chain or string loosely, allowing the pendulum to dangle from it, while you ask your question. The pendulum responds by swinging in a certain direction. You don't jiggle the pendulum but rather allow it to move of its own accord.

> Different stones appeal to different people. A dreamy sort of person may respond best to a hematite or onyx pendulum that helps her stay grounded, whereas someone who isn't particularly intuitive might benefit from using one made of a sensitive stone, such as amethyst or moonstone.

Most of the time, if the answer to your question is "no," the pendulum will swing from side to side. A back-and-forth movement generally means the answer is "yes." However, it's a good idea to check with your pendulum before you ask any questions to determine which direction will indicate yes and which will indicate no. The motion isn't always the same for everyone.

Once you establish the significance of different directions, it's time to pose your question. Keep it simple and direct. Try to hold your hand still—you may want to rest your elbow on a table or other surface to provide support—and give the pendulum a chance to respond. Sometimes it will start swinging right away, but at other times it may take a few moments. If the pendulum swings in a diagonal line, it can mean that the matter is uncertain or that your question can't be answered at this time. If the pendulum doesn't move, you can try asking another question or phrasing the same question in a different manner.

Your pendulum might swing in a circular motion. Usually, if it moves in a clockwise direction, the situation you're asking about is favorable. If the pendulum circles in a counterclockwise direction, conditions seem unfavorable.

Once again, it's wise to confirm in advance which direction means what, to make sure you and your pendulum are both on the same page.

When you use a pendulum, you're doing a form of dowsing. Most people think of dowsing as a way of searching for water that's hidden underground. When you use a pendulum in the manner described above, however, you're dowsing your own inner wisdom. You can use a pendulum to dowse for just about anything, including underground springs or buried treasure. If you don't want to actually walk the land in search of your quarry, you can dowse a map. Hold the pendulum over a map of a particular area and ask, "Is this where [whatever you're looking for] is located?" If the response is no, try another area. Keep at it until the pendulum says yes. You could even dowse a map of a city where you wish to find an apartment—the process is a lot faster and less hassle than pounding the pavement.

FACT

Some pendulums are designed with chambers that can be "loaded" with particular substances to aid the dowser's search. Open the chamber and insert a small amount of whatever you're seeking—gold, water, oil, and so on. The pendulum, thus programmed, will lead you to that substance.

It's a good idea to cleanse your pendulum before using it. One way to do this is to hold it under running water for a few moments. If you prefer, place the pendulum on a windowsill and let the sunlight clear away any unwanted vibrations. Store your pendulum in a small pouch or wrap it in a piece of silk cloth to protect it.

Other Oracles

Almost anything can be an oracle. As a child, you may have pulled petals off a daisy to find out if the person you had a crush on loved you in return. Every time you flip a coin before making a decision, you're consulting an oracle. Some people randomly open a favorite book or religious text and consider the first passage they read to be inspired guidance.

Although some forms of divination may seem too simple or too strange to be dependable, remember that the oracle device is merely an aid to help you bypass your limited left-brain logic and access a wealth of knowledge that exists elsewhere. In fact, you are probably exposed to oracular incidents every day without ever realizing it.

Here's an example. A woman had gotten lost while driving late at night. Without a map and unable to spot any familiar landmarks, she became panicky. Suddenly a truck pulled in front of her, and she noticed the name of the supermarket chain "Safeway" painted on the trailer. She took this as a sign, and when the truck turned off the road a few miles later, she followed it. Soon she found herself on a street she recognized and was able to safely navigate her way home.

"The entire world is our mirror. The number of psychic vehicles is infinite. They depend only on the imagination of the person doing the reading."—Sarvananda Bluestone, Ph.D.

Many people might discount this incident, or others like it, as a mere coincidence. But once you start paying attention to such events, however small or subtle, you'll begin to notice that something or someone seems to be communicating with you. That's what divination is all about: receiving guidance from a source other than ordinary intellect, often through another vehicle.

Scrying

The term scrying means seeing intuitive images in a glossy surface. Crystal balls and magic mirrors aren't the only tools for scrying although they're the ones that turn up most often in fairy tales and myths. You can gaze into any reflective surface—even bathtub water or the hood of a well-waxed automobile—and watch the future unfold before you. Of course, the shiny surface doesn't contain the images you view, anymore than a movie screen does. Instead, what you see is your own thoughts, which you've projected there.

The most famous scryer was Nostradamus. The great psychic sat for hours at a time, staring into a bowl of water as visions of the future appeared before him. The notorious and often baffling quatrains he wrote to explain his visions supposedly predict events well beyond the twenty-first century.

ALERT!

In the beginning, spend only about ten minutes at a time scrying. Don't try to scry when you're tired or upset. If you don't get results right away, don't get discouraged. Try again another day. Trust your impressions, even if they don't make sense immediately.

To scry, relax your mind as you gaze into a glossy surface. Allow impressions to bubble up from your subconscious. A genuine crystal ball works well because it contains all sorts of natural irregularities, foggy wisps, and reflective planes that help trigger the imagination. Some people prefer to gaze into a candle flame or smoke rising from a fire. Others watch the changing shapes of clouds as they drift by. Whatever device you choose, the important thing is to keep an open mind. Don't doubt yourself or try to analyze what you see too closely. Just observe the images that present themselves to you. Write down your feelings as well as any visions you receive; they may mean something later on, even if you don't understand them right away.

Hand Analysis

Most people think the palm is the only part of the hand that can be read, but the fingers and back of the hand offer a wealth of information, too. In fact, everything about your hand—the skin's color and texture, the shape of the fingernails, the spaces between the fingers—provides insight into your temperament, character, and strengths and weaknesses, as well as your past and future.

The "other" hand (the one you don't ordinarily write with) shows your inherent traits and potential. Some hand readers say it also contains information about your past lifetimes. Your dominant hand reveals how you've developed your abilities. It also bears witness to important experiences in this lifetime.

The fingers are one of the most significant factors in hand analysis. Each finger is linked with a planet and the god who, according to the ancients, resided there. Hand analysts believe the finger embodies the qualities associated with that planet and god. The little finger, for instance, is called the Mercury finger; it represents your communication abilities as well as your thinking processes, which are Mercury's province. Long, graceful fingers denote a sensitive, creative, intuitive individual. Short, stubby fingers with square nails are the mark of a practical, down-to-earth person. Flexible fingers show you are adaptable and receptive; stiff fingers suggest you tend to be rigid and don't make changes easily.

FACT

Compare the skin on the hands with the skin on a person's face. The hands reveal who an individual really is; the face, on the other hand, shows how a person presents himself to the world. If a marked difference is apparent, it's likely that the person's inner and outer personalities are also quite different.

Most palms contain at least three major lines: the head line, the heart line, and the life line. Generally speaking, long, deep, unbroken lines indicate that the life areas associated with them are active and well developed. Faint lines show a lack of energy or involvement in the related area. Chained or broken lines describe disturbances or confusion. Contrary to popular belief, a long life line doesn't necessarily mean you'll live to be a hundred, but it does suggest you'll enjoy a rich, full life. Events that occur in the course of your life will register as distinctive marks on the related lines. A head injury, for example, will show up on your head line; a divorce will produce a mark on your heart line.

The mounds and valleys on the palm also tell stories. A fleshy, firm mound indicates energy is being channeled into the areas of life that correspond to that mound. A flat or flabby mound shows a lack of vitality or enthusiasm. For instance, if your mound of the moon (the bottom quarter of your palm, opposite the thumb, between your wrist and little finger) is well developed, it's likely that you possess a keen intuition and strong emotions.

Your hands continue to change throughout your life, and not only because of age, injuries, or general wear-and-tear. You can chronicle your life by photographing or photocopying your hands every few years and comparing the differences.

Chapter 5

Predictive Systems

What if you want to look more than a few months into the future? Is there a way to discern what's likely to happen years from now? Absolutely. The two most reliable and comprehensive predictive systems are astrology and numerology. Both have been used for millennia to provide insight into the past, present, and future. You don't have to be psychic to excel at astrology or numerology. With training, dedication, and practice, virtually anyone can develop the skill necessary to understand and use these systems.

Numerology

When you balance your checkbook or tally your points at the end of a game of bridge, you don't think of numbers as anything more than a way of keeping score. But numbers are more than a convenient form of measurement. They also possess secret meanings that early metaphysicians employed as a means of communicating occult information. The mystical and symbolic qualities inherent in numbers also make them important in spell-working.

"Those who deepen themselves in what is called in the Pythagorean sense 'the study of numbers' will learn through this symbolism of numbers to understand life and the world."—Rudolf Steiner

The Greek mathematician and philosopher, Pythagoras, who lived in the sixth century B.C.E., is usually credited with having developed the system of numerology that's used today. The study of numbers, known as gematria, is also based in esoteric Judaism and the Qabalah. This practice attaches a number equivalent to each letter in a word. Although gematria was initially connected with the Hebrew language, its tenets can be applied to any language.

Table of Number-Letter Correspondences

1	2	3	4	5	6	7	8	9
A	B	C	D	E	F	G	H	I
J	K	L	M	N	O	P	Q	R
S	T	U	V	W	X	Y	Z	

Additionally, each number possesses certain characteristics or resonances. The numbers on tarot cards depict these inner meanings graphically, and indeed, there's a strong link between tarot and numerology. Numbers also play key roles in astrology, feng shui, and other magical practices.

Numbers and Their Meanings

0	Wholeness, all and nothing
(1)	Beginnings, individuality, initiative
2	Polarity, partnership, duality, balance
3	Creativity, self-expression, expansion, positive developments, good fortune
(4)	Form, stability, permanence, order
(5)	Change, instability, communication
6	Give and take, cooperation, love, beauty, harmony
7	Retreat, introspection, rest, spirituality
8	Material mastery, manifestation, responsibility, sincerity, practical matters
9	Transition, completion, fulfillment, abundance
11	Humanitarianism, higher knowledge, insight
22	Spiritual power, wisdom, mastery beyond the physical realm

In casting spells, these numeric associations become significant, as you'll soon discover. The number three, in particular, is often used to seal, complete, or activate a spell. Because three points are necessary to form a plane, this number signifies bringing an intention into the physical realm, literally making it three-dimensional.

What's in a Name?

To someone who understands numerology, a name reveals a great deal about a given individual. Numbers define your personality, your role in life, and to some extent your destiny. If you change your name, as many actors and writers do, your life will change, too.

What does your name say about you? To find out, write down your full birth name. Then refer to the table of number-letter correspondences above and assign numbers to the letters in your name. Numerologists consider vowels to have different meanings than consonants. Therefore, you'll want to distinguish between the numbers that relate to vowels and those that relate to consonants; for example:

1	6					6			9		6
H	A	R	O	L	D	J	O	H	N	B	I	S	H	O	P
8	9		3	4	1		8	5	2		1	8		7

The next step is to add the numbers, starting with the vowels. In the name above, the vowel numbers total 28. The sum of the consonants is 56. To produce a single-digit number as shown in the table of number-letter correspondences, add the digits in each two-digit number together until you get a single-digit number. For example, if you add 2 + 8 (the vowel total) you get 10; you'll need to add 1 + 0 to reduce the sum to a single-digit number: 1. Repeat this procedure for the consonants. When you add 5 + 6 together, the result is 11. You could add 1 + 1 to get 2, but numerologists usually don't reduce the double numbers.

Double numbers—11, 22, and so on—are called master numbers. These numbers are considered to resonate at a higher vibration that reflects a higher level of consciousness. People whose names contain master numbers may experience greater challenges, responsibilities, opportunities, and achievements in their lives.

Your Soul Urge

The sum of your vowels is considered the soul urge. Sometimes called your motivation number, it corresponds to your inner desires, the fundamental urge or energy that propels you to act. It indicates who you are at your deepest level, your innate abilities, emotions, hopes, needs, and dreams. In astrology, this correlates with your moon and its position in the birth chart.

If your soul urge number is one, as in the example above, you tend to be independent and self-motivated. If two is your number, you're likely to be cooperative and flexible, willing to consider other people as well as yourself.

Your Outer Personality

The number that results from the sum of your consonants is called your outer personality number. This is the face you show to the world and corresponds to your sun in astrology. Your public image, the way you behave in social situations, and the way you like to view yourself are all described by this number.

For example, if your outer personality number is three, you're sociable and expansive, and you express yourself in creative ways. If the sum of your consonants is four, you tend to be practical, dependable, and orderly.

Your Destiny

Numerologists call the sum of all the letters in your name your destiny number. Although this may sound rather fatalistic, it really shows your objective in life or your life work. Many people express this through their careers, but it could be more accurately thought of as your "work" not your "job." An artist, for instance, might earn a living as a computer programmer, even though his true *raison d'être* is to create works of beauty.

If your destiny number is five, your purpose in life is to teach others, to communicate ideas, and to encourage change and personal growth. A person whose destiny number is six may devote herself to nurturing a family and providing a comfortable, beautiful home for others to enjoy.

Life Cycles

Perhaps you've noticed that different years appear to have particular themes, qualities, or "flavors." Some years tend to be filled with activity and change, while others seem comparatively quiet. A year of contemplation and study might be followed by a year of travel or career advancement. One of socializing may be followed by one of retreat and solitude.

As in astrology, the predictive side of numerology begins with your birth date. To find this baseline number, add together the month, day, and year of your birth to produce what's called your personal year. Let's say you were born on September 6, 1970. You'd do the math this way:

$$9 + 6 + 1 + 9 + 7 + 0 = 31$$

Again, you want to reduce the sum to a single-digit, so add $3 + 1 = 4$.

From this point, you can track the cycles of your life to see what lies ahead.

FACT

Your personal year runs from one birthday to the next, not from January 1 to December 31. Personal years can be determined by adding the month and day of your birth to the current year or any other year you want to know more about. From the viewpoint of numerology, you experience nine distinct cycles, each lasting a year.

The following table briefly describes the essence of the nine yearly cycles and indicates where you are likely to focus your attention during those years.

Personal Year Cycle	Your Focus for the Year
1	New beginnings, action, independence, self-interest
2	Cooperation, partnerships, balance, developing plans
3	Expansion, travel, creativity, opportunity, personal growth
4	Stability, building, organization, financial matters, security
5	Communication, change, movement, sharing ideas
6	Give and take, balance, domesticity, love, comfort, beauty
7	Rest, retreat, withdrawal, introspection, healing
8	Manifestation, responsibility, power, managing resources
9	Fulfillment, completion, endings, transition, wisdom

Want to know what's in store for you in 2012? Add the month and day of your birth to the year 2012. Using the example above, you'd get $9 + 6 + 2 + 0 + 1 + 2 = 20$, which reduces to 2. This means you'll be in a "two year" in 2012, which suggests that cooperation, partnership, and balancing the polarities in life should become priorities for you.

Astrology

For thousands of years, people have gazed at the stars and considered how the heavenly bodies affected life on earth. Some researchers believe the pyramids were erected as astrological/astronomical observatories. Stonehenge, built about 4,000 years ago, is a tool for the accurate prediction of the solstices, eclipses, and other celestial events. Throughout history, the wealthy and powerful, as well as ordinary individuals, have sought guidance from astrologers. Financier J. Pierpont Morgan once commented on his use of astrology, saying, "Millionaires don't use astrology; billionaires do."

Contrary to popular belief, astrology does not consist of the daily horoscopes you see in your local newspaper. Like Chinese fortune cookies, those are fun to read but not particularly useful. Real astrology is an ancient, complex, and fascinating scientific art that takes many years of study to understand. Marc Edmund Jones, one of the greatest astrologers of the twentieth century, once said that he'd studied astrology for fifty years and had barely scratched the surface.

Astrology can tell you what career is right for you, where the best place is for you to live, how you'll get along with another person, what health issues you're likely to experience, and a whole lot more. You can use astrology to solve crimes or make savvy financial investments. Contemporary astrologers are continually discovering new ways to use this ancient practice—there's probably no limit to its possibilities.

The Birth Chart

When someone asks, "What's your sign?" she's really asking "Where was the sun positioned in the sky on the day you were born?" Astrology divides the sky into twelve sectors and links them with the signs of the zodiac. From Earth, the sun appears to travel through all twelve sectors during the course of a year, spending about thirty days in each sign. This is the simplest (and most simplistic) form of astrology, usually called sun sign astrology. It has

Zodiac Wheel

some validity, but at the same time this method is too general to offer much insight.

Like most of the arts and sciences, astrology contains many different branches and many schools of thought. The one most people are familiar with is called natal astrology. A natal or birth chart is based on the date, time, and place of your birth. An astrologer calculates the positions of the sun, moon, planets, and other significant heavenly bodies to produce a blueprint of your innate talents, life challenges, potentials, traits, and characteristics. The birth chart thus provides a detailed and amazingly precise picture of you.

ALERT!

Because human beings are mainly concerned about what's happening on Earth, most astrological charts are based on a geocentric perspective, that is, from the vantage point of Earth. From this perspective, the sun appears to travel across the sky, though of course that's not really the case. Heliocentric astrology considers the positions of the planets and their cycles as if they were begin viewed from the sun.

The sun isn't the only heavenly body that has a sign associated with it. The moon, planets, and asteroids—everything in the sky, in fact—were also positioned in zodiac signs at the moment of your birth. You not only have a sun sign, you also have a moon sign, a Mercury sign, a Venus sign, and so on. Each body possesses its own inherent energy, nature, and mode of expression, and each governs a particular area of your life. Venus, for instance, rules relationships. The zodiac signs color the energies of these bodies and influence their expression. Therefore, a person with Venus in Taurus will experience relationships differently than someone with Venus in Sagittarius.

A birth chart resembles a wheel with twelve spokes or a pie cut into twelve pieces. Each of these pieces is called a house. (These divisions are determined by mathematical calculations too involved to cover here, but you can find many good books devoted to the subject.) The houses represent the areas in your life: money and material resources, partnerships, home and family, and so on. The heavenly bodies fall into one or another of these houses. Astrologers look to see which bodies occupy which houses in order to understand how things are likely to play out for you in the various parts of your life.

The relationships between the sun, moon, and planets are significant, too. Depending on their positions at the time of your birth, some celestial bodies will likely form special connections, known as aspects, with each other. When two or more bodies are linked by an aspect, they influence each other. Some connections are harmonious and supportive, but others cause stress and challenges.

"Astrology [shows us] that there is a rhythm to the universe and that man's own life partakes of this rhythm."—Henry Miller

Of course, there's a great deal more to natal astrology than this chapter has touched on, but these are a few of the basic details to remember. The birth chart is the starting point for predictive astrology. From here, an astrologer can look at the positions of the heavenly bodies at any given time in the future or calculate other types of charts and give you a good idea of what lies ahead.

Predicting the Future

For predictive purposes, Western astrologers examine the movements of the celestial bodies in relationship to a natal chart. As the relationship between Earth and the heavens changes, your life changes, too. Astrologers use a variety of methods to calculate and predict these changes, including transits, solar returns, and progressed charts.

Transits refer to the passage of the sun, moon, and planets through your birth chart at any given time. As the heavenly bodies move, they activate factors in your natal chart, causing you to feel or behave or experience life in certain predictable ways. For instance, if Uranus transits your fourth house, which corresponds to the home, you might relocate. If it hits your natal Venus, the planet of relationships, you might get divorced. Because the planets closest to Earth move more rapidly than those farther away, the influences of their transits are felt for a shorter period of time. Outer-planet transits can affect you for months, even years.

FACT

You can look up the exact positions of the sun, moon, and planets on any given day in a book called an ephemeris. These tables of planetary motion list the heavenly bodies according to the signs and degrees in which they're located on every day of the year. Usually the data are arranged by month and grouped into a volume that covers a year, a decade, or even an entire century.

A solar return chart can be drawn up each year to give you an overview of your personal year, which means from one birthday to the next. This chart is based on the precise moment in any given year when the sun is in exactly the same place (relative to the Earth's position) as it was at the time of your birth. To construct a solar return chart, use the month, day, and time of your birth, but instead of your birth year, use the year you want to know about. If you are living somewhere other than the place where you were born, calculate the chart for the place you're living now.

A solar return chart can be read separately or in connection with the natal chart. It shows what areas of your life will be emphasized during the year and lets you predict broad patterns that will prevail. Often, it will support the information presented by transits or progressions. Many people find lunar return charts valuable, too. These charts are calculated for the moment when the moon returns to the exact position it occupied in your natal chart, which it does at least once a month. Because the moon is especially important in magic work, lunar charts can help you pinpoint the most auspicious times for casting certain types of spells.

Progressions also provide an excellent way to predict broad patterns for a year. In this type of astrology, your chart is advanced a day for every year you've been alive. Let's say you were born on March 11, 1965. To see what the year 2015 would hold for you, you would count forward fifty days, and then calculate a chart for that date. What you have now is a progressed chart that lets you see what to expect during the fiftieth year of your life. You can also use progressions to examine particular years in your past.

Other types of charts can be cast to reveal various things about the future, too. Each chart offers its own unique data and insights. A horary chart answers a specific question, such as "Should I take this job?" or "What will my life be like if I marry this person?" An astrologer calculates the chart according to the date, time, and place where he or she understands the question—the seeker's birth information isn't relevant. Patterns and symbols contained within the horary chart answer the question and usually provide related information as well. Because horary charts don't follow the same rules as natal charts, and because they also require a great deal of astrological expertise to interpret, they aren't used as widely as other types of charts.

Event charts provide information about a situation or event. For example, you might want to know how a certain election will turn out. You could calculate a chart for the date and time the polls close. The chart would reveal not only who will win the election but also the conditions surrounding the election and what effects this will have on the city, state, or nation. Astrologers often cast charts for presidential elections, and they study the transits to these charts along with the birth charts of the candidates. You can do an event chart for just about any occurrence: a plane crash, a Super Bowl game, a medical procedure, a college graduation, or a marriage.

A Time for Magic

By now you've probably noticed there are many ties between magic and astrology. When doing magic spells, it's a good idea to take astrological influences into account in order to choose the most auspicious times to perform spells and rituals.

ALERT!

Every four months, Mercury goes retrograde for approximately three weeks and appears to be moving backward. Because Mercury rules communication and thinking in general, your mind might not be as clear as usual during retrograde periods, and your ability to communicate with others may be hampered. Usually, these aren't good times to do magic, as confusion and mistakes can occur.

Aligning yourself with planetary energies that support the nature of your spells can improve their effectiveness. Venus's influences, for instance, can enhance love spells. Jupiter's positive vibes can be an asset when you're doing spells for career success or financial growth.

Moon Magic

In early agrarian cultures, our forebears planted crops and bred animals in accordance with the moon's cycles. Today, the moon's influence on fertility, crop cycles, the ocean's tides, and mundane affairs is still evident. In terms of casting spells, the moon is the most important of the heavenly bodies to consider. Magicians often time their spells to correspond to the movements of the "lesser light," perhaps because the moon rules intuition and the emotions, two parts of the psyche that strongly influence magic.

As you probably know, the moon's cycle consists of approximately twenty-eight days. Its waxing phase—the two weeks between the new and full moons—represents a period of growth. This is the best time to do spells designed to encourage increase, attraction, or prosperity. If you wish to attract a romantic partner, improve your finances, or boost your career options, do magic during the moon's waxing phase. As the moon's light grows, so will your blessings.

On the other hand, if your goal is to end something or decrease its role in your life, do magic while the moon is waning. As the moon's shape diminishes, so will the matter about which you're concerned. This two-week period is perfect for spells that involve such things as breaking old romantic ties, losing weight, eliminating bad habits, and reducing responsibilities at home or work.

Because the new moon supports the inception of new ideas, plans, projects, relationships, and activities, this phase augurs well for spells that involve beginnings. The full moon, two weeks later, will show the development of whatever you initiated during the new moon when the seeds you planted under the new moon bear fruit. In the bright light of the full moon, you can clearly see how your goals are shaping up and what steps you need to take (if any) to bring them to fruition.

The moon's sign can influence a spell, too. Do love spells when the moon is in Libra, money spells when it's in Taurus, and travel spells when it's in Sagittarius. The moon remains in a sign for about two and a half days and completes a circuit of all twelve of the zodiac signs each month. Check an ephemeris to determine which days will support your intentions.

FACT

Despite the many sophisticated scientific developments in modern-day agribusiness, the *Farmers' Almanac* still publishes information about lunar cycles. It's not uncommon for farmers who employ advanced technical methods to also believe that the moon influences planting and harvesting cycles. Magicians, too, realize that you can reap greater harvests if you sow seeds (physically or symbolically) when the moon's position supports growth.

Power Days

The ancients believed that a particular deity and/or planet governed each day of the week. You'll notice that the names of the days derive from the heavenly bodies and the gods and goddesses who rule them.

Day of the Week	Ruling Planet/Deity
Monday	Moon
Tuesday (*Mardi* in French)	Mars
Wednesday (*Mercredi* in French)	Mercury
Thursday	Jupiter (Thor, in Norse mythology)
Friday (*Vendredi* in French)	Venus (Freya, in Norse mythology)
Saturday	Saturn
Sunday	Sun

In order to tip the odds in your favor, try to align the type of spell you're doing with the most propitious day of the week. Most love spells, for instance, should be done on Friday. Perform spells to bring success or money on Thursday.

Magic by the Numbers

Keep numbers and numerological cycles in mind, too, when you're doing magic spells. Remember, numbers are symbols, and your subconscious quickly recognizes the inherent meanings within symbols. And, as already discussed, numbers possess specific vibrations that can enhance your spells. Refer to the table on page 67 to determine which numbers are best suited to your intentions.

Lucky Numbers

Here's an easy way to incorporate the power of numbers into your spells. Decide which number relates to your objective. Two, for example, is the number of partnerships, so it's the logical choice when you're doing love spells. If you're making a love talisman, place two items in a pouch, perhaps a piece of rose quartz and a red rosebud. Or burn two candles, one to represent each person in the relationship.

You can also tie your intentions into knots. Let's say you want to stabilize your finances. The best number for this purpose is four. You could make a money charm and secure the pouch with a gold ribbon. Tie four knots in the ribbon and concentrate on your goal each time you tie a knot. Or tie a ribbon around your bills, using four knots to limit the outflow of money.

Your Days Are Numbered

When doing spells, consider the personal year cycle you're in at present. You'll get the best results if you time your spells to correspond to the nature of your current cycle. Spells to promote creativity, for instance, will be more successful if done during a three year than during a four year. Love spells can benefit from the energy present during a two or a six year.

Of course, you may not want to wait until the ideal year rolls around to perform a magic spell. If time is of the essence, you could do a spell when the month, day, and year add up to a number that corresponds to your intention. Let's say you're working on a group project and want to ensure that the participants cooperate effectively. Six is the number of give and take. Therefore, May 1, 2007 (5/1/2007) would be a good time to do your spell because the numbers add up to fifteen and reduce to six.

The day of your birth is also an auspicious day. If you were born on the eighth of the month, eight is one of your lucky numbers. By doing spells on the eighth of any month, you tap the fortunate aspects of your birth number.

In Chapters 11 through 19, you'll find spells that utilize the power of numbers and astrological influences to enhance their effectiveness. As you become adept at magical work, you'll discover your own original ways to bring these energies into your spells and rituals.

Chapter 6

Many Types of Magic

Magic and magicians exist everywhere, and they always have. Archaeologists believe the animal images found on cave walls, such as those at Lascaux, France, may have been painted by shamans more than 30,000 years ago to bring hunters good luck. Medieval tradesmen, members of secret guilds that spawned the Freemasons, worked a type of magic when they created the famous rose windows for Europe's great cathedrals. Today, as in ancient times, magic is alive and well and being practiced in myriad forms throughout the world.

Shamanism

One of the earliest depictions of a shaman was found in France, in the cave of Les Trois Freres. Estimated to be at least 15,000 years old, it shows a sorcerer disguised as a bison and armed with a bow. Originally, the term *shaman* referred to a Siberian medicine man, but it can apply to anyone who engages in shamanistic practices, regardless of the era and society in which the person lives. In simple terms, a shaman is someone who understands both the spirit world and the natural world and who uses that knowledge of these worlds to provide healing, guidance, and protection to his people.

In *Elements of Shamanism,* Neville Drury writes, "The sorcerer was a master of wild animals—able to control their fate through his hunting magic, an adept at disguises, and a practitioner of animal sacrifice . . . the Paleolithic hunter-sorcerer was a precursor of the archetypal native shaman with his animal familiars, his clan totems, and his belief that he could transform his consciousness into an animal form."

FACT

In the 1970s, the bestselling books of Carlos Castaneda introduced readers to the concepts of shamanism. Castaneda wrote about his five-year apprenticeship with a teacher whom he called Don Juan, and described his experiences in what he termed "nonordinary states of reality." He also discussed shapeshifting, a shamanic practice that involved projecting his own consciousness into animals and plants.

English anthropologist Sir Edward Taylor termed this kind of belief system animism, from the Latin word *anima,* which means soul. It fits the world of prehistoric humans, who believed everything—not just humans, but animals, plants, stones, clothing, weapons, and the Earth itself—had souls. According to this philosophy, the human spirit was as malleable as air, capable of entering other people, animals, and even objects.

Other Realities

From the shamanic perspective, the physical world is only one facet of reality. Many other realms exist, and it's possible to travel to these other realities at will. Shamans have learned to erase the barriers that ordinarily separate the physical and nonphysical realms in order to "walk between the worlds."

Often this is accomplished via astral projection, a technique that allows the spirit to journey freely while the physical body remains in a trance-like state. The spirit is also able to temporarily leave the body during sleep and to explore the nonphysical planes. In these other levels of reality, the shaman might meet entities that once occupied human bodies as well as gods, goddesses, and other beings that have never incarnated. When journeying in this way, shamans may seek the assistance of spirit animals or other guides to provide protection and direction.

Native American Shamanism

Among the indigenous people of North, Central, and South America, shamans have long served as medicine men, midwives, visionaries, and healers. These shamans worked with the forces of nature, the deities and ancestors in the spirit realms, and totem animals to ensure the well being of their tribes. Their close connection with the Earth and their understanding of celestial patterns underpinned their magical practices.

Traditionally, each tribe established special affinities with certain animals, which became the tribe's totems or sacred animals. These animal guardians conveyed protection, guidance, healing, and insight, and they assisted the shamans' personal spirit guides in magical work. Shamans can also reach across the worlds into the spirit realm to seek the aid of the ancestors—entities no longer in the physical realm—in matters concerning their people.

As seers and diviners, Native American shamans use drumming, dancing, herbs and botanical substances, fasting, and other practices to induce altered states of consciousness. While in these trance states, the shamans journey beyond the limitations of matter and space to pursue knowledge, communicate with entities in the spirit world, effect healing, and observe the future. Dreams, too, provide access into other levels of reality. Shamans also confront harmful energies operating in the etheric or spirit realm in order to diminish their powers in the earthly sphere or to exorcise them from the bodies of human beings.

You, too, can employ drumming, dancing, visualization, and other shamanic techniques to journey into the spirit world. The beings you meet there—your own relatives now deceased, spirit guides, animal guardians, and others—are usually willing to provide advice and insights. Treat them with respect and, perhaps, bring them gifts when you go to meet them. In time, you can develop special relationships with congenial entities that will serve as your teachers.

Celtic Shamanism

Although the Celts themselves didn't use the word *shamanism,* their spiritual paths encompassed many of the practices and perceptions of shamans the world over. Instead, the Celts referred to their wise men and women as *filidh* (vision poets), *taibhsear* (vision seers), and *awenydd* (inspired ones).

Caitlin and John Matthews, two British authors who have written extensively about Celtic spiritual traditions, explain that shamans are individuals who "act as walkers between the worlds, interpreters of the spirit realms." These individuals, known as the *aes dana,* journey to what might be considered parallel universes and converse with spirit beings residing there in order to gain wisdom, healing advice, and other knowledge that can benefit people on Earth.

Celtic shamans explore what's known as the Otherworld, which is essentially a place of wisdom, creativity, and imagination, similar to what C. G. Jung called the collective unconscious. Dreams, visions, poetry, music, and other forms of creative inspiration derive from the Otherworld. Shamans may also visit the faery realm, the image world or etheric template from which life on Earth evolves.

Spirit Animals, Guides, and Guardians

Shamans consider all creatures great and small to be teachers and guides. Animals, birds, reptiles, and insects—both in the physical world and in the spirit realm—possess certain powers and qualities that they willingly lend human beings. Bears, for instance, are known for their strength, protectiveness, and loyalty. Swans embody grace and beauty.

According to shamanic tradition, all human beings have a spirit or totem animal that serves as a guardian and helper throughout their lives. Some say the characteristics of your spirit animal live within you. For example, if your spirit animal is a cat, you may be clever, quick, and curious. You can call upon your animal guardian whenever you need help, and it will lend its unique abilities to you.

ALERT!

Pay attention whenever you see an animal, bird, reptile, or insect, especially if the sighting happens at a time or in a place that seems out of the ordinary. It may be a message that you need to integrate that animal's innate characteristics into your own life.

One concept suggests that animal guardians are the spirit forms of creatures that once lived on earth and that after death moved into the spirit realm, where they now act as teachers and guides. At times, they may appear to you as physical beings. Other times, they show up in your dreams to convey messages. Spirit animals often accompany shamans when they journey into nonphysical realms of experience. In certain situations, a shaman might assume the form of an animal, bird, reptile, or insect in order to perform a specific task or role. This is called shape shifting.

Power Objects

According to anthropologist Michael Harner, founder of the Foundation for Shamanic Studies in Mill Valley, California, power objects are ordinary objects that can be used in a medicine bundle. Many people collect power objects—a special memento from a trip, a pretty feather found in a field, a smooth stone taken from a riverbed—without realizing it. In a sense, a power object is a mnemonic tool for the shaman. When he handles it, he is able to recall his magical experiences.

Power objects may be displayed on your altar or in another special place in your home. Shamans often put them in a medicine bundle, a packet or pouch that contains a number of treasured items that evoke spiritual connections. Quartz crystals have been prized as power objects among shamans of nearly every culture and geographic location. Because quartz crystals are considered living rock—actual life forms—they possess special abilities that can assist the shaman's work and should be treated with respect.

"When you start your own medicine bundle, it is desirable to acquire at least one quartz crystal to put into it," Harner advises. "Such crystals are the center of power in many shamans' medicine bundles or kits. Their power diffuses through the bundle and helps to energize and maintain the living aspect of the power objects."

"If you have a visionary experience or sense power at a particular location, look about you and see if something distinctive is lying there for you to put into your bundle."—Dr. Michael Harner

Crane bags serve a similar purpose for Celtic shamans. The items gathered in a crane bag represent otherworldly powers. Usually, these are encountered during a shamanic journey; however, objects with special significance might be given as gifts or acquired in other ways. A medicine bundle or crane bag should not be opened, nor should the objects contained within it be idly shown to anyone else. Shamans guard these treasures carefully and may pass them down to subsequent generations of magic workers.

Druid Magic

The word *druid* derives from the Indo-European root *drui,* meaning "oak," as well as "solid and true." Originally, druids served as the bards, teachers, healers, judges, scribes, seers, astrologers, and spiritual leaders of the ancient Celts. They conducted rites and rituals, divined the future, healed the sick, kept the history of their people, and addressed legal matters within their communities. These wise men and women were highly revered and wielded authority second only to the king's.

Much of what's known today about the early druids has been handed down through oral tradition, folklore, legends, songs, and poetry. As the Romans and Christianity moved into Ireland and Britain, the conquerors destroyed the druids and their tradition. Thus, most of druidic history remains shrouded in mystery.

FACT

Maya MaGee Sutton, Ph.D., and Nicholas R. Mann, authors of *Druid Magic,* explain that in contemporary Irish dictionaries, the word *draiocht* means "magic" as well as "spells." Its root, *draoi*, translates as "magician," "sorcerer," or "druid." This suggests a strong connection between the druids and the practice of magic.

Modern-day druids follow some of the beliefs and practices of their early ancestors. With little actual information available about the old ways, however, neo-druids interpret the spiritual tradition by blending ancient with contemporary wisdom. A reverence for nature, knowledge of astrology and divination, healing, and shamanic journeying continue to be part of today's druidic practice.

Tree Magic

The druids consider trees to be sacred. Oaks, in particular, have long been linked with druid spirituality. Sacred rituals were—and still are—performed in oak groves. Trees are believed to embody wisdom that can be passed along to human beings. The Celtic World Tree, which connects the Upper, Middle, and Lower Worlds, or realms of existence, is a symbolic composite of all species of trees and incorporates all their qualities.

Each tree possesses certain characteristics and unique properties that druid magicians use. Rowan trees, for instance, offer protection. Oaks confer strength and endurance. Holly, with its spiked leaves that can withstand even the harshest winters, symbolizes courage. Willows are associated with divination and intuition. Poplars represent death and rebirth.

Trees play an integral role in the druids' magical practice, and they can help you as well. The early Celts often burned the wood of sacred trees in ritual fires, a practice that continues today, especially at Beltane and Yule. Here are a few other suggestions:

- Tie ribbons on the branches of trees to attract blessings.
- Hang the boughs of trees associated with protection above the doors to your home.
- Include the bark or leaves of trees that represent your intentions in talismans or amulets.
- If you're skilled at herbalism, use bark, roots, and leaves in healing poultices or teas.
- Or just sit under a tree and let it convey its wisdom to you.

Ogham

Each of the twenty letters in the ancient Celtic tree alphabet Ogham (pronounced *oh-am*) corresponds to a tree. B, or Beth, for instance, is linked with the birch; N, or Nion represents the ash. The letters look like a series of

Ogham Script

straight and angled lines, or notches, cut along a central line or stave.

A word or phrase written in Ogham looks a bit like a tree limb with branches sprouting from it. Throughout Ireland and Britain you can see standing stones engraved with Ogham glyphs. Early Celtic manuscripts also feature Ogham script.

Another unique characteristic of Ogham is that it can be signed with the fingers. Using a part of the body—the torso, nose, or leg—as a center dividing line, you can extend your fingers on either side to form letters.

Because the Celts and Druids considered trees to be sacred, the Ogham letters also serve as mystical symbols. Like the Norse runes, discussed in Chapter 4, Ogham glyphs can be inscribed on pieces of wood or stone and used as an oracle. You can also draw a single letter or write a phrase in Ogham and add it to a magic charm. For example, the letter L, which corresponds to the rowan tree, could be included in a protection amulet.

Wicca

Few spiritual paths have been so maligned, and for so long, as witchcraft. During the "burning times" in Europe and North America, tens of thousands of people—some accounts say millions, mostly women and girls—were executed as witches. Even today, many practicing witches hide their beliefs for fear of persecution.

An Anglo-Saxon word, *wicca* means wise. Some Wiccans and witches practice in groups or covens, but others observe their beliefs in a solitary fashion. Like the druids, Wiccans revere nature and attempt to live in harmony with the Earth and the cosmos. Although Wiccans observe certain customs, rituals, and practices, it is a flexible and living religion, with no dogma, no sacred texts, and no laws save one: Do no harm.

The eight Wiccan holidays, known as sabbats, mark the passage of the sun through the sky and are celebrated when the sun reaches certain degrees in the astrological calendar. These dates align with the old Celtic holy days: the solstices and equinoxes, and the cross-quarter days that fall halfway between these four spokes in what's known as the Wheel of the Year.

Magic is central to the practice of witchcraft. When casting spells, witches work with the forces of nature, with divine powers, and with their own inner wisdom. Wiccan magic relies heavily on symbolism. An object may represent a person or an intention. An herb might symbolize a particular emotion, and a candle of a certain color could stand for a desired outcome. The person casting the spell imbues the symbols with power.

Although many people erroneously connect witchcraft with black magic, Wiccans are less likely than non-witches to practice the black arts because they understand the boomerang effect of misusing power. As the Wiccan Rede states, "What ye send forth comes back to thee." Like their ancestors in pre-Christian Europe, today's Wiccans focus on magic that involves healing, protection, the knowledge of plants, and divination through the tarot, astrology, runes, a pendulum, or other oracles.

A New Look at an Old Religion

Wicca is actually a new religion based on an old one. Its heritage dates back to the "Old Religion" of pre-Christian Europe, especially that of the early Celts. Its roots also dig deeply into prehistoric times and the ancient fertility goddesses worshiped by Paleolithic peoples. However, Wicca itself developed in the twentieth century and gained a following during the 1960s and 1970s as feminism emerged. Like all belief systems, Wicca continues to evolve, and various branches, each with somewhat different views, already exist.

"Spells . . . go one step further than most forms of psychotherapy. They allow us not only to listen to and interpret the unconscious, but also to speak to it, in the language it understands."—Starhawk

Although Wicca is a pagan religion, not all pagans are witches. Originally, *pagan* was a derogatory term used by Christians to describe country people who upheld the old religions. Generally speaking, pagans take a polytheistic view of divinity and recognize the sacred in nature. Additionally, Wiccans consider themselves witches, but not all witches are Wiccans.

Revering the Goddess

Perhaps the main reason for Wicca's rapid growth is that it's one of the few spiritual paths that honors both feminine and masculine deities. For women, many of whom were raised in patriarchal religions, Wicca offers balance and equality. "In Wicca, the Goddess is seen as the creator of all that is," explains Debbie Michaud in *The Healing Traditions & Spiritual Practices of Wicca*. "She represents the power of the feminine, and a way to connect to all life on this planet."

A male witch is not called a warlock (a Scottish term that means "oath breaker"). Instead, he is also a witch. Although women outnumber men in Wicca, men are welcome and even encouraged to follow this spiritual path. Some covens are headed by both a high priestess and a high priest.

The Goddess is depicted in three aspects—maiden, mother, and crone—that signify the three phases of womanhood. Wiccans also see Mother Earth as a manifestation of the Goddess. God, the masculine principle, is considered to be the Goddess's equal and is often viewed as her consort; both energies must be present for wholeness to exist. The Goddess is linked with the moon, the God with the sun. Many Wiccan rituals and sabbats are based on the changing relationships between the Earth and these heavenly bodies.

Ritual Magic

Also called high or ceremonial magic, ritual magic evolved out of the teachings of early mystery schools in various parts of the world. The Hermetic Order of the Golden Dawn, an organization that formed in the latter part of the nineteenth century as a secret society, has greatly influenced this type of magic and its practice today. The group's philosophy is founded on the Hebrew Qabalah and the doctrines of Hermes Trismegistus, and draws upon the belief systems of the Freemasons, Rosicrucians, Gnostics, and others.

More formalized and intellectualized than Wicca and other pagan spiritual paths, ritual magic involves study of the Qabalah, astrology, alchemy, tarot, and many other subjects. It emphasizes the use of ritual and ceremony, along with mental training, to facilitate spiritual enlightenment, healing, extrasensory powers, and understanding of the cosmic order. Carl Weschcke, president of the publishing company Llewellyn Worldwide, has called this field of magic "spiritual technology."

The Importance of Ritual and Ceremony

Both religious and secular ceremonies include rituals in their observances. Rituals focus the mind and remove the practitioner from the everyday world into a magical one—that's the main reason for enacting them. Rituals rely on symbolic associations that the magician's senses and subconscious mind intuitively understand. Gestures, diagrams, postures, words, images, sounds, scents, and colors all play symbolic roles in magic rituals and ceremonies.

Ritual magic often involves elaborate and carefully orchestrated practices that are designed for various purposes. Purification rituals, for instance, cleanse the mind, body, and energy field. Protection rituals, such as the Lesser Banishing Ritual of the Pentagram, define sacred space and prevent unwanted influences from interfering. Rituals of evocation invite otherworldly entities to assist you or might bring an aspect of yourself into visible manifestation. The rituals themselves are magical acts; however, other facets of magic, such as spell-working or consecrating magical tools, may accompany a formal ritual.

The Qabalah

The Qabalah (sometimes spelled Kabbala, Cabala, and other ways) is a body of collected teachings that underlies Judaism mysticism. The Zohar is considered the Qabalah's central book. The Qabalah includes four sections that cover doctrines, magical practices, orally conveyed wisdom, and techniques for working with words, letters, and numbers.

The Tree of Life as described in the Qabalah plays an important part in ritual magic. It shows the stages of development and pathways to spiritual enlightenment. Usually it's depicted as a geometric design with ten spheres called sephiroth (which represent emanations of God) connected by

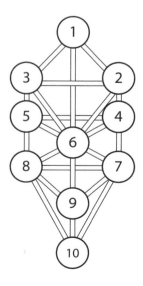

The Tree of Life

twenty-two lines or paths. The diagram symbolizes the descent of God into matter and the ascent of humanity back to the Divine.

Sex Magic

Mystical rites, rituals, and ceremonies involving sex have been practiced in numerous cultures, East and West, for longer than anyone can document. Early Celts engaged in sexual activity, particularly during the spring planting season and on Beltane, as a form of sympathetic magic to encourage the land's fertility. Temple priestesses in ancient Greece combined sex and mysticism. Tantric yoga channels sexual energy toward spiritual goals and also promotes health and longevity. Early Jewish mysticism contained sexual components in its rituals and spirituality. In Wicca's Great Rite, a couple invites the God and Goddess to enter their bodies during sex, and the act is considered sacred.

Western sex magic is rooted in the teachings of Sufis, who supposedly shared their knowledge with the Knights Templar during the Crusades in the Middle East. The Templars brought these practices back to Europe, where they were incorporated into other mystical and occult philosophies.

Magic's notorious bad boy, Aleister Crowley, did much to promote and influence the course sex magic has taken in the West. Crowley learned sex magic while traveling in India and Africa, and he emphasized its practice through the organization he headed, the Ordo Templi Orientis (OTO).

Like other types of magical work, sex magic's objectives are varied, ranging from healing to spell-working to spiritual enlightenment. Franz Mesmer used sexually induced trances to facilitate various types of healing. The British poet William Blake, a Freemason, wrote about a facet of sex magic that involves sexual activity between humans and spiritual beings. In kundalini yoga, sexual energy is raised and directed throughout the body to nourish the charkas and encourage healing on every level. Because sex magic's power comes from blending male and female energies with divine forces to produce wholeness, it can also be an effective way to consciously create virtually any circumstance you desire.

Tapping Creative Energy

Sex magic taps the powerful creative force inherent in sexual activity for specific purposes other than human reproduction. According to sex magic's tenets, this creative force, which is responsible for all human and animal life, can be directed to create abundance, success, healing, and so on.

Sexual energy can provide the fuel to propel all forms of manifestation. The result of magical coupling is known as a "magickal childe." This means an effect is imprinted on the spiritual plane that will eventually materialize in the physical world. As in other types of magic, the participants mentally create an image of the intention they wish to bring into being. Then they engage in sex while holding this image in their minds. At the moment of orgasm, the image is released into the cosmos to be acted upon by divine forces and finally "birthed" on the material plane.

This is only one of many sex magic practices, but it's a relatively easy and effective method. Other forms, such as tantric yoga and astral traveling during sexual trance, require more extensive mental, physical, and spiritual expertise.

Charging Charms

The creative energy raised during sex magic can be used to empower charms and other magic tools. The easiest way to do this is to fashion a talisman or amulet in the usual manner, as described in other chapters of this book. Then keep the charm near you (or wear it) while engaging in sexual activity. Remember to hold your intention clearly in your mind throughout the act.

You can also charge charms with a mixture of male and female fluids (called elixir) generated during magical sexual activity. Anoint a talisman or amulet with these fluids, just as you might anoint a charm with essential oils. The creative force permeates the charm and imbues it with additional power. Magicians sometimes use sexual fluids to charge magical tools, too.

Feng Shui

Based in Taoism and the teachings of Confucius, feng shui (pronounced *fung shway*) has been practiced in China for more than two millennia. Its objective is to direct the flow of vital energy, known as chi, through the environment in order to create balance and harmony. According to Eastern philosophy, chi is the enlivening force in the universe that animates all life.

FACT

In the last decade or so, feng shui has gained popularity in the West, and it is now used by many interior designers and architects. Large corporations, including Coca-Cola, Sony, Shell, Procter and Gamble, as well as thousands of small businesses and individual homeowners in the United States have applied feng shui's techniques to attract money, health, success, happiness, and other benefits.

Also known as the art of placement, feng shui includes both esoteric and practical aspects. The mystical part involves the use of symbolism to magically produce results. The practical side incorporates the principles of interior design to enhance the beauty and efficiency of your living space. One of the reasons feng shui has become so widely accepted is that you don't need to understand or believe in the mystical facets in order to reap its material rewards.

Your Home Is a Magical Environment

Numerous schools of feng shui exist, but the one practiced most often in the West uses a tool called a ba-gua to analyze your home or workplace. The ba-gua divides space into nine sectors called gua, each of which corresponds to an area of your life: money, relationships, health, and so on. By simply looking at the interior of your home—how you position furniture, your color scheme, where clutter tends to collect, and so on—a feng shui practitioner can discern which areas of your life are in good shape and which are causing difficulties.

Ba-gua

Feng shui sees everything in your home as a reflection of you. The goal is to get chi to flow smoothly through your living space so that it energizes your home and the people who live there. By altering certain things in your home, you can literally change your life. Let's say, for example, the section of your home that's linked to relationships is cluttered. This suggests confusion or obstacles are present in your primary partnership. By cleaning out the clutter, you can actually clear up some of your relationship problems.

Feng Shui's Magical Cures

To remedy imbalances, feng shui recommends using various cures that are largely symbolic but that may have practical sides as well. The ten principal cures are light, moving objects, living things, sound, color, heavy objects, images, scent, and electrical items. Each cure has specific purposes and applications. Moving objects, such as wind chimes and fans, circulate chi and keep it from stagnating in places. Heavy objects, such as stones or statuary, hold down chi and prevent it from moving too quickly through your home.

Many feng shui cures are simple and inexpensive to implement. You can combine two or more to create the effects you desire. Feng shui is extremely flexible. For every problem, you can usually find several cures to correct it. As in other forms of magic, your intention is key to the success of feng shui.

Huna

Huna, the spiritual and magical belief system of the ancient Polynesians, was brought to the public in England and North America by Max Freedom Long in the first half of the twentieth century. Huna means "secret," and its priests are called kahunas or keepers of the secret. Fascinated by the Hawaiian kahunas who performed miraculous healings, firewalking, and other feats, Long formed a society known as the Huna Research Associates to study this form of magic.

According to huna's tenets, the human psyche is composed of three nonphysical selves, entities, or levels of consciousness. The low self, akin to the subconscious, is called *unihipili,* which means "spirit." It is considered to be a primitive part that can be guided by the middle self, or *uhane.* *Uhane* means "the spirit that talks" and refers to the everyday conscious self and the rational mind. The high self, or *aumakua,* which means "utterly trustworthy parental spirit," is the divine part of the individual that ties you to the Godhead.

These three selves are linked to one another and the physical body by etheric material called aka cords. These cords serve as conduits that allow mana, or the life force (manufactured by the low self), to flow between the selves. Communication between the selves occurs via the aka cords, too. In magical work, the middle self creates an image of a desired condition and conveys it to the low self. The low self then sends mana to the high self to use in carrying out the intentions of the middle self. A "braided cord" called aha connects everybody's high selves together, allowing contact between individuals to take place. Healing, protection, and other magical work can be done, even at great distance, by channeling energy and intentions along these cords.

Voodoo

When people hear the word *voodoo,* they often envision dolls stuck with pins, zombies, and hideous rituals carried out in darkness. But voodoo is simply a belief system. Voodoo was first brought to Haiti by African slaves sometime during the sixteenth century. It emerged in Louisiana two hundred years later.

Voodoo involves the interaction of humans with spirits. Legba, the spirit in charge, serves as a mediator between human beings and the spirit world. Other loa, or high gods, include Damballah, a snake god imbued with virility; Guede, goddess of love; and her darker sisters, jealousy and vengeance. Many lesser gods and innumerable spirits play parts in voodoo's elaborate rituals and spells.

In a traditional voodoo ceremony, worshipers work themselves into a frenzy through music, chanting, and dancing, sometimes accompanied by various forms of drugs and alcohol. During an altered state of consciousness, worshipers become possessed by one of the spirits and collapse to the ground, writhing and speaking unintelligibly. Once possessed, a worshiper is believed to be able to bring about a cure, good fortune, or some other human desire. During a typical ceremony, animal sacrifices are offered to the loa to win their favor.

FACT

François "Papa Doc" Duvalier, the dictator who ruled Haiti with an iron fist for many decades, is believed to have been a *houngan*—a voodoo priest—who capitalized on the local superstitions to maintain control over his little kingdom. He called his secret police the *tontons macoute,* which means "itinerant magicians," and the license plate on his car was said to consist of magical numbers.

The dark side of voodoo, however, is what has captured the collective imagination. The extremes of voodoo's black magic can include control over others, ritual murders, and cannibalism. Some practitioners curse the recent dead and turn them into zombies, reanimated corpses who are slaves without wills of their own.

Santeria

Often referred to as a Cuban mystery religion, the word *santería* literally means "the worship of saints." A blend of Catholicism and Nigerian paganism that evolved centuries ago, when Yoruba slaves were taken from Nigeria to Cuba, *santería* consists of a panoply of saints, or *orishas*, which are a combination of Catholic saints and Yoruba gods and goddesses. Many of these *orishas* resemble mythological gods. For example, Elegguá, a messenger of the *orishas* and the guardian at the gates, sounds a lot like Mercury. Oshún, the *orisha* of love and marriage, is the equivalent of Venus. Changó, the patron saint of fire, thunder, and lightning, could be compared to Zeus.

Over the centuries, some of the *orishas* became associated with saints of the opposite gender, so they actually have two names. Changó also goes by the name of St. Barbara, the Virgin Mary of the Middle Ages. Obatalá, the patron saint of peace and purity, is also known as Our Lady of Mercy.

When an initiate to the religion becomes a *santero* (or *santera,* if she's female), he agrees to "worship the saints, to observe their feasts, obey their commands, and conduct their rituals," writes Migene Gonzalez-Wippler, author of *The Santería Experience.* "In exchange for this absolute submission, he gains supernatural powers, protection against evil, and the ability to foresee the future and even to shape the future according to his will."

Casting spells is part of a *santero*'s work. As in other magical practices, there are spells for virtually anything and everything. A spell to overcome an enemy requires the use of a snake's skin as well as snake oil. Ingredients for such spells can be found in a *botánica,* a Hispanic religious goods store. A *santero* often keeps icons or statues of the *orishas* and other saints on his altar, along with flowers, a bowl of water, and a bottle of Florida water (a type of cheap cologne used in many of the spells). The darker side of santería, known as mayomberia, is a type of black magic.

Alchemy

Simply put, alchemy is the art of producing change or transformation. The alchemist uses magic to change something of a lower quality into a substance that's more purified or perfected. Turning lead into gold is a common image associated with alchemy that symbolizes the transformation process in human consciousness from ignorance to enlightenment.

"A scientist will find alchemy of interest as a form of early chemistry, the psychologist will see it as a way of mapping the human psyche through symbolic descriptions, and the mystic will interpret it as a quest for divine knowledge."—Cherry Gilchrist, *The Elements of Alchemy*

Alchemy dates back at least 2,000 years and is linked with Asian, Arabic, and Western mystery schools. Like many occult traditions, its origins aren't clear, and its present-day expressions are varied. Ancient Chinese alchemists focused on the secrets of longevity, whereas the Greeks and Romans showed more concern for the chemical aspects of the art. During the Renaissance, the Rosicrucians and other mystical orders helped to blend alchemy's philosophy into other branches of learning.

Producing the Philosopher's Stone is alchemy's objective. Although the stone is said to be a substance similar to gold and to possess its own powers to effect transformation, the term doesn't refer only to a physical object. Combining, distilling, and transmuting physical substances through chemical processes symbolizes the process of spiritual transformation; the metals used represent the human qualities being perfected. By blending internal and external alchemy, the alchemists believed immortality could be achieved.

Chapter 7

Magnificent Magicians

Throughout history, magicians have practiced their art in diverse ways, sometimes openly, among elite circles of influential people, but more often in secret. Religious and political institutions, feeling threatened by a power they didn't understand, frequently persecuted magicians and forced them to go underground. Arcane knowledge has survived nonetheless, resurrected and enlivened by talented individuals past and present. Here are a few who have had an impact on magic's evolution through the ages.

Merlin

A book about magic and spells doesn't seem complete without a discussion of Merlin, the most enigmatic figure in magical lore. Like most legendary figures, Merlin, Arthur, and the rest of the colorful cast of Camelot were probably a blend of fact and fiction. Few other legends, however, have captured the collective imagination in quite the way this one has.

In the romantic version of Merlin's life, his mother was raped by an incubus and sequestered in a tower for the duration of her pregnancy. When Merlin was born, he was covered completely in thick, black hair. His mother supposedly pleaded with the midwives to let him be baptized immediately and named for his maternal grandfather, Merlin (or Mellin). This baptism apparently negated the evil influence of his nonphysical father, from whom he inherited his gift of prophecy and magical powers.

From the moment he drew his first breath, Merlin was precocious, a prodigy of unimagined talent. At the age of eighteen months, speaking in full sentences, he assured his mother that she wouldn't be burned at the stake because of him. When the judge at her trial condemned her for not naming Merlin's father, Merlin himself argued with the judge, claiming that he knew his father was an incubus. But God, he said, had granted safety to his mother by giving Merlin himself the ability to see the future. His mother was subsequently released into the custody of her confessor and became a nun.

Merlin's association with Arthur began even before Arthur's birth, when Merlin prophesied that Arthur would rise to power and become Britain's greatest leader. He served as Arthur's tutor, arranged for the sword-in-the-stone contest that confirmed Arthur's noble bloodline, and convinced the mystical Lady of the Lake to present King Arthur with Excalibur, the legendary magical sword. Some versions of the legend also say that Merlin created the Round Table and advised Arthur throughout his reign in Camelot.

"Merlin was the great 'guru' of the Arthurian world. He had the whole program in mind."—Joseph Campbell, *Transformations of Myth Through Time*

Even the death of Merlin is shrouded in mystery. One account tells that when Arthur was wounded in his last battle at Camlann, Merlin accompanied him to the Isle of Avalon to heal his wounds. There the magician supposedly fell so deeply in love with the Lady of the Lake that he taught her all his magic. She became so powerful that Merlin became no match for her and she imprisoned him in a crystal cave to prevent him from enslaving her.

If Merlin did die, where is he buried? No one seems to know, a fitting end to such a legendary figure. One popular belief about Merlin is that he never died—that he is, in fact, alive and well and living in the forest of Brocelinade. In this account, Merlin looks like a young man because he knows the secret of the elixir of life. He lives with the beautiful fairy, Vivien, the legendary Lady of the Lake. Supposedly the enchanted forest of Broceliande still exists, but it is only visible to those who believe in magic.

The Freemasons

Throughout history, the Freemasons have been accomplished craftsmen who concerned themselves with honest labor conducted in the service of a divine being whom they referred to as the Great Architect of the Universe. No one knows how old the order is. Its members are said to have worked on King Solomon's temple. During the medieval and Renaissance periods, this select guild built the great cathedrals in Europe and Britain. Secret information, in the form of symbols, was interwoven into the architecture of these structures; therefore only tradesmen with special skill, knowledge, and morality were deemed capable of conveying this wisdom. Masonic symbolism even appears on the dollar bill and in the wording of the Declaration of Independence.

Freemasonry describes itself as "a science of morality, veiled in allegory and illustrated by symbols." Its physical lodges, rites, and literature are rich with symbolism. The symbols represent objectives, states of mind, and other conditions; when a brother sees a symbol, he is instantly reminded of a facet of the Masonic system. When someone is initiated into the order and follows its doctrines, he is said to make a "symbolic pilgrimage." Members advance through three classes, or stages of learning, to become adepts. Rather than concerning itself with doing magic spells, the Masonic system seeks to promote friendship, virtue, and spiritual transformation, not only for its members, but ultimately for humanity in general.

FACT

A number of America's founding fathers, including Thomas Jefferson, Benjamin Franklin, and Henry Knox were Freemasons. Since the order's inception, presidents, military leaders, industrialists, literary figures, and movie stars have been Masons, including Franklin D. Roosevelt, John Glenn, General Douglas MacArthur, and Clark Gable.

John Dee

The noted English mathematician, scientist, astrologer, clergyman, navigation expert, and occultist John Dee served as adviser to Queen Elizabeth I and to Britain's parliament during the sixteenth century. One of the most learned men of his day, Dee gained fame throughout Europe for his many skills. He also authored a number of books on occult subjects as well as mathematics and science.

During the early 1580s, Dee began communicating with angels, whom he said dictated several books to him, some in the Enochian (angelic) language. These manuscripts were published posthumously as *The True and Faithful Relation of What Passed for Many Years between Dr. John Dee and Some Spirits*. The scryer and noted alchemist Edward Kelley served as an intermediary between Dee and the angelic realm. For five years, the two men engaged in "spiritual conferences" with the angels and traveled through Europe together.

In addition to his occult contributions, Dee also advanced the fields of cartography and navigation, and he was instrumental in promoting what would become Britain's colonization of the New World. He devised methods of preserving old manuscripts. His personal library in Mortlake was among the most extensive in England and a resource center for many scholars.

Dee managed to bridge the seemingly contrary fields of science, magic, and religion, and he moved in the highest social and political circles. But he ran into problems in 1555 when he was accused of practicing sorcery against Queen Mary, which amounted to treason. He was acquitted, and he so impressed the Catholic Bishop Bonner who had prosecuted him that the two became close associates.

The Rosicrucians

The Rosicrucians date back to the early 1600s, when three short books were published anonymously in Kassel, Germany. The first book in the trilogy, *Fama,* related the story of Christian Rosenkreuz, who supposedly came from a noble German family. When he was sixteen, he set out for the Holy Land and then studied with holy men in Arabia and Egypt. He eventually returned to Germany, where he selected seven disciples, and together they compiled a massive library of arcane knowledge. He died at an advanced age—some accounts place his age at 120, others at 150—but most agree that he died because he wanted to and not because he was sick.

Fama presented alchemy as the transmutation of the soul rather than the transmutation of base metal into gold. The second book in the series, *Confessio Fraternitatis,* provided the purpose of the secret brotherhood. It claimed that the pope was the anti-Christ and that he could be overthrown if people cooperated with the brotherhood to bring about a spiritual awakening. The third book, *The Chemical Marriage of Christian Rosenkreuz,* is a hermetical romance about death, spiritual rebirth, and the perfection of man. Probably the most important of the three books, its occult knowledge influenced the Golden Dawn.

The early Rosicrucians made impressive claims, including the ability to summon spirits and render themselves invisible, as well as to heal the sick and attract riches. The English mystic Robert Fludd, astrologer William Lilly, and several other celebrated thinkers of the 1600s became members of a Rosicrucian society that formed in London. Their objective was to elevate mankind through spiritual means, the alchemy of the soul.

Count Saint-Germain

Sorting fact from legend in the life of the enigmatic Count (or Comte de) Saint-Germain is tricky. By some accounts, his mother was the widow of Charles II of Spain; by others, he was the son of the prince of Transylvania. Either story would place his birth in the 1690s. A talented painter and violinist, he traveled widely in Europe during the eighteenth century and amazed people with his skills as a magician and seer. The charismatic count also moved in influential political circles, in France, England, the Netherlands, and Italy.

The count specialized in alchemy, turning base metals into gold. He claimed to know how to cause pearls to grow in size and supposedly could take several small diamonds and merge them into a single, large stone.

ALERT!

The count's death is as mysterious as his birth. Although he supposedly died in 1784, according to Freemason documents, he represented the Masons at a meeting in 1785. Theosophist Annie Besant claimed she met Saint-Germain in 1896, at which time he would have been 200 years old.

Saint-Germain professed to know the secret of eternal youth, an objective of alchemy. Voltaire described him as "a man who never dies, and who knows everything." The count's charm, plus his extensive knowledge of secret societies, led people to believe he'd been present at ceremonies that occurred a century earlier. This may explain the rumors that he'd been born much earlier than the late seventeenth century. Long after his death, numerous people insisted they'd seen him alive in various parts of the world, perhaps supporting the alchemist's claim.

Eliphas Lévi

Born in 1810 as Alphonse Louis Constant, Lévi was the son of a shoemaker. Raised a Catholic, he eventually turned away from the priesthood because he realized he couldn't live as a celibate. He married a sixteen-year-old girl, who subsequently left him for the Marquis de Montferrier, the owner of several radical journals for which Lévi wrote.

Lévi believed that magic was essentially a power of the mind, an untapped and unexplored resource that everyone possesses, and that ritual magic's purpose was to train practitioners to direct their wills toward achieving what they desired. Will, however, required desire and passion to fuel it.

As a result of his association with the Marquis, Lévi met a Polish nobleman, Joseph Maria Hoene-Wronski, a student of the Jewish Qabalah. Lévi became Wronski's initiate in hermetic magic. When Wronski died, Lévi studied the nobleman's manuscripts and changed his name from Constant to Lévi. He then wrote several books on magic, including *Transcendental Magic* and *The Dogma and Ritual of High Magic,* which reflected his study of the occult. His theories subsequently influenced the founders of the Hermetic Order of the Golden Dawn and sparked a revival of interest in the occult in France during the nineteenth century.

Colin Wilson classifies Lévi and Aleister Crowley as "the most important representatives of the modern magical tradition." And yet Lévi didn't make much money from his writings while he was alive. After his death, the books gained popularity among followers of ritual magic. One of those students was Crowley, who believed he was the reincarnation of Lévi.

The Golden Dawn

The Hermetic Order of the Golden Dawn began in 1887, when William Wescott found a cipher manuscript in a bookshop. The manuscript, which contained magical theories based on the Qabala, alchemy, astrology, and the work of Eliphas Lévi, were deciphered, and the following year Wescott, along with S. L. MacGregor Mathers and William Woodman (all British Freemasons as well as members of the Rosicrucian Society of England) founded the English branch of Die Goldene Dammerung. The order's principles and doctrines were influenced by the beliefs of the Freemasons and Rosicrucians, as well as the contents of the cipher manuscript. The actual rituals for the order were written by MacGregor Mathers and William Butler Yeats, who was one of its most prominent members.

FACT

In its heyday, which lasted about fifteen years, the Golden Dawn was favored by sophisticated occultists interested in magic. A. E. Waite, Dion Fortune, Aleister Crowley, and numerous other noted occultists belonged to the original group.

In the late 1930s, Israel Regardie first published the rituals and teachings of the Golden Dawn. This extensive collection served to revive interest in the order and provided information about various other branches of magical practice. Ritual magic, as presented by the Golden Dawn, has been called a "structured experience" of magic that offers tools for developing spiritual awareness in order to accelerate the evolution of human consciousness. Its complex teachings drew upon the ideas and traditions of numerous ancient cultures and melded them into an intricate, multilayered, and meticulously ordered system.

Like the Freemasons, the magicians of the Golden Dawn employed an extensive array of symbols from various mystical traditions. Sigils (discussed in Chapter 3) and magic squares were applied in spell-working. Carefully choreographed physical movements and symbolic gestures were used to direct energy. Symbols derived from astrology, alchemy, tarot, ancient languages, and many other subjects also played roles in the Golden Dawn's magical practices.

"Mathers's vision for the Golden Dawn was that the magicians in his order could follow the mythic pathways on the Tree of Life and grow in spiritual awareness as they ascended through each life."—Nevill Drury, *The History of Magic in the Modern Age*

The most important symbol for the Golden Dawn is the Tree of Life from the Hebrew Qabalah. This geometric figure contains ten spheres, called sephiroth, which represent levels of spiritual development, joined by twenty-two lines or pathways. This key symbol indicates the stages of personal transformation that a magician must go through to achieve illumination.

Aleister Crowley

The most notorious member of the Golden Dawn, Crowley has been billed as the greatest magician of the twentieth century. Initiated into the order in 1898, he tried to take control two years later and was ousted. He subsequently formed his own secret society, called Astrum Argentinum, or Silver Star, and became a Freemason. In 1914, he joined the Ordo Templi Orientis (Order of the Templars of the Orient, or OTO) and later became its head.

A charismatic figure who excelled at publicity, Crowley was a relentless self-promoter. He grabbed headlines by shocking the public. He was branded "the king of depravity" and referred to himself as "The Beast." Much of the negative press concerning Crowley stemmed from his involvement in sex magic (discussed in Chapter 6), which appalled Victorian England.

In 1920, after inheriting a modest sum of money, Crowley consulted the I Ching about where he should go to carry on his magical activities. Based on the oracle's advice, he established a temple at Cefalù, a port in northern Sicily. For a period, the retreat enjoyed a steady stream of visitors eager to study under the legendary Crowley. When he returned to England, Crowley authored a number of books including *The Book of Thoth, Diary of a Drug Fiend, 777, Equinox, Moon Child, Libra*, and *The Blue Equinox*.

Although many questions surround Crowley's ideas, ethics, and activities, he was well versed in spiritual traditions and occult knowledge. His influence on the field of sex magic, in particular, remains unparalleled, and much of what's practiced today is rooted in Crowley's pursuits.

FACT

In partnership with Lady Frieda Harris, Crowley created the Thoth tarot deck, which today, nearly a century after its inception, remains one of the most popular decks. Based on *The Book of Thoth,* it contains vivid imagery along with symbolism from the Qabala, astrology, and various magical systems.

Madame Blavatsky and the Theosophists

Helena Petrovna Blavatsky, the enigmatic founder of theosophy, was a Russian-born medium whose followers included many noted individuals, among them Thomas Edison, William Butler Yeats, Annie Besant, Rudolf Steiner, and Krishnamurti. Even Mahatma Gandhi visited Blavatsky. Many of the details about Blavatsky's life are simply conjecture. What is known, however, is that she was born in 1831 and married a Russian general when she was sixteen. She abandoned him eventually and took off for Constantinople. After this, she supposedly traveled extensively and worked at a variety of unusual jobs. On July 7, 1873, she landed in New York City, one of a wave of immigrants.

She hooked up with Henry Steel Olcott, a colonel and a student of the occult, and together they founded the Brotherhood of Luxor in 1874, which evolved into the Theosophical Society a year later. Her concepts, put forth in her books *The Secret Doctrine* and *Isis Unveiled,* were allegedly conveyed to her by her spirit guides. Theosophy, which means "divine wisdom," combines ideas from the Greek mystery schools, the Essenes, Gnostics, Hindus, Buddhists, Christians, Neoplatonists, and many more.

Blavatsky proposed that human life on earth began millions of years ago, on the legendary continents of Atlantis and Lemuria. According to her, seven types of people—the great races, as she called them—would evolve over the course of humankind's history, and that currently five of those types have appeared. She believed in the doctrine of reincarnation and taught that humans are immortal beings comprised of subtle energy bodies—astral, etheric, and mental—in addition to a physical one.

In the late 1870s, Blavatsky moved her society to India, the spiritual home of her guides and masters. The Theosophical Society flourished and, at its peak, boasted something between 50,000 and 100,000 followers worldwide.

Dion Fortune

The magical name of Violet Mary Firth, Dion Fortune (Deo Non Fortuna, which means "by God and not by luck") figured prominently in the Golden Dawn and the Theosophical movement. From the early part of her life, she expressed a keen interest in psychology and was influenced by Freud, Alfred Adler, and Jung, but she felt a special affinity for Jung's theory of archetypes and his investigation into mythic images and symbols.

She wrote several books, the best known being *Applied Magic, The Esoteric Philosophy of Love and Marriage, The Mystical Qabala,* and *Psychic Self-Defence.* She also authored novels that contained magical themes and information. In her writings, Fortune discussed a divine "Inner Light" that resembled a higher manifestation of Freud's libido. In her second book, she discussed the connection between sex and the life force, and she recommended dedicating this energy to a god form. In both her fiction and non-fiction works, Fortune expressed a knowledge of sex magic. Her books, however, upset MacGregor Mathers's wife Moina, who expelled Fortune from the Golden Dawn for revealing the order's secrets. *Psychic Self-Defence* grew out of Fortune's belief that Moina Mathers was attacking her magically, and it provides information about warding off such assaults.

One of Fortune's major contributions was her departure from the male-dominated archetypes of the Golden Dawn and her exploration of feminine archetypes. Her novels are perhaps the only literary works of her time that present a feminine view of sex magic. She went on to establish her own occult society, which became known as the Society of the Inner Light, in London. She died in 1946.

Rudolf Steiner

Best known as the founder of the Waldorf schools, Rudolf Steiner was an Austrian-born philosopher whose numerous contributions to society included biodynamic agriculture, eurythmy (a form of harmonious rhythm which he called the "art of the soul"), anthroposophical medicine, and a unique, complex vision of the structure of the universe.

From an early age, Steiner underwent experiences of the spiritual world. For the first quarter of the twentieth century, he devoted himself to verifying his experiences and sharing his knowledge with others. He taught that the spiritual and natural worlds are not separate; human beings only think there's a schism because they have been conditioned to limit their perception.

In Steiner's view, human beings share the world with countless non-physical beings. He believed anyone could develop an awareness that would allow the person to witness these beings and to experience other realms of existence. His book *Knowledge of Higher Worlds* presents techniques designed to heighten perception of nature and the cosmos.

In 1902, Steiner became head of the Theosophical Society's German branch and began lecturing throughout Europe on what he called "spiritual science." His lectures and writings over the next two decades, on subjects such as karma, reincarnation, and the spiritual influences in the evolution of the world, have been published extensively. Steiner broke with the Theosophists and formed the Anthroposophical Society in 1912. Over the next few years, the society under Steiner's direction built the first Goetheanum in Dornach, Switzerland, as an organizational and cultural center. On New Year's Eve 1922, arsonists burned the center; a second Goetheanum was completed five years later, after Steiner's death.

Steiner founded the Waldorf schools in Stuttgart, Germany, in 1919. The schools continue to operate today in sixty countries. The unique educational system attempts to educate children's souls and spirits, as well as their minds, through a combination of the arts, social and spiritual development, physical movement, and academics.

Wilhelm Reich

Reich, an Austrian-born psychiatrist, would not have considered himself a magician or occultist. Yet in his work with the life force, which he called orgone, he traversed the same territory and uncovered many of the same secrets that magicians had known about for centuries. What makes Reich's discoveries significant is that he approached the etheric realms and spiritual forces from a scientist's perspective, offering objective evidence for mystical experiences.

"Reich also understood the nature of energy and how the human body gives access to that unitary, planetary energy which we see active in the formation of hurricanes and in the aurora borealis, through sex and bodily sensation. What makes sex magick possible is that all living systems have the capacity to store a charge of energy."—Donald Michael Kraig, *Modern Sex Magick*

Best known for his contributions in the field of psychology, particularly his book *Character Analysis*, Reich was a colleague of Freud's in the 1920s. In 1933, Reich published an insightful analysis, titled *The Mass Psychology of Fascism*, describing the role psychosexual conditions played in fascism and Hitler's rise to power. This book drew heat from the press, the psychological community, and the Nazis. Reich's Jewish background and his criticism of the Nazis necessitated his exodus from Germany, first to Scandinavia and then, in 1939, to the United States.

Reich emphasized the significance of sexual energy as the life force responsible for mental and physical health. He proposed that repressed psychosexual energy could produce physical blocks, a condition he called "body armoring," that led to physical illnesses including cancer and arthritis. He presented these ideas and the results of his scientific studies of human sexuality in his book *The Function of the Orgasm*. His concepts and experiences show that he had a keen understanding of sex magic, although he didn't use that term and it's unclear whether he knew about such practices within occult orders.

While living in Scandinavia, Reich began extensive studies of how orgone operated in the body and in the environment. He believed cancer was caused by the depletion of orgone energy. As a result of his experiments, he attempted to capture, heighten, and direct this "primordial cosmic energy" for healing purposes. In 1940, after relocating to Maine, he began building orgone accumulators, wood-and-metal boxes in which an ill person sat while orgone was channeled through her body.

To collect orgone from the atmosphere, Reich designed a "cloudbuster" that allowed him to produce rain. His experiments with orgone attracted UFOs, which led him to theorize that orgone fueled these crafts (discussed in his most controversial book, *Contact with Space*). These unconventional ideas caused many people to claim he'd gone mad. In 1947, the U.S. Food and Drug Administration outlawed the sale of orgone accumulators. When Reich disobeyed the injunction, he was sentenced to prison and the FDA burned several tons of his publications. He died in jail of heart failure in 1957.

Carlos Castaneda and the Shamanic Revival

The elusive Castaneda was largely responsible for a revived interest in shamanism during the 1960s, when his first book, *The Teachings of Don Juan: A Yaqui Way of Knowledge*, became a bestseller. This book, like the others that followed, detailed Castaneda's five-year-long apprenticeship with Don Juan Matus, a Yaqui Indian *brujo* (a medicine man, sorcerer, and healer), beginning in Arizona, then in Sonora, Mexico.

Castaneda's shamanic training included the use of three hallucinogenic plants: peyote, Jimson weed, and psilocybin mushrooms. "The importance of the plants was, for Don Juan, their capacity to produce stages of peculiar perception in a human being," wrote Castaneda in his first book. Castaneda termed these peculiar perceptions "states of nonordinary reality," intended to teach him about the acquisition of power and wisdom. His altered states of reality also aided Castaneda in finding a "magical ally" who would enhance his powers and ultimately enable him to gain complete control over his physical body, so he could shapeshift or project his consciousness into animals and plants.

Part of the fascination with Castaneda's books lay in the author's mysterious nature. According to some sources, his real name was Carlos Arana or Carlos Aranha, and he came from either Peru or Brazil. He changed his name when he became an American citizen in 1959. Beyond that, not much is really known about Castaneda. Even his death is veiled in mystery. Still less is known about Don Juan. Did the sorcerer really exist? Were any of his adventures real? Or were the stories Castaneda chronicled meant to be mythic, their messages holding collective truths about the human condition?

Michael Harner

Anthropologist Michael Harner, who started the Foundation for Shamanic Studies in Mill Valley, California, began his shamanic apprenticeship in the late 1950s with the Jivaro Indians of Ecuador. In 1960, the American Museum of Natural History sent Harner back to the Amazon to study the Conibo Indians in Peru. When he expressed an interest in learning about the Conibo's religious beliefs, he was told that he must first drink *ayahuasca,* the "soul vine," a sacred drink of the shamans made from a hallucinogenic plant.

"In a sense, shamanism is being reinvented in the west precisely because it is needed."—Michael Harner, *The Way of the Shaman*

During his experience, Harner experienced a vision of Earth before life existed on the planet. Reptilian creatures showed Harner how they had created life on Earth, and hundreds of millions of years of evolution were condensed into his single vision. After the experience, Harner sought advice from an old blind shaman who had made many journeys into the spirit world and already knew what Harner had witnessed. Michael Talbot, author of *The Holographic Universe*, believes that experiences like Harner's, through paths such as shamanism, may actually be "sophisticated accounts of the cartography of subtler levels of reality."

Terence McKenna

Before his death in 2000, Terence McKenna spent twenty-five years studying what he called "the ethnopharmacology of spiritual transformation" and the subtler levels of reality. He was an expert on the ethnomedicine of the Amazon basin, the author of a number of books, and an international spokesperson for the development of a global consciousness.

In *True Hallucinations*, McKenna writes about an expedition that he and his brother, Dennis, and several other people took to the Amazon basin in 1971, in search of the mythic shamanistic hallucinogen of the Witoto. The experience led to McKenna's theory that psilocybin, the psychoactive ingredient in the *Stropharia cubensis* mushroom, is the missing link in the development of consciousness and language itself.

During his stay in La Chorrera in the Amazon, McKenna experienced a close encounter with a UFO that caused him to believe the UFO was "a reflection of a future event that promises humanity's eventual mastery over time, space, and matter." A later visit to La Chorrera inspired his theory of time, based on the I Ching, that he termed the "timewave," a kind of metaphysical calendar. McKenna also believed that the World Wide Web is a route to global consciousness. Although some people discount McKenna as a drug-crazed madman, his original ideas and experiences with other levels of existence provide food for thought and further exploration.

Lynn Andrews

Before she gained an international reputation for her work in shamanism, Lynn Andrews was an art dealer in Los Angeles. A search for a Native American marriage basket she'd seen in a photo took her to Manitoba, Canada, where she met Agnes Whistling Elk and Ruby Plenty Chiefs. The meeting led to Andrews' initiation into the Sisterhood of the Shields, a group of forty-four women of power from indigenous cultures throughout the world.

When Andrews returned to California, she'd changed so dramatically that she felt she no longer fit in. She flew back to Canada and pled with Agnes to continue teaching her. But the old woman replied, "Go write a book and give away what you have learned. Then you may come back to me." Andrews did exactly that. *Medicine Woman*, the first of many books detailing Andrews' experiences, reads like a spiritual thriller and provides shamanic insights from a woman's perspective.

Starhawk

Among the most respected figures in Wicca and contemporary Earth-based spirituality, Starhawk was born Miriam Simos, to parents of Russian-Jewish descent. She studied film at UCLA and won early recognition as a novelist. A long-time political activist, she has devoted herself to encouraging nonviolence, environmental awareness, world peace, and anti-globalization, and is considered one of the foremost voices of ecofeminism.

A practicing witch, Starhawk is best known as the author of the classic text on Goddess-centered religion, *The Spiral Dance: A Rebirth of the Ancient Religion of the Great Goddess*, a collection of history, philosophy, spells, and rituals that was first published in 1979. Her teachings include the principle of immanence, which means that "the Goddess, the Gods, are embodied, that we are each a manifestation of the living being of the earth, that nature, culture, and life in all their diversity are sacred." In this and many other books, she also emphasizes the connection between human beings and the Earth, stating, "What affects one of us affects all."

"Unless I have enough personal power to keep commitments in my daily life, I will be unable to wield magical power. To work magic, I need a basic belief in my ability to do things and cause things to happen. That belief is generated and sustained by my daily actions."—Starhawk

Starhawk helped found the Reclaiming tradition of witchcraft, whose goal is to "unify spirit and politics." To this end, she lectures internationally, gives classes and workshops, and conducts public rituals in Earth-based spirituality. She lives in California, where she continues to write, teach, and promote understanding of contemporary witchcraft, magic, and pagan spiritual paths.

Sai Baba

Called a miracle worker or "Godman" by some, Sathya Sai Baba was born in 1926 in Puttaparthi, a small village in India's Anantapur district. In the 1960s, as Westerners began journeying to India for spiritual reasons, his reputation and following grew. From humble beginnings, he has become an internationally known guru to millions of people worldwide and the head of 1,200 spiritual centers around the globe. Some confusion, however, surrounds his early life, perhaps due to language barriers and difficulties with interpretation.

Rather than preaching the dogma of any one religion, Sai Baba teaches that all paths lead to God. He emphasizes the value of love, truth, peace, right conduct, compassion for all beings, service and charity, devotion to God, and nonviolence. He professes to be the incarnation of Shiva, Shakti, and other Hindu gods, but points out that this is also true of everyone.

FACT

Sai Baba's daily materializations of *vibuthi* (red holy ash), food, and pieces of jewelry have captured the attention of audiences of both seekers and skeptics. What Sai Baba describes as an act of divine creation is what magicians call the art of manifestation.

Using personal will and thought forms in connection with cosmic powers, Sai Baba is able to manipulate energy to produce a material result. Many accounts also testify to his miraculous healing powers as well as his ability to levitate, vanish, change the color of his garments, and control the weather.

In recent years, Sai Baba has been attacked in the press for alleged sexual misconduct, yet he continues to receive support from India's prime minister and other high-ranking officials in the Indian government. He and his followers are dedicated to providing service to the poor in India and other countries. His philanthropic projects include free educational opportunities, free health care at hospitals he established in his home town, where he still lives in an ashram, and in Bangalore, clean water programs, an airport, a railway station, and more.

Masaru Emoto

In the late 1980s, Japanese scientist Masaru Emoto began looking at water in a new way. His experiments involved directing words into water ("imprinting" it), then freezing it and viewing the ice crystals under a microscope. The words could be spoken, thought, or written on paper and taped to a bottle containing the water. What he discovered was that words and ideas could visibly alter the water's structure.

Just as each snowflake is unique, Emoto found that each word or emotion produced a unique shape. When the words *love, gratitude,* and *peace* were projected into the water, it froze into beautiful shapes. Thoughts such as "I hate you" caused distorted, broken forms. The vibrational energy contained in human thoughts changed the physical appearance and the molecular shape of the water. Interestingly, it didn't matter what language was used. The words *love, amour, amore,* and the kanji symbol for love all generated similar snowflakes.

Emoto published his findings in several books, including *Messages from Water* in 1999 and *The Hidden Message in Water* in 2004, which document his research with photographs. His studies were also featured in the controversial film *What the Bleep Do We Know.* Although traditional scientists have questioned his discoveries, Emoto's work reflects a basic principle of magic: Thoughts, emotions, and images create physical results.

Chapter 8

Ingredients for Spells

As any good cook will tell you, the key to great food lies in the ingredients and how they are combined. The same holds true for spells. The lists in this chapter are by no means comprehensive, but they provide enough information so that eventually you can design your own spells. You don't need to run out and buy everything on these lists. A good way to start is to select a few staples that seem to fit the kinds of spells you want to do. As you become more proficient at casting spells, you'll compile your own lists of what works and what doesn't.

Essential Oils and Incense

For thousands of years, aromatic oils, gums, and resins have been used for both medicinal and cosmetic purposes, as well as in sacred rituals. Ancient Chinese and Indian texts describe the therapeutic, philosophical, and spiritual properties of aromatics. The Bible discusses special oils for anointing and healing; aromatics were so highly prized that the Three Wise Men gave them to Jesus at his birth. The Egyptians employed scent in all areas of life, from seduction to embalming.

Scents affect the limbic system, the portion of the brain associated with memory, emotions, and sexuality, which is why certain smells reawaken memories or stimulate the libido. A whiff of a certain perfume, of sea air, of fresh-baked apple pie and, presto, a panoply of memories unfolds. Because aromas immediately trigger moods, impressions, and associations, they can be assets in spells and rituals.

Essential Oils

Essential oils are extracted from plants instead of being concocted from synthetic substances, as is the case with most modern perfumes. From the perspective of magic, essential oils are preferable to other scents because they contain the life energy of herbs and flowers.

Magicians use essential oils in myriad ways. Dressing candles is a popular practice. To dress a candle, choose an oil that relates to your intention. Pour a little oil in your palm and rub it over the waxy surface to add the properties of the scent to the candle. When the candle burns, the essence is released into the atmosphere to help manifest your intent. If you choose to make your own candles, you can incorporate essential oils into the mix.

Some essential oils can irritate skin or cause allergic reactions. A few oils are toxic. Research the oils you want to use before applying them to your skin or adding them to a ritual bath. Don't ingest them!

Essential oils can also heighten the power of an amulet or talisman. Rub a little oil onto the charm or put a drop on a piece of paper and place it inside the charm. Magicians sometimes anoint their tools with essential oils to charge them. Of course, wearing fragrant oils is probably the most common way to enjoy them. You can even draw symbols on your body with essential oils to provide protection or to attract desired energies.

Incense

In Latin, *incense* means "to make sacred." For centuries, churches and temples have used incense to clear the air and to send prayers to the deities. In Buddhist belief, burning an offering of incense invokes the Buddha into a statue of the holy being. The best incense is made from pure gums and resins, without synthetic binders.

Incense is often used to purify sacred space. Sage is the most frequently used herb for this purpose, but you can burn pine, frankincense, or eucalyptus if you prefer. Before performing a spell or ritual, a magician may cast a protective circle by lighting a stick of incense and walking around the area in a clockwise direction, allowing the smoke to mark the space. You can also charge charms with incense by holding the amulet or talisman in the smoke for a few moments.

Essential Oils and Their Magical Properties

Acacia	Meditation, purification
Almond	Vitality, energy booster
Amber	Protection
Basil	Protection, harmony
Bay	Love spells, prophetic dreams
Bayberry	Money spells
Cedar	Prosperity, courage, protection
Cinnamon	Career success, wealth, vitality
Clove	Healing, prosperity, increased sexual desire
Eucalyptus	Healing, purification

Frankincense	Prosperity, protection, psychic awareness
Honeysuckle	Mental clarity, communication
Jasmine	Love spells, passion, to sweeten any situation
(Lavender)	Relaxation, peace of mind, healing, purification
Mint	Money spells
Musk	Love spells, vitality, to stimulate drive or desire
Patchouli	Love spells, protection, career success
Pine	Purification, protection, strength
Rose	Love spells, to lift spirits
Rue	Protection
Sage	Cleansing, wisdom
Sandalwood	Connection to the higher realms, knowledge, safe travel
Vervain	Money spells, fertility
Ylang-ylang	Aphrodisiac, love spells, to heighten passion or feminine power

Herbs, Flowers, and Other Botanicals

Botanicals are to spells what CDs are to CD players. Herbs, flowers, leaves, roots, bark, and seeds are staples in magic charms. Raw ingredients can also be blended into candle wax, burned in ritual fires, or used in combination with plant oils. You may wish to concoct your own massage oils with specially selected herbs, or you can fashion poultices, ointments, and lotions from your favorite plants. Of course, kitchen herbs can be mixed into magical recipes and ingested as part of a ritual or spell.

ALERT!

Use herbs and flowers with care. Some are toxic or poisonous, and some may irritate skin or cause allergic reactions if handled or inhaled. If you're not sure which herbs are edible, do some research before you ingest.

Ideally, you'll want to grow your own botanicals or acquire wild-crafted plants that are free of pesticides and other chemicals. If that's not possible, you can find much of what you'll need in a good-sized supermarket.

Herbs and Their Magical Properties

Acacia	For meditation, to ward off evil, to attract money and love
Aloe	To soothe burns or skin ailments, for digestion and internal cleansing
Angelica	For temperance, to guard against evil
Anise	For protection; burn seeds as a meditation incense
Balm	To soothe emotional pain, mitigate fears
Bay	For purification, divination, psychic development, heightened awareness
Basil	For protection, balance, purification, divination
Burdock	For purification, protection, psychic awareness, to ward off negativity, aphrodisiac
Catnip	For insight, love, happiness
Cayenne	To stimulate courage, sexual desire, or enthusiasm
Cedar	For wealth, abundance, success
Chamomile	For relaxation, peace of mind, as a digestive aid, to bless a person, place, or thing
Cinnamon	For financial and career success, love spells, mental clarity
Cinquefoil	To stimulate memory, aid communication, for divination or psychic dreams
Clove	For success, prosperity, to remove negativity, to numb pain
Clover	For love spells, psychic awareness, luck
Comfrey	For protection, cleansing, endurance
Daisy	To attract good luck
Elder	For protection, healing rituals
Fennel	For protection
Foxglove	To heighten sexuality (poisonous)
Frankincense	To aid meditation, psychic visions, mental expansion, purification

Garlic	For protection, healing, to lift depression
Ginger	For love, balance, cleansing, to speed manifestation
Hawthorne	For success, happiness, fertility, protection
Jasmine	For love, passion, peace, harmony, to sweeten a situation or relationship
Kava-kava	To heighten psychic awareness, to calm anxiety
Laurel	For success and victory
Lavender	For relaxation, spiritual and psychic development, purification
Marigold	For happiness, psychic awareness, success in legal matters
Marjoram	For acceptance of major life changes
Mint	For prosperity, to speed up results
Mugwort	For divination, psychic development and awareness, good for washing crystals
Myrrh	For protection, healing, consecration
Nettle	To mitigate thorny situations such as gossip and envy
Parsley	For prosperity, protection, health
Rosemary	For protection, love, health, to improve memory
Rue	For protection, to strengthen willpower, to speed recovery from illness and surgery, to expel negativity
Sage	For cleansing and purification, protection, wisdom, mental clarity
Sandalwood	For consecration, spiritual communication, travel spells, success
Skullcap	For relaxation before magical practices
Thyme	To focus energy and prepare oneself for magical practice
Vervain	For protection, divination, creativity, self-confidence, to remove negative energy
Willow	For love, protection, conjuring of spirits, healing, dowsing
Wormwood	For spirit communication, to enhance psychic ability (poisonous if burned)
Yarrow	For divination, love, protection, to enhance psychic ability

Gemstones and Crystals

Long before people began prizing gems for their monetary value, they used them as magic charms. In early societies, only rulers, members of royal families, priests, and religious leaders wore gems. According to Nancy Schiffer, author of *The Power of Jewelry*, our ancestors believed gemstones were "capable of human feelings and passions so that they could express jealousy and shock." Today, adornment is the primary reason for wearing precious and semiprecious gems; however, a growing number of people (especially magicians) realize that crystals and gemstones can also be used for healing, spell-working, divination, shamanic journeying, meditation, and dowsing.

Each stone has its own unique properties and energies that can be tapped for doing spells. As a rule, clear stones are best suited for mental and spiritual issues, translucent or cloudy stones for emotional situations, and opaque stones for physical matters. Gems may be used alone or in combination with other stones or crystals to facilitate the results you desire.

FACT

Birthstones, which resonate with the qualities of the zodiac signs to which they correspond, were originally worn to enhance, balance, or modulate a person's own innate characteristics.

Quartz crystals, which frequently play roles in magical work, are a combination of silica and water formed under certain conditions of pressure, temperature, and energy. These crystals possess amazing abilities to retain information, amplify energy, and transmit vibrations. As a result, they're often used in watches, computers, laser tools, television and radio equipment, and many other practical implements. In metaphysical applications, the properties of these crystals make them ideal for healing, storing knowledge, sending energy and thought patterns, and increasing the power of any substance with which they come into contact. People who work with crystals believe they are actually unique life forms that possess innate intelligence and many diverse powers. Hold one in your hand and see if you can feel it resonate.

It's a good idea to cleanse your gemstones and crystals periodically. Wash them in running water, with mild soap if you like, then let them sit in the sun. This removes any unwanted vibrations as well as dust. You can also purify crystals energetically by gently rubbing them with a piece of citrine. It's a good idea to clean your crystals before using them in a magic spell or ritual. You also should wash them if they've been exposed to any strong emotions or unsettling events.

FACT

Some of the best lapis lazuli comes from Chile, where it's inexpensive and often carved into animal figures. Shamans there use it in their spiritual practices. The most coveted lapis is a deep bluish hue, with almost no white flecks in it.

The relationship you establish with your stones and crystals will be unique to you. In time, they'll become your good friends. You may choose to designate certain stones for certain purposes. Treat them with respect and they'll speak to you. The guidelines provided below will give you a starting point for working with the magical properties of stones. With time and practice, you'll develop your own ideas about which stones are best to use in which spells.

Stones and Their Magical Properties

Amber	For physical and psychic protection
Amethyst	For meditation, enhancing and remembering dreams, calming emotions, increasing psychic ability
Aquamarine	For clarity and mental awareness, encouraging spiritual insight, stimulating creativity
Aventurine	To attract wealth or abundance
Bloodstone	For healing, strength, and physical protection
Carnelian	To stimulate passion, sexual energy, courage, and initiative

Stones and Their Magical Properties *(continued)*

Citrine	For clearing vibrations from other stones and crystals
Coral	To attract love or increase affectionate feelings, to enhance self-esteem, to calm emotions
Diamond	To deepen commitment and trust, especially in a love relationship, to absorb and retain energies and vibrations, for strength and victory
Emerald	To aid clairvoyance and divination, to promote healing, growth, mental and emotional balance
Hematite	For grounding, to help stabilize emotions
Jade	For prosperity, to enhance beauty and health
Jasper	Red jasper is good in love spells to stir up passions; brown jasper is excellent for healing purposes; poppy jasper breaks up blockages that prevent energy from circulating through the body
Lapis lazuli	For opening psychic channels, dealing with children, to stimulate the upper chakras; ancient Egyptians used it to charge power meridians on the planet
Moldavite	To energize psychic talent, to quicken spiritual evolution, to open the upper chakras; moldavite is regarded as an extraterrestrial stone because it resulted from a meteor collision with the earth nearly 15 million years ago
Moonstone	To enhance the vividness of dreams and dream recall, to calm emotions
Onyx	For banishing and absorbing negative energy, grounding and stabilizing, to help break deeply ingrained habits
Opal	For protection, to encourage psychic ability and visions, to attract love
Pearl	To strengthen self-esteem, for balance in love relationships, to increase femininity
Quartz (clear)	To retain information, to amplify the energy of other stones, to transmit ideas and energy, for psychic awareness

Stones and Their Magical Properties (continued)

Rose quartz	To attract love and friendship, for emotional healing and balance, to amplify psychic energy
Ruby	To stimulate the emotions, passion, love, to open your heart to divine love
Sapphire	To increase spiritual knowledge and connection with the Divine, for wisdom, insight, and prophetic vision; star sapphires provide hope and clarity of purpose
Smoky quartz	For endurance, to hold problems until you are ready to deal with them
Tiger's eye	For abundance, self-confidence, the freedom to follow your own path
Tourmaline	Green and black tourmaline are good for cleansing, healing, and absorbing negative vibrations; pink and watermelon tourmaline attract friendship, love, and fulfillment; use them to transmit messages and energy
Turquoise	For protection, healing, prosperity, to ease mental tension and emotional anxiety

Power Objects

The custom of using magic charms is rooted deep in antiquity. Myths, legends, and literature from cultures around the world mention talismans and amulets, tokens and totems. These were designed to attract love, ward off evil, and provide health, wealth, and happiness to their wearers. Museums display extension collections of artifacts that are believed to have served as power objects for our Stone Age ancestors. The early Egyptians placed charms in the tombs of royalty to ensure safe passage into the world beyond. Ancient Greek soldiers carried amulets into battle to protect them. Aztec priests used gemstones to invoke the deities and for prophesying.

Once sealed, a magic charm, amulet, or talisman should never be opened.

Good-luck charms are as popular today as they were in ancient times. Even people who don't believe in magic often give special significance to certain treasured objects, regardless of whether those objects have any monetary value. Is it just superstition, or do these items really work?

From the perspective of magic, your belief imbues an amulet or talisman with power. As we've already said, your mind and your intentions are the force behind all magic. Charms, however, draw upon the vibrations of their ingredients as well, especially gemstones, botanicals, and other natural substances that contain their own vital energies. The blending of mind and matter, in this case, can produce a very potent power object indeed.

Talismans

A talisman is designed to attract something its owner desires. Gemstones and jewelry have long been favored as talismans. The Chinese, for example, prize jade and wear it to bring health, strength, and good fortune. For centuries, women of different cultures have worn lockets that contain locks of their beloveds' hair.

You can also combine several items that relate to your objective; refer to the tables on pages 123–130 or the books recommended in Appendix B for ideas. Slip the selected items into a cloth or leather pouch and wear it as a talisman. Or you can place meaningful objects in a wooden box and set it on your altar to attract the object of your desires. A talisman can be made for yourself or for someone else. It's usually best to fashion a talisman while the moon is waxing. Check an ephemeris to make sure the planet that rules your intention is in direct motion at the time, too.

Amulets

Amulets are used to repel an undesired energy, condition, or entity. Protection amulets are among the most common and ancient tokens. During the Crusades, ladies gave opals to soldiers to keep them safe in battle. Ancient Egyptians wore the Eye of Horus to protect them and placed this symbol in tombs to guard the souls of the deceased.

Many people cast a circle around the space where a talisman or amulet will be made, to prevent unwanted energies from tainting it. When you're finished, charge the charm by sprinkling it with saltwater and/or holding it in incense smoke for a few moments.

An amulet may be a single stone or a combination of several ingredients known for their ability to ward off harm. You can wear an amulet or place it where it will safeguard something you value. The Celts hung rowan branches and Middle Easterners put eye amulets at the doors to their homes to ward off evil. Usually it's best to make amulets when the moon is waning.

Charms

Early charms were verbal spells, but the word "charm" is often used to refer to any magic spell, amulet, talisman, etc. A charm is frequently something you create specifically for yourself. Fashion it for a particular intention, with only one purpose per charm. Don't make a charm to win the lottery *and* to attract a lover.

Amulets or talismans may be a single gem or object, however charms generally contain more than one item. Each item should be something that relates to your intention and holds special meaning for you.

FACT

Use natural fabrics for amulet, talisman, or charm bags. Silk is a good choice because it protects the contents from outside vibrations. Cotton, because it's a porous material, allows the vibrations generated by the ingredients in your charm to move into the world more freely. The cloth's color should be one that relates to your intention (see Chapter 3).

Place the chosen ingredients in a cloth pouch. Tie the appropriate number of knots to hold your intentions in place (see Chapter 5), then charge the charm according to your favorite method. Carry the charm with you until your intention manifests. Then burn the charm in a ritual fire to show gratitude.

Chapter 9

Tools of the Trade

Although you don't really need any tools to perform spells and rituals, most magicians employ several special pieces of equipment as aids in their magical work. Each of these tools has its own, unique purpose. The four primary tools—the wand, pentagram, chalice, and athame—relate to the four elements. They're also pictured as the four suits of the tarot. Consider your tools sacred and don't let anyone else handle them or use them to practice magic.

9

Wand

The best known of all magic tools, the wand has gained even greater recognition through the Harry Potter stories. But while the scene in which Harry receives his wand is amusing, it's not accurate—the magician selects the wand, not the other way around. Until you imbue your wand with power, it's just an ordinary rod. Another misconception is that magicians use wands to turn people into toads or make them invisible.

A wand's real purpose is to direct energy. Aim it at the heavens to draw down cosmic power. Point it toward a person, place, or thing to which you intend to send energy. Use your wand to draw a protective circle around a place where you'll perform a spell or ritual.

The wand represents the fire element. A symbol of masculine power, it appears as the suit of wands (sometimes called rods or staves) in the tarot. In astrology, it's linked with the zodiac signs Aries, Leo, and Sagittarius.

ALERT!

Store your wand—and all your magic tools—in a safe place, such as an altar, trunk, or chest when you're not using it. Wrap it in a silk cloth or put it in a wooden box to protect it from dust, dirt, and ambient vibrations.

You can purchase a wand or make one yourself. Traditionally, wands were made from wood, but if you're skilled at metalsmithing you could fabricate one from iron, brass, or gold. The Druids preferred hazel or yew, but apple, ash, and oak are good choices, too. Rather than cut a wand from a living tree, find a branch that's fallen off. Cut it to a length of more than six inches, peel away the bark, and shape the tip into a point (it needn't be sharp). Decorate your wand with red or golden gemstones, ribbons, feathers, or objects that hold special significance for you. Affix a single-terminated quartz crystal at the pointed end. You may wish to paint or carve symbols on your wand, too.

Charging your wand transforms it from a stick of wood to a magical tool. Choose a day when the sun and moon are in fire signs (Aries, Leo, Sagittarius). Anoint your wand with one of the following essential oils: cinnamon, sandalwood, clove, musk, or almond. Then hold it in the smoke of a ritual fire for a few moments. Place it in the sun for a day to let it soak up solar rays. Speak to it and direct it to perform your will. Then wrap it in a piece of red silk and store it in a safe place until you're ready to use it.

Pentagram

The pentagram is a five-pointed star with a circle around it. An important symbol of protection, it's often used in magic ceremonies. Sometimes it's drawn in the air as part of a circle-casting ritual, sometimes pentagrams are positioned at the four compass points. In ceremonies it may be painted with essential oil on the foreheads of the people taking part in the ritual. Many magicians, especially followers of Wicca, wear pentagrams as protection amulets. Some hang a pentagram beside their front doors to keep their homes safe. If you have an altar, you may wish to place a pentagram there where it can continue sending out protective vibrations to your home and your housemates.

Pentagrams

A representative of the earth element, the star stands for the five "points" of the human body: the head, arms, and legs. It is linked with the feminine force, therefore it's best to choose a pentagram made of silver, a feminine metal ruled by the moon, or copper, which is ruled by Venus. In the tarot, the symbol appears as the suit of pentacles (sometimes called coins or discs), and astrologers associate it with the earth signs Taurus, Virgo, and Capricorn.

Since the 1800s, the Texas Rangers have worn badges shaped like pentagrams over their hearts. This powerful protection symbol may have saved more than one lawman's life. Today, Texans prominently display pentagrams on their homes, businesses, and public buildings, although most people don't realize the symbol's true meaning.

Pentagrams can be used in conjunction with other magic tools and charms. You might choose to adorn your wand, chalice, or athame with a pentagram, for instance. Carve a pentagram on a candle as part of a protection spell. Embroider one on an amulet pouch or draw one on a piece of paper and slip it inside a charm bag. This attractive symbol can also serve as a decorative motif for jewelry or clothing.

On a day when the sun and moon are in earth signs, charge your pentagram by anointing it with essential oil of mint, pine, patchouli, amber, or basil. Place it in a waterproof container, and bury it beneath a tree for a week. At the end of the week, dig it up and tell it how you want it to work with you. Either wear your pentagram or wrap it in green silk and store it in a safe place until you're ready to use it.

Chalice

Some people say the Holy Grail was actually a magic chalice. The chalice is also associated with the feminine force; its shape clearly suggests the womb. In rituals and rites, participants often drink a ceremonial beverage from a chalice. You could choose to drink special potions you've concocted from your chalice, too.

Many chalices feature long stems, especially those designed to be passed from hand to hand in rituals. Silver, because it's a feminine metal ruled by the moon, is a good choice for your magic chalice. Some people prefer crystal, colored glass, or ceramic chalices—the choice is entirely yours. Decorate it with meaningful symbols, if you wish, or leave it plain. You could also have one chalice for large gatherings and a smaller one that you reserve for private spells and rituals that involve only a magical partner.

Choose a day when the sun and moon are in water signs to charge your magic chalice. Sprinkle it with water you've collected from a spot that's special to you, as if "baptizing" it. Speak to your chalice and tell it how you want it to serve you. Then wrap it in a piece of blue silk and store it in a safe place until you're ready to use it.

The Chalice Well in Glastonbury, England, is a sacred site for Celts and followers of Goddess religions. Many people believe it is the final resting place of the Holy Grail. For 2,000 years, this well has been in constant use and has never been known to run dry. A symbol of the life force, the well is revered as a gift from Mother Earth to her children.

In the tarot, the chalice relates to the suit of cups. In astrology, it's linked with the water signs Cancer, Scorpio, and Pisces.

Athame

This ritual dagger is usually a double-edged knife about four to six inches long. Wiccans, however, sometime prefer crescent-shaped athames that represent the moon. If you decide to purchase a vintage dagger for your magic work, make sure it hasn't drawn blood in the past.

Except for perhaps inscribing symbols in candle wax with the dagger's point, you won't actually cut anything physical with your athame, so it needn't be sharp. When chopping up herbs, flowers, and spices to include in spells, use a regular kitchen knife instead.

The athame's main purpose is to symbolically clear away negative energies from a space you'll use in spell-working. It can also be utilized to slice through obstacles, again symbolically. Some people prefer to cast a circle with an athame instead of a wand. This tool represents the air element. In astrology it corresponds to the zodiac signs Gemini, Libra, and Aquarius; in the tarot it appears in the suit of swords.

Before you use it in spells and rituals, charge your athame by holding it in incense smoke—carnation, cinnamon, or ginger is best—for a few moments. If you wish, decorate the hilt with gemstones, crystals, feathers, and/or symbols that are meaningful to you. The best time for consecrating your ritual dagger is while the sun and moon are in air signs. When you've finished, wrap your athame in yellow silk and store it in a safe place until you're ready to use it.

Candles

The term candle comes from *candere,* a Latin word meaning to shine. Candles represent hope, a light in the darkness, a beacon that shows the way to safety and comfort. Regardless of whether you believe in magic, the concept of illumination carries both a practical meaning—visible light that enables us to carry out our daily tasks—and an esoteric one—an inspiration or awakening that enlivens our mundane existence and expands our understanding.

"There are two ways of spreading light, to be the candle or the mirror that reflects it." – Edith Wharton

Candles are essential ingredients in many spells. They symbolize the fire element and spirit, the energizing force that activates spells and rituals. In addition, they provide a focal point for your attention, helping you to still your mind. And their soft, flickering light creates an ambiance that shifts you out of your ordinary existence.

Magicians usually keep on hand a supply of candles in a range of colors. Chapter 3 discussed color symbolism. When you cast spells, it's important to remember these color connections. If you're doing a love spell, for example, burn a red or pink candle that represents passion, affection, and the heart. Prosperity spells call for green, gold, or silver candles, the colors of money.

Candles can enhance just about any spell. Many magicians set candles on their altars: white, red, or gold to symbolize male/yang/god; black, blue, or silver to represent female/yin/goddess energies. Some formal rituals involve carefully placing candles in specific spots and moving them according to prescribed patterns.

FACT

Five thousand years ago, the Egyptians formed beeswax into candles similar to the ones used today. Beeswax candles with reed wicks have been discovered in the tombs of Egyptian rulers, placed there, perhaps, to light their journey into the realm beyond.

You can cast a circle with candles, too. Simply position them around the space where you plan to perform a magic spell or ritual, then light them in a clockwise manner, beginning at the easternmost point. As mentioned earlier, you may choose to dress your candles with essential oils and/or carve words or sigils into the wax. More complicated spells require forming candles into shapes that represent your intentions.

Most people are familiar with a very simple and popular candle spell: blowing out candles on a birthday cake. Because cosmic energies are generally auspicious on your birthday, this is an ideal time to do magic spells. But in most instances, it's usually better to snuff out the candle than to blow it out, and some spells recommend letting the candle burn down completely.

Other Tools

You may choose to add a few other tools to your magical toolbox. Many magicians use ribbons to tie up charms and for other types of spells. (This will be discussed in more detail in later chapters.) You might wish to keep on hand a selection of ribbons and cords in a variety of colors—the colors should correspond to your intentions (see Chapter 3).

If your money seems to be going out faster than it's coming in, try this quick fix. Tie green ribbons around every faucet in your home. Tie three knots in each ribbon, and as you do this, say aloud: "As water flows, my wealth grows."

The bell, another pretty and popular tool, is often rung to signal the different steps in a ritual. The lovely sound can also help to clear sacred space because it dispels stagnant vibrations in the air.

Although many people consider the cauldron a witch's tool, it's symbolically a larger version of the chalice. You can mix brews and potions in a cauldron, if you like. Some people even use it for cooking magic meals over an open fire. If you prefer, you can build a fire inside your cauldron and drop requests, written on paper to petition the deities, into the flames.

The sword, a larger version of the athame, is generally used to banish unwanted energies from a ritual space. Like the dagger, it can also let you symbolically cut through obstacles in your path, but it's never wielded as a weapon.

Keeping a Grimoire

Also known as a Book of Shadows, a grimoire is a magician's secret journal of spells and rituals. Here's where you keep a record of the magic you perform, the ingredients and tools you use, and your results. It's a bit like a cook's personal collection of favorite recipes. You may wish to write your spells in a large, elegant book bound in leather or in a simple loose-leaf notebook. What's inside is more important than what's outside. If you like, decorate the pages with symbols and designs you find appealing.

Date your entries. You can include moon phases, the zodiac signs in which the sun, moon, and planets were positioned at the time you did the spell, and any other relevant data. For instance, you might want to make note of the time of day and place where you performed a spell or ritual. Make sure to write down your intention in doing the spell and, if you choose, the name of the person for whom it was enacted.

ALERT!

Remember, your grimoire is a very private and secret record. Don't let anyone else look at it, except perhaps a trusted magical partner with whom you work regularly. Store it in a safe place, so that your information won't accidentally fall into the wrong hands.

Be sure to describe your results and reactions. You'll probably do your favorite spells many times, so it's a good idea to make comments each time you repeat one. If you vary a spell at any time, note that too. Some spells take a while to materialize; if possible, keep track of results that develop over time.

Creating an Altar

An altar is a special place you create to hold the objects you use in your magic practice. Your altar could be a simple shelf, table, trunk, or cabinet, or it might be something more elegant and elaborate. It can be a permanent fixture or a portable one you can easily move when necessary. You can locate your altar inside your home or outdoors. Choose a spot that feels right for you, where you'll be able to enjoy peace and privacy. If you wish, dowse to find a place that resonates with positive vibrations.

This place is yours. You can display whatever you want on your altar: fresh flowers, incense, candles, statues, figurines, crystals, or whatever else pleases you. You might like to drape your altar with a decorative cloth and hang meaningful artwork above it. This is a good place to store your grimoire, tarot cards, runes, pendulums, gemstones, botanicals, and other ingredients you will use in spells. Depending on how large your altar is and how much room you have, you could even house ritual clothing and jewelry there.

ALERT!

Some people like to place their ritual tools on their altars; others store them inside. Don't just leave one or two implements out on your altar, however. Lay out all four principal tools (wand, pentagram, chalice, and athame) to establish a balance of elemental energies.

At different times of the year, you might enjoy decorating your altar for special ceremonies and sabbats. Don't feel that once you've created an altar it must remain the same way forever. In fact, it's a good idea to move things around periodically and to make changes that reflect the changes taking place in your life.

Chapter 10

A Guide to Successful Spell-Working

A few fundamental concepts underlie all magic: One, that thought empowered by emotion and will produces an outcome in the material world; two, that other realms of reality beyond Earth exist, populated by various entities and intelligences; and three, that magic blends your intention with the creative energy of a higher force. Regardless of which path appeals most to you—the formalized rituals of the Golden Dawn, the nature-based spirituality of Wicca, or the otherworldly journeying of shamanism—your magic will be safer and more effective if you follow some basic guidelines.

10

Magic and Miracles

Both magic and miracles defy the generally accepted laws of nature. They make lies of physical limitations. But that doesn't mean magic and miracles aren't natural or real. All it means is that the generally accepted ideas most people hold are too narrow. Newtonian physics postulated that the reality of the material world was distinct and separate from human beings' perception of it. Today's quantum physicists are showing that when you look at something, your perception and interaction with that object literally changes it. That's the view magic takes, too.

FACT

People who don't believe in magic or miracles are less likely to experience them than those who do believe. Even if hardcore skeptics do witness a miracle or magical result, they probably won't realize it.

The main difference between magic and miracles is that unlike miracles, magic is intentionally and consciously directed. When you do a magic spell, you choose an objective and design your thoughts and actions so as to bring about that objective. Miracles occur as a result of putting yourself in a state of receptivity and allowing a force greater than your conscious mind to produce a result, without predetermining what that result will be or how it will come about. Magic is active; miracles are receptive. In both instances, however, you serve as the conduit through which energy flows. In other words, you're the catalyst for whatever results.

Spiritual Guidance

At some point, your magical practice is bound to entail spiritual guidance. Many practitioners have guides upon whom they call for help, illumination, intervention, and advice. The Freemasons performed their magical work under the watchful eye of the Architect of the Universe. Pagans call upon the assistance of various gods and goddesses when doing spells. Shamans seek the aid and protection of totem animals. Whatever terms you use, and whatever power you choose to believe in, you'll need to align yourself with forces beyond your consciousness to perform magic.

Spiritual Assistance in Spell-Working

When some people do magic, they think of themselves as a co-creators with Divine Will. They consider Divine Will to be the animating force in the universe. You could call it God, Goddess, Spirit, Creator, or Source if you prefer. No matter how you view it, your job as a magician is to connect with this force, channel it through your mind and body, and shape it with images, words, and movements to bring about the desired outcome.

Magicians often use magic wands and other tools to direct spiritual energy. In many tarot decks, the Magician card depicts a man in a ritual stance, holding his arm above his head with his wand pointed at the heavens. This gesture draws down the divine force, so he can use it to work magic.

You'll also want to request spiritual protection while you are operating in magical realms. When shamans journey to other worlds, they go in the company of a totem animal guardian, just as a traveler to a foreign country might solicit the knowledge and direction of a native guide. Your spiritual guardian prevents other entities from harming you or interfering with your intentions.

This guide can also serve as a facilitator who helps you achieve your goal in the most expedient and correct manner. At the end of a magic spell, it's a good idea to turn over your intention to a higher power by saying something like, "This is done in harmony with Divine Will, my own True Will, and for the good to all." By doing this, you allow the spiritual force—which has a broader vantage point and understands factors you may not be aware of— to effect results in the best possible way.

Contacting Your Spirit Guides

There are many ways to connect with your guides, including meditation, guided imagery, visualization, dreams, relaxation techniques, and even a simple request. In theory, your guide is an entity or personality that accompanies you through your life. Some people call this entity a guardian angel. If you don't believe in angels, then think of this guide as your higher self, or as an evolved spirit who has your best interests at heart, or even as someone you love who has passed on. A guide may even be the soul of someone you knew in a past life.

Brian Weiss, a Miami psychiatrist and author of *Many Lives, Many Masters* and several other bestselling books, refers numerous times to the "masters." He defines them as evolved beings that are no longer in physical form, although they may have been human at one time.

You may wish to place an image—a statue, icon, or painting—in a place where you'll see it often, to remind you of your guide's presence and to keep you connected. Some people even tattoo their bodies with an image that reminds them of their guide.

Some people make offerings to their spiritual guardians. Burning incense is a traditional offering among Buddhists. This is a good way to begin a meditative session in which you seek to communicate with your guide. If you have a favorite essential oil that relates to your guardian, you might wish to dab some on your wrists or third eye to awaken your intuition. You can also light different-colored candles to invite your guide to join you.

Your spirit guardian can provide assistance in any situation or problem. Bestselling author and medical intuitive, Caroline Myss, recommends asking, "Why is this happening? How can I best respond to it?" "From this position," she writes, "you will be receptive to guidance and the clearest level of insight."

Purification

Before you begin a magic spell or ritual, you'll want to remove any unwanted energies from your person and from the sacred space where you'll be working. Some magicians take ritual baths before performing magic. Pour a few drops of a cleansing essential oil, such as pine, sandalwood, citrus, or eucalyptus, into your bathwater. If you like, burn candles and play relaxing music. Clearing your mind in this way also enables you to put the cares of the day behind you so they don't distract your attention.

To clear the area where you'll perform your spell or ritual, light a sage wand (a bundle of dried sage, tied together) or a stick of sage incense. Waft the fragrant smoke around the space until you feel the air is cleansed of any harmful, disruptive, or unbalanced energies. If other people will participate in the ritual with you, purify them before they enter the sacred space by waving the sage smoke around their bodies (front and back). You might also wish to draw a pentagram with essential oil on each person's forehead.

You can use a ritual dagger or sword to disperse negative energies, too. Hold your tool parallel to the ground with the point facing out while you walk around the space you are sanctifying. Or sweep the area clean with a broom—not just the floor, but the air as well—as Wiccans sometimes do. Some people ring bells, singing bowls, or chimes to chase away unwanted vibrations.

Casting a Circle

Think of Stonehenge, a great circle of stone megaliths. Or consider the enormous ditch in nearby Avebury, England, that is 1,200 feet in diameter, and the ring of standing stones within it. Stone circles like these dot the landscapes of Britain and Ireland. Circles symbolize both wholeness and protection, which is why magicians usually perform spells and rituals inside the perimeter of a magic circle.

When you cast a circle, you work on several levels simultaneously. At a physical level, you're defining the boundaries for your magical work, separating it from ordinary space. At a spiritual level, you're imbuing the space with your personal power and erecting a psychic barrier to keep out any unwanted energies.

In *The Spiral Dance,* Starhawk describes the circle as "the creation of a sacred space . . . Power, the subtle force that shapes reality, is raised through chanting or dancing and may be directed through a symbol or visualization. With the raising of the cone of power comes ecstasy, which may then lead to a trance state in which visions are seen and insights gained."

If you wish, you can draw a circle with flour, sea salt, sticks of burning incense, candles, feathers, flowers, or, of course, stones. But you needn't use a physical substance to cast a circle; you can simply envision a wall of white light surrounding you instead. You can cast a circle outdoors or inside. The circle should be large enough to accommodate the number of people who will be doing magic inside of it, as well as any objects that will be in the circle and your work area (such as a table, altar, or fire pit).

Bring all the ingredients you'll need and everyone who'll participate in the spell or ritual into the area before you cast the circle. Once inside, no one should leave the circle until the spell or ritual is finished. Cast your circle in a clockwise direction, so that when it's completed you'll be inside it. Begin at the easternmost point of the space where you'll be working (use a compass to find this point, if necessary). Move clockwise to the south, then the west, and the north, and finally come back to the east again to close the circle.

Many people place a symbolic item at each of the circle's four compass points. Here are some suggestions, but feel free to choose objects that hold meaning for you.

Direction	Element	Corresponding Color	Symbolic Objects
East	Air	Yellow	Wind chime, flag, feather, incense
South	Fire	Red	Candle, lantern, torch, rod/pole
West	Water	Blue	Cup or bowl of water, bell
North	Earth	Green	Stone, plant, coin, bowl of salt

When you're finished performing your magic, open the circle. This signals an end to the spell or ritual and releases the power you've generated into the world, where it can manifest. To open the circle, go to the east and trace another circle, this time walking in a counterclockwise direction.

At the end of a ritual, Wiccans often open a circle by holding hands and chanting or singing together: "The circle is open, but never broken. May the peace of the Goddess be forever in your heart. Merry meet, and merry part, and merry meet again."

Calling in the Four Directions

This part of the circle-casting ritual invites the guardians of the four directions to be present and to lend you their protection and power for the term of the ritual. Some people envision these guardians as angels: Raphael guards the east, Michael the south, Gabriel the west, and Uriel the north.

As you walk around your circle, stop at each compass point and "call in" the energy of that direction. Facing out, petition the entity by saying something like:

Guardian of the (eastern, southern, western, northern) sphere,
now we seek your presence here.
Come, (east, south, west, north), come. Join this rite tonight.

Another technique involves standing in the center of the circle, facing east, while you say aloud:

Before me Raphael, guardian of the east.
Behind me Gabriel, guardian of the west.
To my right Michael, guardian of the south.
To my left Uriel, guardian of the north.

Your invocation can be as simple or eloquent as you wish. Use your imagination. At the end of the spell or ritual, remember to release the energies you've called in and thank them for assisting you. Here's a simple releasing statement, but you can say whatever expresses your own feelings.

Guardian of the (east, north, west, south) we thank you.
Return home now, harming none, and let there be peace between us.
Hail, farewell, and blessed be.

Because you'll be opening the circle by moving counterclockwise, you'll release the energies of the four directions in the reverse order from the one you used to invoke them.

The Four Elements Technique

This technique combines the four elements—fire, earth, air, and water—to cast a circle. First, fill a bowl with saltwater, which symbolizes earth and water. Beginning in the east, walk in a clockwise direction, sprinkling the saltwater on the ground to define a circle as you say "With earth and water I cast this magic circle." Next, light a stick of incense, which represents fire and air (smoke). Again, start in the east and walk clockwise around the circle, trailing the fragrant smoke behind you while you say "With fire and air I cast this magic circle."

If you prefer, two people can perform this circle-casting ritual together. In this case, one person holds the bowl of saltwater, and the other carries the stick of burning incense.

Circle Casting with Candles

You'll need twelve candles in rainbow colors for this method. Position a yellow candle in the east, a red one in the south, a blue one in the west, and a green one in the north. The other candles can be colors that represent your intention, such as green for money or pink for love. Or you might choose seven candles to coordinate with the colors of the seven chakras, plus a white candle for protection. Arrange these eight candles so that they complete the circle.

Begin at the east and light the twelve candles one at a time in succession, working in a clockwise direction. When you've finished your spell or ritual, extinguish the candles in reverse order to open the circle.

Manifestation

You probably manifest things daily and don't even realize it. Perhaps you simply take these magical happenings for granted, or, as happens in many instances, you don't notice them at all. But in order to attract what you want consistently, you need to become aware of how manifestation occurs and begin to observe even the smallest things you're causing to manifest. This requires paying close attention to your thoughts and feelings throughout the day.

Manifestation means making something materialize in the visible world. As you already know, your thoughts are the seeds from which the fruits of your life grow. Everything that happens to you is the result of your thoughts taking form, or manifesting. And as simplistic as it may sound, like attracts like. Positive thoughts and energy tend to attract positive things: smiles from other people, compliments, favors, opportunities, good health, and abundance. Conversely, angry, negative thoughts and emotions lead to unpleasant things: rudeness from others, disappointments and frustrations, losses, even injuries and sickness. Good luck doesn't just happen; you create it yourself.

Focusing on Your Intention

Confused or unclear thoughts produce muddled, delayed, or unpredictable results. To bring about what you truly want, you need to be able to really focus on your intention. One way to do this is to collect pictures of the outcomes you desire. Place these images where you'll see them often.

For example, Elizabeth needed a computer but didn't have the money to buy one, so she cut out a photo of the model she wanted from the manufacturer's literature and taped it on her desk at home. Shortly thereafter, she got a new job. Her boss, without consulting with her, bought her a computer to use at home—exactly the model she'd been envisioning.

Make your own manifestation book, a loose-leaf binder with pictures of all the things you intend to manifest—a home, a new job, good health. Look through it often to focus your mind on your objectives. Keep updating it as necessary, adding pictures that represent new wishes and removing pictures that depict things you've already manifested.

You could also write a list of the things you intend to bring about. Although there's no limit to how many intentions you can manifest, most people can't focus their minds on a large number of ideas simultaneously. Therefore, it's usually best to include no more than ten things at a time on your list. Read through your list first thing in the morning and last thing at night. As soon as you manifest something on your list, remove it and add another wish.

Writing and Burning

Identify your most important objective, the one wish you most want to come true. Write this intention on a piece of paper. Remember to state it as an affirmation, in a positive way and in the present tense (see Chapter 2). After you've written it, read your affirmation aloud. Then burn the paper, releasing the thought into the cosmic web. As the smoke rises up to the heavens, ask that your wish be acted upon by Divine Will (or whatever higher force you choose) and brought into manifestation now, in a way that's for the good of all.

Ideally, you'll only have to do this once per wish. If you harbor any doubt or don't feel your power is strong enough, however, you might have to repeat the writing and burning ritual several times before you see measurable results.

Letting Go

Once you do a spell, let it go. Trust that your intentions will manifest at the right time, in the right way. Don't worry about whether you did everything just right. Don't keep doing the spell over and over, for this indicates doubt. Don't get impatient if you don't see results immediately—some things may take a while. Letting go means getting your ego out of the way and believing with all your heart and mind that the seeds you've planted will bear fruit.

The Power of Words

As discussed in Chapter 2, words produce vibrations that echo through the cosmic web and create effects in the visible world. Words also act as verbal symbols that embody your intentions. Uttering chants, affirmations, and incantations serves two purposes: to focus your mind during spells and rituals, and to project your objectives out into the universe.

Pay attention to any words you speak in connection with "I AM." Because this statement is imbued with creative power, it has a profound effect on you. Never say things like, "I am stupid" or, "I am afraid" or, "I am incapable of doing something." Such expressions are likely to manifest the conditions you've described.

Magicians use certain words and phrases for special purposes. These words contain secret meanings beyond their obvious, everyday ones. "I

AM," for instance, represents the divine spark, spirit, or life force within you that links you to the creative source of the cosmos. When you say this, you affirm your indestructible and eternal nature and accentuate the divine power within you.

Some magicians prefer to speak words from Sanskrit, Arabic, or other ancient languages. In many of their ceremonies, ritual magicians intone god names taken from the Hebrew language. The vibrations in these sounds produce a physical result known as harmonic resonance, which can be felt on other planes of existence. One of these words, YHVH, is an abbreviation for the word Jehovah and is considered most sacred. The vowels have been removed because the actual name is said to be unspeakable.

Wiccans often greet one another with the words "Merry meet." Another phrase, "Blessed be," may be spoken as a welcome, at the end of a ritual, in parting, or any time you want to wish someone well. This simple blessing contains the vibrations of love, and it thus attracts positive energy, dispels harmful vibrations, and confers protection.

Ending a Spell or Ritual

Spells, like books, have a beginning, middle, and end. Properly concluding a spell or ritual is just as important as doing the other parts. These final actions seal your spell, activate it, and allow you to step back into your everyday world. Perform the following before you open the magic circle (as described on page 151).

Binding a Spell

The number three represents creativity, form, and manifestation in the three-dimensional world. Therefore, you can end a spell by repeating a statement three times or performing a gesture three times. For instance, you could tie three knots to close a charm bag or pass a talisman through incense smoke three times.

It's customary to close a spell with a definitive statement. The phrase, "So mote it be," is often used by Wiccans to bind a spell. If you prefer, you can say "So be it now" or, "So it is done" or, "Amen." In her book *The Spiral Dance*, Starhawk offers this closing statement you can use to bind a spell:

> *By all the power*
> *Of three times three,*
> *This spell bound around*
> *Shall be.*
> *To cause no harm,*
> *Nor return on me.*
> *As I do will,*
> *So mote it be.*

To make sure your spell only brings about positive results, say something in conclusion like, "This spell is done for the good of all, harming none."

ALERT!

When you perform a spell for another person, the vibrations you activate produce a ripple effect throughout the cosmos. Therefore, the energy generated will have an impact on you as well. Magicians believe that whatever you send out will return to you, like a boomerang, but multiplied threefold; thus, you actually receive more than you give.

Gratitude

Gratitude is the final step in doing a spell. Always end every spell by showing gratitude to whomever you see as the source or creative power in the universe. Even before you see results, say thank you. Gratitude has two purposes in magical work. It indicates that you fully believe your intention will be manifested, and it acknowledges the help you receive from forces outside yourself.

An expression of gratitude may be as simple as saying "Thank you" at the close of a spell. Some people like to make an offering of some kind. Others demonstrate gratitude for the help they've received by giving help to someone else. How you choose to show your gratitude is less important than the intention behind it. Sincerity is what really matters.

Chapter 11

Prosperity and Abundance Spells

Do you define prosperity as a dollar amount, such as a cool million, for instance? Or do you think of it as a condition or a state of being, such as living comfortably? Does *abundance* mean having more of everything or having enough of everything? These distinctions may seem trivial, but before you begin doing prosperity and abundance spells, you need to be absolutely clear in your own mind about what these concepts mean to you.

Your Perceptions about Prosperity and Abundance

If you were to conduct an informal survey among your friends and acquaintances, you might be surprised to discover how differently various people view prosperity and abundance. Their responses would probably cover a wide spectrum of conditions: to have more money; to be in a better job; to enjoy a happy marriage or romantic relationship; to write a bestselling novel or screenplay; to own a house; to be self-employed; to be able to travel.

"Your state of wealth externally is an extension and testament of your state of wealth internally. How clear and certain you are in thoughts of wealth is evidenced externally." —David Cameron, *A Happy Pocket Full of Money*

Over time, your concepts about what constitutes prosperity might change. Once you own the house or your novel hits the bestseller lists or you find the ideal relationship, you'll likely develop new ideas about money and abundance.

Prosperity Exercise

Take a few minutes to define what prosperity and abundance mean to you today, right now, in this moment. Make a list of ten things you desire and that would make you feel prosperous if you had them. Now find an object that represents each entry on your list. Select these objects with care—you're going to use them to work magic.

Let's say that your wildest dream of personal prosperity includes you getting your pilot's license. Perhaps you haven't yet accomplished this goal because you didn't have enough money for lessons or an airplane. Any number of objects might represent your dream: a model airplane, a photograph of the type of plane you would like to fly, or a child's plastic toy plane. The point is to choose something that immediately connects you to the feeling.

When you've collected all ten items, one for each entry on your list, put them in a place where you'll see them often: your desk, a mantelpiece or windowsill, or your altar. Each time you look at them, you'll be reminded of your dreams of abundance and your intention to attract prosperity into your life.

Prosperity Consciousness

Do you think you're worthy of prosperity? Do you believe you are inherently valuable? Do you trust the universe to provide for you and always give you whatever you need? Or do you constantly worry about paying bills and fear poverty? Do you believe that money is evil? Do you think you can't be both rich and spiritual?

FACT

Money and material bounty are the earthly expressions of a universe that is infinitely abundant. Everyone can tap into that abundance without depriving anyone else. It boils down, once again, to belief in yourself and in the universe's ability to provide.

Prosperity consciousness means you wholeheartedly believe you deserve to have whatever you desire. You know that your good fortune doesn't detract from anyone else's—the universe's warehouse of goodies is infinite. You welcome riches and abundance of all kinds into your life. You use money to enrich your life and the lives of others. If you don't have prosperity consciousness, you'll need to develop it before you can successfully do a spell for prosperity.

Louise Hay devotes a chapter to prosperity in her book *You Can Heal Your Life*. She provides a list of negative money beliefs and then shows you how to change any of these beliefs that you may hold. To be prosperous, she writes, it's necessary that you do the following:

- Feel deserving
- Make room for the new
- Be happy for other people's prosperity
- Be grateful

To these, she adds, "Love your bills." At first this seems crazy. Love your Macy's bill? Your electric bill? Your mortgage payment? But the more you think about it, the more sense it will make. After all, a bill is simply an acknowledgment that the company trusts that you can and will pay, a sort of cosmic honor system. The lender has faith in you. Why resent that?

Creating New Beliefs

If you're like most people, your beliefs about money and prosperity were instilled in you long ago, perhaps by your parents, a religious institution, or the society in which you lived. If these deeply entrenched attitudes are preventing you from attaining the level of abundance you desire, they must be eliminated and replaced with new ideas.

Each time you notice yourself saying or thinking something that undermines your prosperity consciousness, such as "I can't afford that," cross it out in your mind's eye by drawing a line through it. Then rephrase the statement in a positive way.

Affirmations are good tools for reprogramming your ideas. Write down one or more affirmations related to abundance and repeat them often. Say your affirmation(s) aloud at least a dozen times a day, until your subconscious gets the message. Here are a few suggestions:

- My life is rich with abundance of all kinds.
- I have everything I need and desire.
- All my bills are paid, and I have plenty of money to spare and share.
- I am happy, healthy, wealthy, and fulfilled in every way.

Try not to concern yourself with how you're going to get that extra money. Just be aware that opportunities will begin to present themselves to you if you continue to say the affirmation. Be alert for signs and patterns that can signal new opportunities. And always phrase your affirmation in the present tense, as if the condition you desire already exists.

While you're building your prosperity consciousness, make symbolic gestures that reinforce your belief in your worth. Donate money to a worthwhile charity. Buy yourself something special. Treat yourself to dinner at your favorite restaurant. Post this quote from Louise Hay's book in a spot where you'll see it frequently: "True prosperity begins with feeling good about yourself . . . It is never an amount of money; it is a state of mind. Prosperity or lack of it is an outer expression of the ideas in your head."

Discover the Source of Your Beliefs

Look back over your life and see if you can determine where your ideas about money and abundance originated. Most likely, you were quite young when this happened. Close your eyes and see yourself as a child again. Witness your child-self's reaction when these concepts were being implanted in your consciousness. How did you feel at the time? Do you still feel the same way? Do you want to change those old beliefs?

Imagine taking your child-self onto your lap. Talk to your child-self and explain that the old ideas are no longer valid for you. This part of you is very receptive and will do its best to please you. Describe the new beliefs you want your child-self to accept and why these updated ideas are better.

Remember something you wanted as a child—a toy, a shiny new pair of shoes, a special outing—but never received because there wasn't enough money. Now, give yourself that thing you wanted as a child. Envision taking your child-self along on a shopping trip or outing. Enjoy your time together.

Be Careful What You Wish For

At some stage in most people's magical work, something invariably happens that brings home the truth of the saying, "Be careful what you wish for. You may just get it." The adage is actually addressing the power of intention. When you ask for wealth or financial freedom, think about the repercussions of that wish. How will your new abundance or financial freedom affect your family? Your relationships with your friends? Your living situation?

You've probably heard stories about people who've won the lottery and how sudden wealth changed their lives. Some of them missed their old jobs, their old neighborhoods, their old friendships. "The Monkey's Paw," by W. W. Jacobs, is a story about what can happen when you make a wish without considering the possibilities. Before you do prosperity magic, think carefully about what you wish for. Changes may be inevitable, and the changes may be what you desire. If you are clear in your intentions, you can direct those changes to your advantage.

Timing Prosperity and Abundance Spells

For each of the spells in this chapter, the most advantageous time to perform the spell is noted. In most cases, you'll be more successful if you do spells for prosperity and abundance while the moon is waxing. The seeds you plant with your spell grow along with the moon. As the moon's light increases, so will your wealth.

Taurus is the zodiac sign of money, material goods, and physical resources. Therefore, an ideal time to do prosperity spells is when the moon and/or the sun is in Taurus. If your spell involves other people's money, insurance, taxes, or litigation, you might be better off casting a spell when the moon and/or sun is in Scorpio.

The best days of the week for doing prosperity magic are Thursday and Friday, the days ruled by Jupiter and Venus. These planets encourage growth, abundance, and good fortune. Sunday—the sun's day—can also be favorable, especially if your career success and public image are involved.

If you know astrology or can consult with an astrologer, look for periods when transiting or progressed Venus or Jupiter influences your birth chart in a positive way. Avoid doing prosperity spells when transiting or progressed Saturn forms difficult connections with the planets and money houses in your chart.

Spell to Create Prosperity Consciousness

Tools:

- 14 green, scented candles
- 1 empty glass container
- An affirmation

When:

- On the new moon

Purchase fourteen green candles scented with pine or cedar essential oils. Votives and tea light candles are good to use for this spell. On the night of the new moon, light one of the candles at your altar or special place. While it's burning, say your affirmation aloud and feel its truth. After five minutes, extinguish the candle and rub your hands in the smoke. Waft the smoke toward your face, your body, your clothes. Remember the fragrance, and associate it with abundance, prosperity, and your new belief. Set the candle aside.

ALERT!

In some countries, green is the color of paper money; therefore, your mind automatically makes a connection between green and wealth. If you live in a country where a different color appears on your currency, use that color to symbolize money instead. Gold and silver, the colors of precious metals, are good choices, too.

Repeat this ritual each day for the next thirteen days, using a new candle each time. Set each spent candle next to its predecessor. On the night of the full moon, after you have burned the fourteenth candle, light all fourteen and let them burn down. Then pour the melted wax left over from all the candles into a glass container, forming a new candle. This new candle symbolizes your new belief about prosperity. Once the wax has solidified, bury it, symbolically planting it in the ground to make your wealth grow.

Tarot Spell to Increase Your Income

Tools:

- 1 green candle and 1 white candle
- 1 deck of tarot cards
- An object that represents your desire
- 1 pen with green ink
- 1 piece of paper

When:

- During the waxing moon

Green is the color of paper money as well as healthy, growing plants. White represents clarity and protection. Put your candles at opposite ends of your altar. Between them, place an object that signifies your desire to increase your income. This could be one of the objects that you chose to symbolize the intentions on your wish list. Or it could be a coin, a dollar bill, a piece of jewelry, or something else that suggests wealth.

From your deck of tarot cards, select the ace of pentacles (sometimes called coins), which indicates new financial undertakings and opportunities. Place it in front of the white candle. In front of the green candle, put the ten of pentacles. Sometimes called the "Wall Street" card, the ten symbolizes a financial windfall. In the middle, between the two candles, place the nine of cups—the "wish card"—and the Star card (from the tarot deck), which symbolizes hope.

Light the candles and say:

The money I spend
or the money I lend
comes back to me
in multiples of three.

Visualize money flowing to you from all directions. The more vivid you can make your visualization, and the more you back it with intense emotion, the faster your wish will manifest. This ritual can be as short or as long as you want it to be. End the spell by extinguishing the candles and giving thanks. Allow everything to remain on your altar overnight.

You can enhance the money-drawing power of the candles by dressing them with essential oils before you burn them. Pour a little oil of pine, sandalwood, mint, clove, or cinnamon—the scents associated with money—in your palms, then rub the oil on the candles.

The next night, repeat the ritual, but with a few changes. Get out your tarot deck again and remove the two and five of pentacles from the deck. You don't want these two cards on your altar. The two of pentacles indicates financial imbalance and can mean you're robbing Peter to pay Paul; the five signifies poverty and debt. Take the remaining cards in the suit of pentacles and place them between the candles. Light the candles. Say the incantation while you visualize and affirm your wish coming true. Then extinguish the candles, leaving everything on the altar overnight.

On the third night, light the candles and give thanks for everything you have (even those things that haven't yet manifested). Repeat the incantation and feel the reality of your increase taking form around you. Let the candles burn down completely.

Feng Shui Wealth Spell

Tools:
- A plant with red or purple flowers

When:
- During the waxing moon

In feng shui, red and purple are considered lucky colors. Plants symbolize growth.

Stand at the door you use most often when going in and out of your home, facing inside. Locate the farthest left-hand corner of your home, from this vantage point. That's your wealth sector. Put the plant in that area to make your wealth grow.

Water, feed, and care for the plant with loving kindness. As you tend it and watch it grow, you'll notice your fortune improves.

Prosperity Brew

Tools:
- Fresh or dried parsley
- Fresh or dried mint leaves
- 1 cup of water

When:
- During the new moon

On the night of the new moon, pour a cup of water into a pot and begin heating it on the stove. Put the parsley and mint in the water and say, "I embrace prosperity and open myself to receive abundance of all kinds." Stir the brew with a wooden spoon, making three clockwise circles to charge the mixture. Bring the water to a boil, then turn off the stove and allow the brew to cool. Strain the water, then pour it on the plant you placed in your wealth sector (see the Feng Shui Wealth Spell) or use it to water other plants in your home or yard.

Goodbye Debt Spell

Tools:
- 1 large iron pot or cauldron
- The five of pentacles from a tarot deck you don't use
- Cedar wood chips, sticks, or shakes

When:
- During the waning moon

Place the cedar inside the pot or cauldron. The cauldron represents creativity and fertility; cedar is associated with prosperity. Set fire to the wood, and when you have a small blaze going, drop the tarot card into the flames. The five of pentacles signifies debt and poverty; as the card burns, envision your debts disintegrating as well. Let the fire burn down completely, then collect the ashes. On the night before next new moon, bury the ashes far from your home.

Money Talisman

Tools:
- 1 strip of paper
- 1 pen with green, gold, or silver ink
- Peppermint essential oil
- 1 green pouch (preferably made of silk or velvet)
- 1 coin (any denomination)
- 3 whole cloves
- 1 pinch of cinnamon
- 1 gold or silver ribbon 9 inches long
- Cedar chips
- Pine or sandalwood incense

When:
- During the waxing moon

On the strip of paper, write an affirmation such as, "I now have plenty of money for everything I need and desire. Riches come to me from all directions." Dot the corners of the paper with essential oil, then fold it three times and slip it into the pouch. Add the coin, cedar, and herbs to the pouch.

Tie the pouch with the ribbon, making three knots. Each time you tie a knot, repeat your affirmation. When you've finished, say "This is now accomplished in harmony with Divine Will, my own true will, and with good to all." Light the incense, and hold the talisman in the incense smoke to charge it. Carry the pouch in your pocket or purse. If you prefer, use the talisman in your place of business. You can put it in your safe, cash register, or money drawer.

Crystal Abundance Spell

Tools:

- 1 quartz crystal
- An image that represents abundance

When:

- On a Thursday when the moon is waxing

Select a magazine picture that symbolizes prosperity to you. Or choose an image of an object or condition you desire—a new home, a sports car, a European vacation—and set it face up on a windowsill where the moon's light will shine on it.

FACT

Some quartz crystals contain bits of greenish mineral matter in them. These are known as "money crystals." If possible, acquire one of these to use in this spell. The amplifying energy of the crystal combined with the symbolism of the color green can enhance your spell.

Wash the crystal in warm water with mild soap to cleanse it of any ambient energies. Dry the crystal, then hold it to your third eye while thinking about your intention; this projects the image into the crystal. Then set the crystal on the picture. Make sure the crystal's point faces toward the inside of your home, to draw abundance from the universe to you. Leave the crystal in place overnight. In the morning, remove the crystal and picture and give thanks for the bounty you are about to receive.

Chapter 12

Love Spells

Love makes the world go round, as the saying goes, and more magic spells are cast for matters of the heart than for any other purpose. Because emotion is one of the key ingredients in magic, it's logical that love spells would be among the most powerful of all. Strong feelings, however, can sometimes cause confusion or throw you off balance. Therefore, use extra caution when performing love spells, and don't let your heart rule your head.

Defining What You Want

What's your reason for doing a love spell? Are you trying to attract a new romantic partner? Looking for your soul mate? Hoping to rekindle the spark in an existing relationship? The more specific you can be, the greater your chances of success.

Keep in mind that a love spell's primary purpose isn't to make someone fall in love with you. Its purpose is to balance your own energy so you attract the partner who is right for you. A relationship results from the interaction of two people, two individual forces—yin and yang—that merge to form a sum greater than the parts.

"Relationships are the Holy Spirit's laboratories in which He brings together people who have the maximal opportunity for mutual growth. He appraises who can learn most from whom at any given time, and then assigns them to each other."—Marianne Williamson, *A Return to Love*

One would think this should be easy, but for many people it's not. Your ideas may be influenced by the expectations of your family, your friends, or the culture in which you live. Your perceptions about the ideal mate might be conditioned by television and movies, books and magazines, and all sorts of societal stereotypes, as well as by unconscious archetypes. Most likely, your conceptions of relationships and what you want in a partner contrast dramatically with the ideas that your grandmother held. The reasons a man in Zimbabwe marries could be quite different from those that unite a couple in Sweden. Even you and your best friend may not agree on what constitutes a good relationship.

Your Love List

Before you do any love spells, make a list of the qualities you seek in a partner. The act of compiling this list will prompt you to really think about your needs, desires, hopes, and priorities, to put energy and intent behind the process of manifesting your objectives. In a sense, your list becomes a spell. Like an affirmation, you state your intentions—what you intend to find in a partner—and focus your mind toward achieving these objectives.

Your list can be as long and as detailed as you choose. As you write your list, be sure to state your desires in a positive way and in the present tense. Here are some examples:

- I now have a partner who respects and values me.
- I can trust and rely on my partner at all times and in all situations.
- My partner and I support and encourage each other's goals.
- My partner and I share a spiritual path.
- My partner and I have many common interests and enjoy one another's company.
- I now have a mate who is willing and able to enter into a committed, loving, primary partnership with me.

Be specific. Consider every angle. Cover all your bases. You might want to let a trusted friend read your list and provide feedback, so you don't overlook anything. A woman made a long and detailed love list that described all the qualities she sought in a mate. Soon afterward, she met the man of her dreams. Unfortunately, he was already married to someone else, a point she'd forgotten to include on her love list.

Defining Who You Are

Before you can attract a romantic partner who's right for you, you have to love yourself. It sounds simple enough, but many people have grown up believing that they aren't worthy or that they aren't attractive or intelligent enough, and they undermine their chances of establishing healthy, happy relationships. So before you start doing love spells, spend a little time uncovering your beliefs about yourself.

If you find that you hold negative beliefs about yourself, try one of author Louise Hay's most fundamental and powerful affirmations: "I love and approve of myself." Say it out loud while staring at yourself in the mirror. Write it down and stick the note on your fridge, your computer, or wherever you'll see it frequently. Yes, you probably will feel a bit foolish at first, but that just means the affirmation is working. When you repeat something often enough, your unconscious mind eventually gets the message.

Online matchmaking services often ask you to create a personal profile. Even if you have no intention of doing computer dating, it can be helpful to write a brief synopsis of yourself, outlining your positive qualities as if you were trying to entice a prospective partner. Write a paragraph that highlights all your assets—don't be shy!

Magic, Free Will, and Manipulation

Love spells tend to be the trickiest of all, the place where many magicians go astray and dabble in black magic. That's not to say they hex their partners or wish anything evil to happen. But the heart isn't rational, and powerful emotions can interfere with good judgment. When you want someone really badly, it can be hard to refrain from using magic to manipulate that person.

What makes a spell manipulative? The main criterion to look for is whether it violates another person's free will. You don't have to actively harm someone to misuse magic. Any time you force or coerce a person through magical means to do something he wouldn't do of his own volition, you're on shaky ground. Whenever your desire to get what you want overshadows your respect for another person's rights, you're leaning in the wrong direction.

The book *Naughty Spells/Nice Spells* by Skye Alexander suggests that before you do a love spell you "Consider the possible consequences—are you willing to accept what happens? Would you advise your best friend to do it? How would you react if someone did it to you? Trust your feelings—if you don't feel right about it, don't do it."

The Right Way to Do Love Spells

Let's say you're interested in a certain individual and want to entice that person into a romantic relationship. Your intention and the way you word a spell can make a big difference in the quality of the outcome. Instead of stating, "Joe and I are now lovers," word your affirmation like so: "Joe and I now enjoy the best possible relationship we can have together." Then, if it's best for the two of you to be lovers, that's what will happen. If, on the other hand, another type of relationship would serve you and Joe better, you'll put yourself in a position to experience what's best for both of you.

ALERT!

When you do a spell to tie a partner to you, you also bind yourself to that person. The bond can be extremely hard to break if you decide later on that your perfect lover isn't perfect after all. Before you do a love spell, be absolutely certain about what you want. Even so, it's wise to turn over the end result to a higher power.

The ideal way is to let the universe find the right mate for you. Instead of fixating on a particular person, do a spell to attract the partner who's right for you. This might turn out to be the individual you've got your eye on, but maybe there's someone even better out there whom you haven't met yet. Doing magic with an open mind and an open heart sends your message into the cosmic web—like posting your request with a magical matchmaking service—so that your perfect partner can receive it and respond.

Doing Spells with a Partner

When it comes to doing magic, two hearts can be better than one—provided you both are in agreement. The blend of yin and yang energies forms a strong, balanced creative force. Doing a spell with a partner to increase the love between you can be a very powerful and beautiful experience. Many couples do magic together to conceive a child or for other joint purposes.

Before you begin, discuss your intentions and your feelings about the spell you plan to do. Each of you should have input in designing and casting the spell. Unless one person is significantly more skilled than the other, try to make your roles in the ritual equal, so that neither partner dominates. Remember, the outcome will affect both of you.

Timing Love Spells

As you already know, each day of the week is governed by a planet, and each planet rules specific areas of life. Astrologers connect Venus with love and relationships, and Friday is Venus's day. In order to tip the odds in your favor, do the love spells in this chapter on Friday, unless stated otherwise.

FACT

Libra is the zodiac sign of relationships. You'll get an added energy boost if you perform a love spell when the moon and/or the sun is in Libra. Taurus embodies the physical side of love, so if you want to turn up the heat in a romance, consider doing your spell when the sun and/or moon is in Taurus.

If you're trying to attract a new partner, do a spell on the new moon. If you want to increase the joy or passion in an existing relationship, or to nudge a budding affair into full bloom, do your spell when the moon is waxing. To end an unfulfilling relationship, do magic while the moon is waning.

If you know astrology or can consult with an astrologer, look for periods when transiting or progressed Venus influences your birth chart in a positive way, or when Jupiter makes a favorable contact with your natal Venus or seventh house. Avoid doing love spells when transiting or progressed Saturn, Uranus, or Pluto forms a difficult connection with Venus, the moon, or the relationship houses in your chart.

Spell to Attract a New Lover

Tools:
- 1 rose-colored candle
- Ylang-ylang, rose, or jasmine essential oil
- List of qualities you seek in a partner

When:
- The first Friday after the new moon

This is your chance to put the love list you compiled earlier to work, magically. On the first Friday after the new moon, dress your candle with essential oil. Pour a little oil in your palm, and then rub it over the entire candle (except the wick). Set your list on your altar or other surface, and set the candle on it. Light the candle.

As the scent of the heated oil is released into the air, vividly imagine your lover. Feel this person's presence there in the room with you. How does this person look, act, speak, and dress? Imbue your vision with as much detail as possible. What type of work does he or she do? What are his or her passions? Continue the visualization for as long as you like, making your mental images as rich as possible.

When you've spent as much time as you feel is necessary, snuff out the candle's flame. Repeat this spell two more times before the full moon. On the night of the full moon, release your wish by allowing the candle to finish burning down completely. Express thanks for the love you are about to receive.

Spell to Attract Your Soul Mate

Tools:
- 1 fresh rose
- 1 ballpoint pen
- 1 pink and 1 red candle (small votive-style candles are best)
- Ylang-ylang essential oil
- 1 copper bowl
- Rose, patchouli, ylang-ylang, or jasmine incense
- A vase of water

When:
- On the new moon, preferably on a Friday

Place the red rose, which symbolizes the love you're looking for, on your altar. Use the ballpoint pen to inscribe the letter X—the Norse rune for love—in the candles. Anoint the candles, which represent you and your soul mate, with the essential oil. (Pink is the color of love and affection, red the color of passion.) Set the candles together in the bowl. Light the incense and the candles, then say:

Winds of love, come to me,
Bring my soul mate, I decree.
As I wish, so mote it be.

Imagine yourself with your soul mate. Make your visualization as detailed and vivid as possible. Feel this person's presence forming in the air around you. Let the candles burn all the way down, so the pink and red wax flows together in the bowl. While the wax is still warm, shape it with your fingers to form a heart, commingling the pink and red. Run cold water into the bowl so the wax doesn't stick, and then remove the wax heart and place it near the door of your home. If you know feng shui, put the wax heart in your relationship sector. Allow the rose petals to dry. Save them for other spells.

Spell to Enhance a Relationship

Tools:
- 2 pink or red candles
- Rose, ylang-ylang, jasmine, or patchouli essential oil
- Deck of tarot cards

When:
- During the waxing moon, preferably on a Friday

This spell is designed to increase the love between you and a partner. Choose candles of a color that signifies what you're trying to accomplish. Pink represents love and affection, and red represents passion. Select the oil you like best.

During the waxing moon, anoint the candles with the essential oil. Put a dot of oil on your heart to open it. From your deck of tarot cards, select the king and the queen of cups (which stand for you and your partner) and the nine of cups (the wish card). Place the candles on the altar, and set the three cards face up between the candles.

Light the candles and state your wish. Be specific. Imagine it coming true. After a few minutes, extinguish the candles and place them in the area where you and your beloved will be spending time together. Whenever you're together in that room, make sure these candles are burning.

Clean Up Your Love Life

This spell is based on the feng shui concept that clutter in your home signifies confusion, blockages, and messiness in your life. It requires no tools and can be done anytime—the sooner the better!

Stand at the entrance you use most often to go in and out of your home, facing inside. Locate the furthest, right-hand section of your home (as seen from your position). This is your relationship area. Notice what's in this space. If it's cluttered, go clean it up. Get rid of old stuff that you don't need or use anymore. In feng shui, old stuff represents old baggage and things from your past that may be holding you back. Organize what you choose to keep so it's neat and orderly.

Pay attention to the things you place in this area, for their symbolism is an important part of the spell. Old, faded, worn-out objects represent a love life that's lost its sparkle. Broken items indicate broken dreams or a physical breakup. Display things in this sector that symbolize what you desire in a romantic relationship or that signify hope, joy, and love.

The Drink of Love

Tools:
- The Lovers card from a tarot deck
- A glass of spring water
- A silver (or silverplate) spoon
- A drop of melted honey or a pinch of sugar

When:
- On a Friday night during the waxing moon

Place the tarot card face up on a windowsill where the moon will shine on it. Set the glass of water on top of the card and leave it overnight. The image of the card will be imprinted into the water. In the morning, use a silver spoon to stir the honey or sugar into the glass to sweeten the water and, symbolically, your relationship. Drink the water with your partner to strengthen the love between you.

Love Talisman

Tools:

- 1 strip of paper
- 1 pen with red ink
- 1 pink or red pouch, preferably made of silk or velvet
- 2 dried rose petals left from the Spell to Attract Your Soul Mate
- A pinch of cocoa
- A pinch of thyme
- 2 apple seeds
- 1 piece of rose quartz
- 1 small pearl
- 1 purple ribbon
- Saltwater
- 1 ritual chalice or cup

When:

- On the first Friday after the new moon

On the strip of paper, write an affirmation such as, "I now have a lover who's right for me in every way and we are very happy together." Fold the paper three times and slip it into the pouch. Add the rose petals, cocoa, thyme, apple seeds, and gemstones.

Tie the pouch with the ribbon, making six knots. Each time you tie a knot, repeat your affirmation. When you've finished, say "This is now accomplished in harmony with Divine Will, my own true will, and for the good of all."

Pour the saltwater into your ritual chalice or cup and swirl it around a few times, in a clockwise direction, to energize it. Dip your fingers in the water, and then sprinkle the talisman with the water to charge it. Carry the pouch in your pocket or purse. If you know feng shui, place the talisman in the relationship sector of your home.

Six is the number of give and take, and it signifies the exchange of energy between two people. Because six is the total of three times two, it represents bringing a wish that involves two people into the three-dimensional realm. When you tie knots, while stating your intention aloud, you fix the energy of your wish permanently into the talisman.

Gemstone Fidelity Spell

Tools:
- An obelisk-shaped piece of rose quartz
- An obelisk-shaped piece of carnelian
- 1 piece of dark blue ribbon
- 1 piece of white silk
- A metal box with a lid, large enough to contain the two gemstones

When:
- When the moon is in Capricorn

The gemstones have two symbolic meanings in this spell. Not only do they represent you and your partner, but rose quartz is a stone of love and affection, and carnelian represents passion. The ribbon's color—dark blue—indicates strength, sincerity, and permanence; the white cloth offers protection.

Wash the gemstones with warm, soapy water, and then stand them side by side on your altar so that they are touching. Imagine one embodying your energy, the other your beloved's energy (it doesn't matter which gem you choose to represent which person). Tie the stones together with the ribbon, making two knots, while you envision you and your partner being connected by a strong bond of love and devotion. Cover the gems with the white cloth and leave them until evening.

Once the moon has risen, wrap up the gemstones in the white silk cloth, and then set the package in the box. Take the box outside and bury it in the ground, preferably beneath an oak or apple tree.

Love Bath

Tools:
- A tub filled with comfortably hot water
- 1 teaspoon of sea salt
- The rest of the rose petals left from the Spell to Attract Your Soul Mate
- A few drops of jasmine, ylang-ylang, patchouli, or rose essential oil
- 1 red or pink candle in a candleholder
- Romantic music

When:
- On a Friday night, during the waxing moon

As you fill your bathtub with water, sprinkle the sea salt into it. Salt acts as both a purifying agent, dispersing any unwanted vibrations, as well as a symbol of the earth element, which is associated with stability, security, and sensuality. Add the essential oil to the bath water, then scatter the rose petals on top. Light the candle and turn on the music. Get into the tub and soak pleasantly, as you think loving thoughts about your partner. If you don't yet have a romantic partner, think positive thoughts about the person you intend to attract. If you have a lover, invite him or her to join you in the love bath.

Chapter 13

Spells for Personal Power

Self-doubt and lack of self-worth are common problems for many people. Self-esteem issues can keep you from achieving success in your career, from becoming financially secure, or from finding the love you desire and deserve. They can even cause illness. Increasing your sense of personal power will help you to enhance every area of your life. You'll also improve your magical power so you can produce better, faster results.

Your Self-Image

Ironically, your self-image probably isn't something you created yourself. It's a patchwork affair made up of bits and pieces you've collected from lots of other people: family, teachers, religious leaders, your culture, and the media. Like donning clothing that's *in* style, rather than in *your* style, the self-image you wear might be uncomfortable or inappropriate. Maybe you even fashioned your self-image without questioning whether or not the garment was right for you.

Tailoring your self-image according to someone else's ideas usually results in unhappiness or frustration. If you see yourself in this picture, perhaps it's time to take a closer look at the person you think you are, the person you'd like to be, and where the ideas you hold about yourself came from.

"Think of yourself like this: There's a universal intelligence subsisting throughout nature inherent in every one of its manifestations. You are one of those manifestations. You are a piece of this universal intelligence—a slice of God."—Dr. Wayne W. Dyer, *The Power of Intention*

Because your mind is the architect of your reality, it's inevitable that your thoughts about yourself and what you deserve will generate material conditions that correspond to your ideas. Look at elements like your life situation, your finances, your job, your relationships, your position in your community, and your health. Your life is your mirror. What you see is a reflection of what you believe about yourself. If you aren't happy with your situation, you can change it by changing your perceptions of yourself.

Remember, nobody else gets to decide whether you're worthy. Only you do. Consider this quote, which comes from Eleanor Roosevelt: "No one can make you feel inferior without your consent." Nor can anyone else limit your personal power without your consent.

Your Self List

Make a list of your ideas about yourself. Consider your physical qualities, mental abilities, talents, job, relationships, lifestyle, and so on. What are your strengths and weaknesses? What things do you feel comfortable with, and which would you like to change?

Look at all areas of yourself. Make "plus" and "minus" categories if you like. Are you good at managing time? Do you have pretty eyes? Are you a skilled cook? Are you compassionate, a good listener, a loyal friend? Are you overweight? Are you always late for appointments? Do you buy things you don't need to make yourself feel better? Are you impatient, judgmental, or indulgent?

ALERT!

Pay attention to your "self talk," or the things you say about yourself. Learn to catch yourself whenever you say something derogatory or self-limiting. Every time you notice you've thought or said something unkind about yourself, stop and replace the criticism with a compliment.

It can help to also examine where the negative ideas you hold about yourself originated. Then, think about how these ideas are undermining your power, happiness, success, and well being. Project into the future. If you changed those ideas, what might happen? Plunge into yourself to delve and discover your true motives, needs, and desires. Once you've done that, work to bring that self-knowledge to full consciousness, into your daily awareness.

Willpower

Your will is the force behind every visualization, manifestation, and spell. It galvanizes you at the deepest levels to achieve something that you desire. You don't simply say the words. You don't just go through the motions. You commit to the path you've decided upon and trust the process that unfolds.

Remember a time in your life when you felt powerful. Bring to mind the feelings that you experienced then, and reconnect with them. Hold these impressions in your mind and heart while you remind yourself that you are still that powerful person inside. Let your willpower energize this image to activate your personal power in the present.

Go with the Flow

Although this phrase implies passivity, what it really recommends it that you put yourself into the stream of cosmic energy that flows through everything in the universe. Alcoholics Anonymous members use the phrase, "Let go and let God."

"We allow ourselves to be led by the Creative, rather than by intellectual calculation . . . by clinging to the Creative and its action, we assist in bringing about the correct result. Through non-action—doing nothing at all—we achieve everything."—Carol K. Anthony, *A Guide to the I Ching*

"Go with the flow" means "Stop resisting, and relax." Swimming is a good analogy. If you relax, the water will buoy you up, but if you flail about, you'll drown. Instead of struggling to figure out everything with your rational mind, allow your intuition to kick in. Trust that the universe, your higher self, Divine Will, Source, or whatever term you prefer has everything under control—all you have to do is stop interfering with the plan. When you hook into something larger than yourself, you discover that the big picture is vastly more complex than you imagined.

The flow of a river is altered constantly by the curvature of the land that contains it, as well as by weather patterns and myriad other factors. In the same way, the purpose of the flow in your life changes as your goals and needs change. By developing an awareness of this deeper stratum of your life, you're better equipped to anticipate opportunities, to deal with challenges, and to fulfill your potential. In short, you are empowered.

Your Field of Energy

Chinese medical practitioners call it *chi*. Hindu mystics refer to it as *shakti*. Yogis label it *prana*. Medical intuitives think of it as an energy field. Occultists call it an aura. Its existence has been recorded since ancient times, as primitive art clearly shows. In the Sahara desert, in the rocky massifs of that harsh terrain, paintings dating back to the ninth millennium B.C.E. depict human figures surrounded by an envelope of light. In the stained-glass windows of Europe's cathedrals, these luminous orbs are illustrated as halos.

The energy field radiates outward from the body, forming a sphere of light that can be several inches or several feet wide, depending on the individual's emotional, spiritual, and physical state at any given time. This vital energy permeates your body and enlivens you; without it, you couldn't survive. Psychics and sensitive individuals can see different colors swirling in the aura, and those colors change as your thoughts and emotions change. Blockages in the energy field often appear as black or dark spots.

FACT

Acupuncturists insert needles into the body along pathways known as meridians, which serve as conduits through which this vital energy or chi flows. The needles stimulate the movement of energy and remove blockages in the chi that can lead to health problems.

In some schools of thought, this energy field is known as the etheric body. It is the energetic pattern from which the denser, physical body forms. Before problems materialize in the physical body, they exist as disturbances in the etheric body. Thus, potential problems can be healed in the etheric field and prevented from solidifying into physical matter.

The Chakras

Chakra (pronounced *sha-kra*) means "wheel" in Sanskrit. According to Eastern philosophy, seven major chakras or energy centers run down the center of the physical body, from the crown of the head to the base of the spine. Psychics and medical intuitives often describe the chakras as resembling spinning wheels of different colors.

The vital energy flows through the chakras and nourishes them. Yoga, acupuncture, visualization, sound, light, and other healing practices can energize the chakras so they function optimally. When the chakras are open and balanced, health, well being, and empowerment result. You'll find more about the energy field and energy centers in Chapter 17.

Energizing the Chakras for Personal Empowerment

Each of these chakras corresponds to a different color and function. By focusing your attention on the various chakras, you can increase the amount of energy flowing through them and remove blockages that can impede the energy.

Let's say that you're going to be interviewing for a job that seems absolutely ideal for you. It offers great hours, great flexibility, the whole nine yards. But you're nervous about the interview, uncertain about what to say or how to say it. A spell to enliven your throat chakra might be just what you need to get through the interview with flying colors.

Here's a list of the chakras and how they relate to personal empowerment.

Chakra	Location	Color	Correspondences
Crown	Top of head	Purple	Spiritual issues
Brow	Between eyebrows	Indigo	Intuition, imagination
Throat	Base of throat	Blue	Communication, self-expression
Heart	Center of chest	Green	Love, courage
Solar plexus	Stomach area	Yellow	Self-worth, confidence
Sacral	Lower abdomen	Orange	Creativity, sexuality
Root	Base of spine	Red	Security, foundations

Determine which area of your life needs work and which chakra corresponds to this area. To energize or balance the chakra, close your eyes and visualize sending light of the related color to that part of your body. If you want to spark your creativity, for instance, focus orange light on your lower abdomen. To strengthen your sense of self-worth, imagine yellow light glowing in your solar plexus.

Timing Personal Power Spells

For each of the spells in this chapter, the most advantageous time to perform the spell is noted. In most cases, you'll be more successful if you do spells for personal empowerment while the moon is waxing. However, if your goal is to eliminate an obstacle or condition that's limiting your sense of power, do a spell during the waning moon.

FACT

Leo is the zodiac sign of self-love, confidence, and leadership. Therefore, an ideal time to do spells for personal empowerment is while the moon and/or the sun is in Leo. If you want to increase your daring or assertiveness, you could do a spell when the sun and/or moon is in Aries.

The best days of the week for doing self-empowerment spells are Tuesday, Thursday, and Sunday, the days ruled by Mars, Jupiter, and the sun, respectively. These heavenly bodies encourage self-esteem, courage, optimism, growth, and leadership ability.

If you know astrology or can consult with an astrologer, look for periods when transiting or progressed Mars, Jupiter, or the sun influences your birth chart in a positive way. However, you may feel a strong need for personal empowerment spells when transiting or progressed Saturn forms difficult connections with the planets in your chart or with the ascendant, imum colei, or midheaven. Saturn contacts often diminish self-esteem temporarily, so you might benefit from doing magic to bolster your confidence at these times.

Spell to Expand Self-Awareness

Tools:

- 1 amber-colored candle
- Frankincense essential oil
- Myrrh essential oil
- An object that represents personal power
- 1 quartz crystal

When:

- Preferably on a Thursday night during a full moon

Thursday is Jupiter's day, and Jupiter encourages expansion. If you can't do this spell on a Thursday, do it during a full moon on any day except Saturday (Saturn's day).

The object that represents your personal power should be something solid and three-dimensional: a stone, for instance, versus a photograph. Select the object with care. The crystal you're using will amplify your desire. The amber-colored candle symbolizes the sun's golden light.

Pick a spot where you won't be disturbed. If possible, do this spell outside, under the full moon. Dress the candle with both essential oils and set it on your right. The object that represents your personal power and the crystal should be positioned directly in front of you. Light the candle, and then open your arms to the moon. Vividly imagine its light suffusing you as you say:

This light is presence,
This light is power.
It fills me
Until I am presence,
And I am power.

Gaze at the crystal and your power object as the moon's light shines on them. Inhale the aroma of the oils for a few moments, and then pinch out the candle's flame. Place your power object on your altar or in a place where you'll see it often. Or, if you prefer, carry it with you and touch it whenever you need a power boost.

Talisman for Self-Confidence

Tools:

- A sigil for the word *power*
- 1 gold-colored pouch, preferably made of silk
- 1 red ribbon
- 1 almond
- A pinch of sage
- 1 acorn
- 1 small piece of topaz, carnelian, or agate
- Sandalwood incense

When:

- Preferably a Sunday or a Thursday, on a full moon

As described in Chapter 3, design a magic sigil by entwining the letters that spell the word *power* so they form an image. Fold the paper three times, then slip it into the gold-colored pouch. Add the remaining ingredients, except the incense. Tie the pouch with the red ribbon, making nine knots. Each time you tie a knot, repeat this incantation:

By the magic of three times three
Divine power flows through me.
I am everything I wish to be.

Light the incense. Hold the talisman in the smoke for a few moments to charge it. Carry the talisman with you to increase your self-confidence. Hold it in your hand whenever you feel a need for a confidence boost. If you prefer, put it on your altar or in a spot where you'll see it often.

Quick and Easy Spell for Empowerment

This spell requires no tools except the belief that magic works and that it can work for you. As you're waking up in the morning, before you open your eyes, when you're still in that drowsy state halfway between dreams and full consciousness, visualize whatever it is that you desire. The first thoughts you have in the morning are very powerful, and they color your experiences throughout the day. Then say your wish silently to yourself, in the form of an affirmation.

FACT

You can do this spell quickly anytime you choose, not just as you're waking up in the morning. The most important factors are the vividness with which you visualize the end result and the intensity of the emotion with which you fuel your desire.

Maybe your intention is to ace an exam. Visualize the end result as vividly as possible: a big red A at the top of your exam sheet. Pour emotion into it. Imagine how excited you'll be when you see the A. Then say to yourself, "I ace my exam," feeling confident that you will do just that. When you get out of bed, forget about it. Release the desire and don't worry. Assuming that you've done your part to get an A on the exam (studied or otherwise prepared yourself), your intention should come true.

Spell for Strengthening Your Self-Worth

Tools:
- 1 ballpoint pen
- 4 yellow candles
- Almond oil

When:
- On a Thursday, Friday, or Sunday night on the full moon

This spell energizes the solar plexus chakra. With the ballpoint pen, draw a circle on each candle and make a dot in the center of the circle. This is the astrological glyph for the sun. Yellow, the sun's color, is also the color associated with the solar plexus chakra, the energy center that's linked with self-worth. Rub almond oil on the candles to dress them. Dab a little almond oil on your solar plexus, too, to energize it.

Place the four candles at the four cardinal directions and stand inside the circle defined by the candles. Starting at the east, move clockwise as you light the candles. When you have finished, spend a few minutes drawing the fire energy from the candles into yourself. Inhale the scent of almond oil and imagine a golden-yellow ball of light glowing in your solar plexus. Let this light expand until it fills you with warmth and confidence.

Pinch your right nostril shut, inhale through the left, and hold to the count of ten. Exhale through the right nostril. Repeat five times, then switch sides. As you do this alternate nostril breathing, imagine your solar plexus chakra being imbued with power.

Spend as much time as you like in the circle of light. When you're ready, extinguish the candles in reverse order from the direction you lit them and leave the circle.

Stretching Your Energy Field

When you say someone has presence, what you're really describing is a person whose energy field is expanded beyond the ordinary range. The energy field is what you react to when you meet a person, even when you see him or her walk into a room. With practice, you can learn to expand your energy field from the usual several inches around your body to as much as several feet.

The field is easy to detect through touch. Stand in front of a mirror and open your arms wide, as if you were about to hug someone. Bring your hands slowly toward your head until you feel a slight resistance. This usually happens when your hands are several inches away from your head. When your energy field expands, you'll feel the resistance occurring farther away from your head.

You can train yourself to see your energy field. Gaze into a mirror in a dimly lit room. It's best if the source of illumination is at your back. If you wear glasses or contacts, remove them. If you have 20/20 vision, gaze at your head in the mirror and let your eyes unfocus, so that your reflection seems hazy. Don't stare into your eyes, but instead look slightly to the side or above your head. You can also do this with another person. Seat that individual in front of a dark cloth and look at the area around his or her head, without trying to focus too closely.

FACT

In feng shui, red is considered to be a lucky color. Yellow is associated with royalty and power. Use these fortunate colors to dress up your entrance and thereby strengthen your self-image. Consider painting the door one of these colors or planting red or yellow flowers in pots near the entrance.

The longer you gaze at your reflection in this way, the more likely you are to see an aura surrounding your head. Some people detect colors, while others simply see a halo of pale light. Now think of something that makes you happy—the memory of your marriage, the birth of your child, the purchase of your first home, getting an offer for a great job, winning an award. Recall the emotions that you felt during this event or experience. Let the emotion fill you completely. As the emotions suffuse your entire being, your energy field will start to expand and the halo will balloon. Positive emotions expand your aura—and your personal power—whereas negative ones contract it.

Become familiar with this joyful feeling so you can recapture it at will. With practice, you can charge your energy field in ten or fifteen seconds. It can be done anywhere, anytime. Your body is the only tool you need.

Feng Shui Spell for Personal Empowerment

Have you ever noticed that the entrances to the homes of rich and powerful people—as well as doors leading into government buildings, successful businesses, and cathedrals—tend to be grand, easily accessible, and well lit? In feng shui, the entrance to your home corresponds to your self-image and identity.

Observe your entryway. Is it attractive and inviting? Or is it nondescript, cluttered, dark, and even difficult to find? To change your image—and the impression you make on others—all you have to do is improve your home's entrance. Install better lighting. Put a large, attractive plant near the door. Paint the door a bright, cheerful color. Affix handsome brass numerals on the door. Hang a decorative wreath on the door. Clear away any clutter or obstacles. Fix broken steps and railings. Remember, this is the first impression your visitors get of you. It's the image you project, so make it as appealing as possible. While you're making these updates, keep your intention in mind—that's the most important part of the spell.

Chapter 14

Spells for Career and Business Success

What does success mean to you? Some people consider themselves successful if they reach the highest ranks of their profession; others see money as a marker of success. In this celebrity-oriented society, fame is often the benchmark of success. In a broader sense, however, success means deriving fulfillment, purpose, and joy from the work you do. According to author Christopher Morley, "There is only one success—to be able to spend your life in your own way."

14

Setting Goals and Intentions

Setting goals is intrinsic to professional achievement. Just as travelers plot a route, companies design business plans to guide them where they intend to go. Without a roadmap of this sort, you can easily get sidetracked or derailed. Some business people recommend establishing a five-year plan, while others opt for longer or shorter terms and update their plans periodically. Many experts suggest that entrepreneurs at least create a mission statement, which describes the business's vision.

Your professional life is intimately connected with your beliefs about self-worth, prosperity, and success. If you feel unworthy, this will be reflected in your income and in your work situation. If, on the other hand, you believe you're valuable and deserving—of a raise, a promotion, of better working conditions—your self-image will be reflected in your outer-world image.

Given what you already know about magic, you can probably see the value of setting a goal, an end result you wish to achieve. Once you've created an image of your goal, you can infuse it with desire and willpower in order to propel your dream toward manifestation. Your goals don't have to be etched in stone, but it's important to at least have a clear view of what you would like to accomplish professionally. As in all areas of your life, the more distinct and vivid you can make your images of career success, the more likely they are to materialize in the way you desire.

Long-Term and Short-Term Goals

Some people sit down every New Year's Eve and make a list of their goals for the coming year. They review their goals quarterly, to get some sense of how far they have come, and revise their goals as necessary. You, too, may benefit from setting a timetable for success and reviewing it periodically.

If you like, you can establish an overall, long-term objective and then break it down into a number of short-term goals or steps that lead to the final destination. Understandably, situations will arise that affect your progress and perhaps even take you in a different direction altogether. Allow flexibility in your plan for the unexpected. Adjust your plan as necessary.

Write It Down

Don't just keep your goals in your head. Instead, write them down in a journal or loose-leaf binder. Writing your goals is the first step toward bringing them into the material world. The very act of putting words on paper takes them out of the realm of imagination and makes them more tangible.

State your objectives in the form of affirmations. Your affirmations might be all-encompassing and general, such as "I now have a job that's perfect for me," or they may be very precise, such as "I am now the president of [company name]." Make a list that includes at least three and not more than ten goals. As soon as you've accomplished one objective, replace it with another.

Read through your affirmations daily, when you first wake up and just before going to sleep at night. Repetition impresses your goals on your subconscious and directs it to carry out your wishes.

Power Symbols in Business

In Chapter 3, you learned the significance of symbols in magical work. In business, as in other areas of life, symbols serve as touchstones and embodiments of your intentions. Logos are particularly important symbols in business. A good logo presents important information about a company at a glance, in a way that words can't. When you see a logo, you understand immediately what that company stands for, even if you don't know what products it makes.

FACT

An object is merely an object until it has, for lack of a better word, *soul*. That soul comes from the person who owns it, touches it, and takes care of it and who, in doing so, imbues that object with the uniqueness of the individual he or she is. Then it becomes a power object.

Take, for example, the typewriter Thomas Wolfe used to write his masterpieces. On the surface, the machine looks tired and worn out, but because Wolfe's fingers pecked at those keys, because that typewriter materialized his creativity, it has become an object of utter power. The same is true of the *Spirit of St. Louis* hanging from the ceiling of the Air and Space Museum. It looks like a fascinating antique, but as soon as you learn it was the plane Charles Lindbergh flew when he crossed the Atlantic, it becomes a symbol of humanity overcoming physical limits to achieve a dream. That, in a sense, is alchemy: transforming a mundane object into a magical tool that makes imagination manifest.

Creating Your Own Power Symbols

Objects absorb and reflect energy, just by virtue of being in the same space inhabited by a certain person. If you're passionate about a particular thing, your energy clings to that inert object and enlivens it. This happens without any effort on your part. Psychics can read your past, present, and future by holding an object you've worn because it has absorbed your energy. When you consciously imbue an object with your passion and intent, the object becomes extremely powerful. Magicians do this with ritual tools, talismans and amulets, and other objects.

A paintbrush is an easily recognizable symbol for an artist. A chef instantly identifies with a tall white hat. A private investigator might see a magnifying glass or a Sherlock Holmes–style pipe as a sign of his profession. What symbols do you associate with your career? Select one that resonates with you and use it in your spells for career success.

Look around your work area. What do you see? With what objects have you surrounded yourself? What do they mean to you? How did they come to you? Do the objects have stories attached to them? Mementos of pleasant experiences, trophies you've won, and family heirlooms that connect you to your personal history are all individual symbols with which you identify. They link you to your own power.

Choose one or two objects that represent your successes. Display these in a place where you'll see them often: your desk, your altar, or your living room. Remember, these objects have been selected for a very specific purpose, not just for decoration. Whenever you want to bolster your sense of success or need some reassurance before facing a career challenge, take a few moments to gaze at these power objects. Touch them and let them remind you of your personal power.

Charms for Career Success

A success charm is similar to a shaman's medicine bundle. The outer container should be made of cotton or silk, in a color that represents your intention. If you're making it for personal power, use a purple pouch with a drawstring closure. If money is your object, use gold or silver. You could choose a color that connects to the chakra you use most frequently in your work. If you do a lot of talking in your job, blue might be the best color for the bag because blue represents the throat chakra, the center of your self-expression.

"Hidden alliances work to move you into your authentic vocation as soon as you begin to commit to it."—Rick Jarow, *Creating the Work You Love*

The bundle should be small enough to carry with you. Keep the number of objects you include in your bag to a minimum; select only items that symbolize something significant and important to you. A bundle can also contain slips of paper on which you've written your desires or goals. If you do a lot of business traveling, for instance, you may want to make a charm that relates specifically to travel. This charm would ensure safe, smooth travel—no canceled flights, no long waits in airport lobbies, no lost bags.

Periodically, you might wish to update the items in your charm bag. Because your charm works its magic on particular projects or issues, consider replacing the items that no longer correlate with your intentions with new power objects. Be imaginative when designing your success charms and have fun making them.

Timing Success Spells

Like other spells, the ones you do for career success will be more powerful if you do them at the right time. In magic, as in other areas of life, timing counts. In most cases, you'll get better results if you do spells for business and career success while the moon is waxing. However, if your goal is to eliminate an obstacle or condition that's blocking your success, or you want to scale down your work-related responsibilities, do a spell during the waning moon.

FACT

Capricorn is the zodiac sign of business, goals, and public image. Therefore, an ideal time to do spells for career success is while the moon and/ or the sun is in Capricorn. Virgo is connected with work, work relationships, and work-related health matters, so if your intention involves these things, do a spell when the sun and/or moon is in Virgo.

The best days of the week for doing success spells are Thursday, Saturday, and Sunday, which are the days ruled by Jupiter, Saturn, and the sun, respectively. These heavenly bodies govern expansion, business, travel, public image, status, ambition, self-image, and leadership ability. The best day for doing each of the spells in this chapter is indicated at the end of the spell.

If you know astrology or can consult with an astrologer, look for periods when transiting or progressed Venus, Jupiter, or the sun influences your birth chart in a positive way. In some cases, transiting or progressed Saturn can also produce career opportunities, especially those you've worked hard to obtain or that involve slow, steady development over a period of time.

Retrograde Mercury

About four times a year, for approximately three weeks at a time, the planet Mercury goes retrograde. This means that from Earth, it appears as if Mercury is traveling backward in its orbit around the sun. Mercury rules communication, the mind, written documents, communications equipment (such as computers and phones), and short-distance travel.

ALERT!

Astrologers usually recommend that you avoid buying computers, telephones, or cars while Mercury is retrograde. They also warn against signing contracts, making investments, or launching a new business venture at this time because you may overlook important details or encounter delays.

When the planet turns retrograde, you're more likely than usual to run into problems in these areas. Computers break down, checks get lost in the mail, and mental errors occur. Many people have trouble communicating clearly. Considering that the mind is the most important part of magic, this obviously isn't a good time to do business spells either. Check an ephemeris to see when Mercury is retrograde, and plan accordingly.

Optimal Times for Setting Goals

Samhain (Halloween) is the pagan New Year. Therefore, this is an ideal time to make your New Year's resolutions and set goals for the coming year. The Winter Solstice, when the sun enters Capricorn, is another optimal date for establishing goals and plans. On this day, the sun is at its lowest point in the sky and daylight hours are shorter than at any other time of the year (in the Northern Hemisphere). The goals you set now will develop and come to fruition as the sun's light grows stronger.

Spell for Clarification

This spell is intended to clarify a goal you have. Quite often, people think they want one thing and later on find that what they wanted was something else entirely. So before you get to the "later on" point, do this simple spell for clarification.

Tools:
- 1 dark blue candle
- A few drops of essential oil of citrus
- Pen and paper

When:
- As you feel the need

Dress your candle with the oil and light it. As the scent of citrus suffuses the air, write down your goal in the form of an affirmation. Keep it simple. Prop the paper on which you've written your goal up against the candle. Gaze into the candle's flame and sit quietly for a few moments, keeping your goal in mind. Imagine that you have already achieved this goal. How does it feel? Are you comfortable with it? How does it affect your family and friends? What is your life like now that you have attained what you wanted?

The more vivid and detailed your imaginings, the greater benefit you'll derive from this visualization. Hold the vision in your mind until your mind starts to wander, then stop. Now read your goal again. Is it what you really want? If not, rewrite it. You may find that you merely need to fine-tune what you've written. If you rewrite your goal, let it sit for a day or two before you look at it again. Then ask yourself if it feels right. Chances are that it will. Once you're certain you've got it right, burn the piece of paper to release your intentions into the cosmic web.

Spell to Get Recognized

Tools:
- 1 ceramic pot

- Potting soil
- 9 seeds for a plant that blossoms with red or purple flowers
- Water

When:
- On a Thursday during a waxing moon

Fill your ceramic pot with potting soil and place nine seeds at various spots in the soil. As you plant the seeds, say aloud:

As I plant these seeds
I draw to me
The one who sees
What I can be.
So mote it be.

Once the seeds begin to sprout, the person who recognizes your genius should appear in your life. Until that happens, lavish your plant with tender loving care. And take every opportunity to make contacts—you never know who might become your "angel."

Spell to Launch a New Venture

Tools:
- 1 piece of yellow paper
- 1 pen, pencil, or marker
- 1 quartz crystal

When:
- Nine days before the full moon

Whether you're seeking a new job, planning to start your own company, or taking on a new project, this spell can help you make a successful start. Nothing can be as frightening as the prospect of starting something new. Most people wonder if they're smart enough, experienced enough, or talented enough to make a go of it. But if you listen to your fears, you'll never know how successful you might have been.

FACT

An aspiring young author had written a book, but he didn't think it was good enough to be published. When he tossed it in the garbage, his wife retrieved the manuscript. Not only was the book published, it became a bestseller and a movie. The author? Stephen King. The book? *Carrie.*

Yellow is the color of optimism and creativity. It also corresponds to the solar plexus chakra, the center of self-confidence. Choose a word that represents your goal or describes the endeavor you are about to undertake. Then design a magic sigil with the letters in that word (see Chapter 3 for instructions) and draw it on the paper. Hold your intention in your mind while you create the sigil and project your thoughts into the drawing. If you like, decorate it with pictures and other symbols that relate to your venture.

Nine days before the full moon, lay your sigil face up on your altar. Set the crystal on top of the sigil. On the night of the full moon, burn the drawing while you imagine yourself succeeding at your new effort, thereby releasing your intention into the cosmic web. Carry the crystal in your pocket, purse, or briefcase if you wish, or set it in your workspace.

Spell to Release Negativity

Tools:
- 1 piece of white paper
- 1 pen with blue ink
- White carnations in a clear glass container
- 1 white candle

When:
- During the waning moon

Occasionally a bad day at work collapses into a really negative situation. This spell breaks the destructive cycle and restores peace. You can't change what has happened, but you can alter your perspective about it, which can soften the impact. Write the following intention on the paper:

I now release (name the situation)
and create new, positive energy to carry me forward.
I trust this is for my highest good
and affirm my commitment to this new path.

Place the paper beneath the vase of flowers. Leave it there until the flowers wilt. When you throw out the flowers, burn the paper to complete the releasing process.

Point of Power Spell

Tools:
- Potted plant with yellow flowers
- 1 piece of malachite or turquoise
- 1 green candle
- 1 purple candle

When:
- Thursday or Sunday during a waxing moon

With this spell, you're affirming that your point of power is in the present. This very moment is your launching pad for the rest of your life. The yellow flowers symbolize self-esteem and optimism. The green candle represents growth and prosperity, and the purple candle signifies wisdom and power. Malachite and turquoise are stones for abundance, success, and good fortune.

Place the plant and gemstone on your altar, between the two candles. Light the candles and say aloud:

My point of power,
like these flowers,
some way, somehow
lies in the now.

Allow the candles to burn down completely. Carry the gemstone with you in your pocket or purse as a reminder that you have the ability to accomplish whatever you desire. Continue to care for the plant with tender loving care. As its flowers continue to blossom, so will your goals.

Feng Shui Spell for Success

Tools:
- Three objects that represent career success
- 1 mirror
- 1 bell

When:
- During the waxing moon

Stand at the door you use most often to enter and exit your home, facing in. From this vantage point, locate the spot halfway between the furthest right-hand corner and the furthest left-hand corner of your home. This sector represents your future, fame, career, and public image. Arrange in this sector the three objects you've chosen to represent your career success. Position the mirror so it reflects these objects, symbolically doubling their impact.

Each day, take a few moments to gaze at these objects. Ring the bell as you do this to activate positive energy in this sector of your home. The sound of the bell also triggers your attention and helps you focus on achieving your goal.

Spell to Get a Raise

Tools:

- 1 ballpoint pen
- 1 gold candle
- Peppermint essential oil
- 1 $20 bill

When:

- During the waxing moon, preferably on a Thursday night, at least a week before the full moon

The bill you use to represent your raise can be of any denomination. It's merely a symbol, though many people like to choose a bill that is a tenth of the amount they intend to manifest. With the pen, inscribe words such as *wealth* or *prosperity* on the candle. You may also include images that represent money, such as dollar signs. Then, dress the candle with peppermint oil, set it on top of the bill, and light the candle. As you gaze into the flame, say aloud:

Element of fire,
Fulfill my desire,
The raise I seek,
I receive this week.

Allow the candle to burn for as long as you can focus on your attention, and then snuff it out. Repeat the procedure each night for a week, and on the last night let the candle finish burning down completely. (If you receive your raise before the week is up, give thanks and discontinue the process.)

Gemstone Talisman for Career Success

Tools:
- Book or list of rune symbols
- Paint or nail polish
- 1 piece of malachite
- 1 piece of tiger eye
- 1 piece of jade
- 1 piece of turquoise
- 1 piece of onyx
- 1 smoky quartz crystal
- 1 gold or silver pouch
- 1 red ribbon

When:
- During the waxing moon

Look through the book or list of rune symbols and select five that represent goals, conditions, or outcomes you desire. Paint one rune on each of the gemstones. Do not paint the quartz crystal. When the paint dries, put all the stones into the pouch and tie it closed with the ribbon. Make six knots in the ribbon, one for each stone, and think about the intentions you've chosen to symbolize with the runes. Carry the talisman in your pocket, purse, or briefcase. If you prefer, place it in a desk drawer, in your business cash register, or on your altar.

Chapter 15

Spells for Your Home

Protection spells for the home are among the oldest forms of magic. The early Celts hung rowan branches over their doors to safeguard their homes. The indigenous people of North America painted totem animals and other symbols on their teepees for magical reasons as well as decoration. In the Middle East, it's common practice to hang an eye amulet near the entrance to your home to ward off evil. It's even possible that the ancient cave paintings in the south of France had magical significance.

Your Home and You

Your home is more than a roof over your head and a place to store your stuff. Sayings such as "Home is where the heart is" and "There's no place like home" express the strong sentiments connected with the home. Owning a home is part of the American dream. For most people, their homes are their most valuable assets. Home is where you go to rest and relax, where friends and family gather to socialize, and where holidays are celebrated and life's passages marked.

The place you live in absorbs and retains your energy. Every home resonates with the unique vibrations of its inhabitants. Antique homes can retain the energetic patterns of all the people who've lived there over the centuries. Some old houses even boast resident ghosts, the energetic residue of deceased occupants who refuse to leave. Because so much of your energy is centered in your home, it's usually the best place to perform magic spells and rituals. You may choose to set up an altar in your home or to designate a special place to do your magical work.

"Houses themselves have a quality, a life, that is picked up by potential buyers . . . When you live in a house that conspicuously belongs to another age, you are to some extent avoiding the contemporary nature of life."—Jane Roberts, *The Unknown Reality,* Vol. 2

In astrology, the bottom-most sector of your birth chart (the fourth house) represents your home. As such, it signifies your foundation, the base upon which all else is built. In feng shui, your home is viewed as a mirror of your life. Everything in your home is considered to be a reflection of you. Simultaneously, every article of furniture, every architectural feature, and every appliance and piece of artwork influences your life. When you look at your home from this perspective, each object and each act takes on magical meaning.

What Your Home Reveals About You

Someone who knows feng shui can walk through your home and instantly tell a great deal about you: your financial situation, your relationships with family members, your health, and more. According to feng shui, your home is a mirror of the people who inhabit it. Each sector corresponds to a part of your life: wealth, relationships, creativity, identity, future, community, helpful people, knowledge, and health. The condition of a particular section reveals the condition of the area of your life that's related to it.

Does clutter tend to accumulate in a particular area of your home? Clutter suggests that the part of your life that's represented by this area isn't functioning smoothly. Clean up the clutter, and you'll simultaneously clear away obstacles in your life.

Like other forms of magic, feng shui involves symbolism. Look at your home with the new eyes of a feng shui practitioner. What images do you see in the various parts of your home? Are the colors and objects in your health sector conducive to well being? Does your relationship sector feature loving, joyful images? Are symbols of prosperity and abundance featured in your wealth sector? If things like furnishings, artwork, and colors conflict with your intentions, change them. You'll be amazed at how quickly your life changes, too.

Your Home's Energy Field

Feng shui practitioners believe that chi, the vital energy that flows through your body, also moves through your home and the landscape. You've probably entered buildings that gave off bad vibes. What you reacted to was the building's energy field and an imbalance in the chi contained within the building. Imbalances occur for lots of reasons, but they can usually be corrected.

How does your home feel? If you're like most people, you don't tend to notice the energy in your own home. Go outside and re-enter, paying close attention to the first impressions that arise. Invite a friend to join you and solicit your friend's responses; they may be more objective than your own. Observe how you feel as you walk through your home, where the energy seems stagnant or heavy, where it seems light and free. Start sensing the vibes in other people's homes, too. Pretty soon, you'll develop an ability to feel where the chi needs some adjustment.

Clearing Bad Vibes from Your Home

The people and pets that share your living space contribute to the overall feeling texture of your home. If someone in your home tends to be overly negative or disruptive, you can neutralize the stressful energy magically. Smudging your home by burning sage periodically is a good way to clear the air.

After an argument, party, or stressful event, it's a good idea to smudge your home with sage. Other people's vibrations—particularly angry or fearful energies—can linger in your home long after the people themselves have gone. These vibrations may have a disruptive effect on you and your family members.

Gemstones absorb vibrations, too. Place a piece of onyx or dark green tourmaline in the disruptive person's bedroom to collect the negative energy. Each week, wash the stone in saltwater to purify it, and then set it in the sun for a few minutes before putting it back in the person's room. A black candle will also transmute harmful energies. Burn a black candle in or near the difficult person's room to absorb the negative energy. Let the candle burn all the way down, and then toss it out.

Timing Spells for Your Home

In astrology, the moon rules the home. Therefore, it's important to pay close attention to the moon's signs and phases when you're doing spells for your home. If your intention is to find a new home, do a spell on the new moon. If you want to sell your home, do a spell while the moon is waning. Protection spells and banishing spells to disperse unwanted energies should be done during the waning moon, too.

FACT

Cancer is the zodiac sign of home and family matters. Consider doing spells for your home while the moon and/or the sun is in Cancer. If you intend to do a spell to protect your home, however, you could do it while the sun and/or moon is in Capricorn.

The best day of the week for doing home-oriented spells is Monday, the moon's day. Unless otherwise noted, the spells in this chapter will be most effective if you perform them on a Monday.

If you know astrology or can consult with an astrologer, look for periods when transiting or progressed Venus, Jupiter, or the sun contacts the moon in your birth chart in a positive way. Also pay attention to planetary influences in the fourth house of your chart.

Good Vibrations Potion

Tools:
- 1 spray bottle
- Saltwater
- A few drops of orange essential oil

When:
- During the waning moon

Fill the spray bottle with saltwater (or add a pinch of sea salt to tap water). Add the essential oil and shake the bottle three times to charge the water. Start in the east and mist each room with this potion to clear away negative energy and fill the air with good vibrations.

Spell to Invite Happiness into Your Home

Tools:
- Lavender-scented incense
- Several houseplants with round leaves
- 1 wreath

When:
- Any time

Light the incense and place it near the front door of your home. Fragrant lavender dissolves stress and promotes serenity. Position the plants throughout your home. Put at least one in each room, and set one on your altar. The round leaves represent harmony and unity. Jade plants are excellent choices because they also attract wealth, prosperity, and good health. Hang the wreath on your door to welcome positive forces into your home.

Consider hanging a festive, seasonal wreath on your door and change it at least four times a year. This practice keeps you in touch with the Earth's natural cycles. Changing the wreath periodically also prevents stagnation and draws new opportunities to you and the occupants of your home.

Continue caring for your plants, watering and feeding them to keep them healthy. Periodically, light incense to keep positive energy wafting through your home.

Spell to Protect Your Home

Tools:
- An image of an animal totem
- Basil leaves

When:

- Three days before the new moon, or whenever you feel the need

Do you have a totem animal? Totems serve as guardians and helpers—you can call upon them to aid you in times of need. Your totem is an animal, bird, reptile, or insect with which you feel a strong sense of kinship and which, to you, represents protective power. Select an image of your totem animal—a figurine, painting, or photograph—and place it near your front door. Say aloud, to your animal guardian:

Protect this home,
High to low,
Fence to fence,
Door to door,
Light to dense,
Roof to floor.

Next, scatter the basil leaves all around the outside of your home. If you live in an apartment, either scatter them around the entire building or place the leaves in a bowl. Set the bowl and your animal image just inside the door to your apartment.

Spell to Sell Your Home

Tools:

- A picture of your house
- 1 pen
- 1 gold candle
- 1 red candle
- A box with a lid

When:

- During a waning moon

Take a photo of your house (or download the realtor's listing sheet for your house and print that out). Write "SOLD" across the picture. Place the candles on your altar and set the picture of your house between them. (Red represents good luck, and gold symbolizes money.) As you light the candles, say, "My house is sold for the price I choose, and everyone is content with the transaction. So be it now." Repeat this spell three times during the waning moon period.

Any problem or issue you can't resolve on your own can be turned over to your guides or higher power by placing it in a box and closing the lid on it. Sometimes called a "God box," this container serves as an incubator for your intention. By releasing your attachment to the matter, you allow it to unfold according to Divine Will.

After completing this part of the spell, place the picture of your house in the box. You are now turning over the process to the universe to enact. Close the lid and stop thinking about it, trusting that all will transpire according to your wishes and in the proper time.

Spell to Honor Your House

To sell your home, you must be ready to release it emotionally. You have to be able to vividly imagine yourself living elsewhere and doing it without regrets. Otherwise, no spell in the universe is going to get your home to sell. Once you accomplish this, make peace with the home where you've been living. Express your gratitude. You may feel odd talking to the walls and floors, but do it anyway. Spend a few minutes in each room, remembering good experiences you've had there. Then get out of the way and let things unfold.

Spell to Find a Home

Tools:

- 1 pencil, pen, or marker
- Glue
- Scissors
- Magazine pictures
- Poster board

When:

- On the new moon

Either sketch the house you're looking for (if you have artistic ability), or find pictures that depict features you seek in your new home. Glue these illustrations to a poster board and hang it where you'll see it often. The goal is to create a visual tool that focuses your mind on your desire. Make it vivid and detailed. Get everyone in your household involved. Kids love doing this sort of thing and often come up with great ideas. The more energy you pour into your intention, the quicker it will materialize.

Spell to Get Settled in a New Home

Tools:

- Sea salt
- 4 small stones
- 1 large stone
- 1 black felt marker

When:

- Just before you move into your new home or as soon afterward as possible

Moving is one of the most stressful and upsetting experiences in life. This spell helps you establish yourself comfortably in your new home and get grounded.

Before you move into a new dwelling, smudge the space with burning sage to chase away the lingering energies of the previous occupants. It's also a good idea to smudge any furnishings you purchase—particularly antiques—to remove the vibrations of former owners.

First, sprinkle a little sea salt in each corner of your new home. Next, draw a pentagram on each of the small stones. Place these stones at the four outer corners of your home, where they'll anchor and protect you. On the large stone, write, "This is [your name]'s home." Put this stone somewhere on your property, either inside or outside, in the place that feels right to you.

Blessing a New Home

Tools:
- Sage
- Broom
- 1 bottle of wine or apple cider
- 1 loaf of freshly baked bread

Begin by smudging your home with sage to clear away any unwanted energies. Then, use the broom to sweep out the vibrations left behind by the former occupants. When this is done, pour the wine (or cider) and slice the bread. The bread and wine ensure that you will always have enough to eat and drink in your new home. Share this magic meal with all who will live in the home with you and/or any friends who will enjoy visiting you there.

Protection Amulet for Your Home

Tools:
- 1 white candle
- A picture of your house
- 1 silver pentagram

- Dried petals from a white carnation
- 1 ash leaf
- 1 quartz crystal
- 1 piece of coral
- 1 moonstone
- 1 piece of amber
- 1 white pouch, preferably made of silk
- 1 black ribbon
- Saltwater

When:

- Any time

Set the candle on your altar and light it. Set the picture of your house on the altar in front of the candle and put the pentagram on it. (An alternative is to draw a pentagram on the back of the picture.) Gaze at the picture and, at the same time, envision a sphere of white light completely surrounding your home. Say aloud, "My home is protected by divine white light. It is safe and sound at all times and in all situations."

FACT

Texans often display the Texas Lone Star on their homes. Few of them realize, however, that this five-pointed star with a circle around it is more than a pretty decoration or a sign of state pride. It's actually a pentagram, a powerful magic symbol for protection.

Place the flower petals, ash leaf, crystal, coral, moonstone, and amber in the white silk pouch. Add the picture of your home and the pentagram. Tie the pouch closed with the ribbon, making eight knots. With each knot, repeat your affirmation while you hold the vision of your home, surrounded by white light, in your mind's eye. When you've finished, sprinkle the amulet with saltwater to charge it. Extinguish the candle. Hang the amulet inside the front door to safeguard your home and your possessions.

Feng Shui Ritual for Three Great Blessings

Tools:
- Sandalwood incense
- 1 bell or gong
- 1 piece of paper
- 1 pen with red ink
- 1 red envelope
- A plant with red flowers

In feng shui, red is considered a lucky color. This spell is designed to attract what the Chinese call the Three Great Blessings: health, wealth, and happiness. Light the incense. Ring the bell or gong three times to dispel any stagnant, unbalanced, or disruptive energies.

On the piece of paper, write an affirmation that states your wishes—the Three Great Blessings or something else—and slip the paper into the envelope. Say your affirmation aloud three times. Hold the envelope in the incense smoke for a few moments while you envision your intentions manifesting. The smoke carries your wishes into the higher realms where they can be acted upon by Divine Will. Then put the envelope underneath the plant. Ring the bell again to activate positive energies. The plant symbolizes growth. Set it in a prominent place in your home and continue to care for it faithfully; as it grows, so will your good fortune.

Chapter 16

Spells to Enhance Creativity

In its broadest definition, creativity is the act of coming up with something new rather than producing an imitation. People tend to think of creativity only in terms of the arts or inventions, but the very act of living involves self-expression and imagination. Everyone is inherently creative. Every day, you come up with new ways of doing things, new ideas, new approaches, new perspectives and insights, and new solutions to problems. The only limits to your creativity are those you set for yourself.

Recognizing Your Uniqueness

Everyone is unique, and everyone has something special to offer the world. Just walk outside on any given day and observe the variety of plant and animal life around you. Two birds may appear to be similar, but they're not the same. A saguaro cactus and an aloe plant share certain attributes, but they are not identical. Even though identical twins look alike, their inner experiences differ and so do their personalities.

"Creative energy is a constant and we can always tap into it . . . It is our resistance to our creativity that causes us to equate it with suffering. It is important to remember that 'effort' and 'suffering' are two different things."—Julia Cameron, *The Vein of Gold*

Your right brain, the hemisphere where creativity resides, is a tireless worker. It churns out ideas twenty-four hours a day, every day of your life, even while you're asleep. People don't always utilize their full creative potential, however, because they're creatures of habit. If something has worked in the past, they tend to keep following that pattern because it requires less effort—and besides, who wants to mess with success? They begin to approach living according to an internal formula: If they do A, then B and C all the way through Z, they can pretty much predict the result. Even though it may feel boring, it's safe.

Let Friends Inspire You

You might not consider yourself to be unique, but ask a trusted friend what she thinks. Your friends probably see sides of you that you don't even realize exist. Perhaps you're trying so hard to be what you think you should be that you overlook what's special and wonderful about you.

Let's take the example of a woman who creates beautiful throw pillows and wall hangings. When her friend complimented her work and asked if her creations were for sale, the designer modestly said, "Oh, I just do them for myself." The friend insisted that the designer sell her one. Soon afterward, a mutual friend bought a wall hanging and another friend invited the woman to display her work at a conference. A reporter saw the pillows there and wrote an article about them in the local newspaper. With a little help from her friends, this woman is gaining a greater appreciation for her creativity and the joy it brings to others.

Stretch your imaginations and inspire one another. By combining your energies and ideas with those of your friends, each person creates more than she might have alone.

Your Talents List

Make a list of ten things you really enjoy doing. Don't think about whether you do them well, whether you earn money from these endeavors, or whether anyone else approves or disapproves. Maybe you love to cook, or perhaps gardening is your thing. You might have a neighbor with a special talent for making people feel welcome who acts as the unofficial greeter for newcomers to the community.

"Almost all of us fear our potentials... Generally, fear's message is that we're not yet ready to be, do or have what we want. The way out of this dilemma is through a change of mind about ourselves—not simply the gaining of technical skills or textbook knowledge."— Marsha Sinetar, *To Build the Life You Want, Create the Work You Love*

Examine your list. These are the places where your creativity abides. But if you're like many people, you may not devote enough time to doing what you love. Instead, you might let other people's needs, job responsibilities, and the demands of everyday living take precedence. As you look over your list, imagine ways you can give these things a bigger place in your life. Maybe you can leave the dishes in the sink and spend an hour writing a poem instead. When you give yourself permission to follow your bliss, as Joseph Campbell phrased it, your creativity will blossom.

Sparking Your Creativity

Look at nature: Every plant and animal is perfectly suited to its purpose. A horse doesn't question whether it should gallop. A rose doesn't doubt that it should blossom. Marsha Sinetar, author of the bestseller *Do What You Love, the Money Will Follow*, urges people to get in touch with their hearts' desires. The idea is that when you're aligned with your true being and doing something that gives you joy, your capacity for success increases. The workload seems lighter. Time flies by.

FACT

Every act of magic is a creative act. Magic requires using your imagination to create something in the manifest world. You are the designer, the architect, the artist who fashions your reality with your visions. Whether or not you realize it, you're doing it all the time.

Getting Out of a Rut

Let's say you're in a rut at work. You detest your job but at the moment, you don't have any other prospects on the horizon. However, you're preparing a resume, putting out feelers, setting things in motion. In the meantime, you can do a little magic, and it starts with simply taking a different route to and from work.

On the first morning that you take the new route, give yourself some extra time. Leave home ten or fifteen minutes earlier than usual. Notice how this route to work differs from the one you ordinarily take. Is it more scenic? More hectic? Is it longer or shorter? Pay attention to any feelings you have during the trip, as well as any thoughts and impressions that surface.

Throughout the day while you're at work, notice if you feel differently about your job. Are you more committed to finding something else to do? Are your thoughts any clearer? Does your boss still rub you the wrong way? Are you less impatient with other people and your situation?

By changing your habitual way of doing things, you're making a symbolic gesture to the universe that you're ready for change. By opening yourself up to new experiences, you allow new people, events, and knowledge to come into your life.

Fear of change can be crippling. But all growth requires change, and resisting change causes pain. Intentionally putting yourself into unfamiliar circumstances forces you to use your creativity rather than relying on old habits. Until you change your habitual ways of thinking and old patterns, your life will remain stuck.

Creativity and Nature

Put on your walking shoes and head for the great outdoors. If you live in a large city, the outdoors is probably a park. In the suburbs you may have a few more choices, but ideally you want to really get away and commune with nature. No convenience stores, no gas stations, no shopping malls, no movie theaters, no traffic.

Use what's available where you live. Look at trees and other plants. Observe the wildlife. Enjoy the smell of the air, the feel of the ground under your feet. Take note of how your thought processes start to change. You may hear some inner grumbling and moaning at first, the usual body complaints like *It's too far, I'm hot, I'm thirsty, I'm hungry,* or *Where's the bathroom?* But when you get past all that—and you will—something magical happens. You can feel the inner shift. Your thoughts begin to flow rather than to sputter. Your rhythm changes. Your gait quickens or slows. You feel lighter, happier, more optimistic. This is exactly the right atmosphere for your creativity to percolate.

Quite often, when you venture into nature simply to see what you'll discover, your imagination is stimulated in unusual and, sometimes, enduring ways. When British biologist and author Rupert Sheldrake was a young boy, his father took him to see the freeing of homing pigeons. "When the appointed time came, the porters opened the flaps and out burst hundreds of pigeons, batch after batch, in a great commotion of wind and feathers," he wrote in *Seven Experiments That Could Change the World*. His fascination with homing pigeons as a boy led many decades later to the first experiment described in his book.

FACT

Julia Cameron, author of *The Artist's Way* and *The Right to Write*, recommends walking every day to get the creative juices going. Mystery writer Sue Grafton runs three miles a day. Annie Dillard's Pulitzer-prize-winning book *Pilgrim at Tinker Creek* describes her retreat to nature to connect with her muse.

Ten Tips to Spur Imagination

Often all your creativity needs is a little nudge. Here are some ways to prime the pump, so to speak:

- Go to a museum or art gallery.
- Read a story or poem and notice how your mind forms images from the words.
- Take a walk and pay attention to everything around you.
- Listen to a CD you've never heard before or attend a concert.
- Take a class or workshop on a subject that's always interested you.
- Write your thoughts in a journal each morning.
- Observe children.
- Go someplace you've never been.
- Brainstorm with friends.
- Turn off the television.

Most important, stop listening to the old tapes in your head that say you can't do it, you aren't creative, you can't make money as an artist, and so on. Just give yourself room to express yourself, to enjoy the process without judging yourself or worrying about the outcome.

Establishing an Environment for Creating

In her essay *A Room of One's Own,* Virginia Woolf stated that "A woman must have money and a room of her own if she is going to write." Many people have trouble making time and space for their creative endeavors. Here's where forming new habits can be helpful.

When you enter your workplace each morning, your mind shifts into work mode. Your environment instantly triggers a change in your thinking and behavior. To get your mind into creative mode, designate a place solely for the purpose of self-expression. It might be a room in your home, an attic alcove, a sunny spot in your yard, or a corner of your garage. If your home doesn't allow you the space you need, find a place elsewhere. You might like to go to a little café near your home to write. Perhaps you could find the privacy you seek in the local library. A walk in a park might stimulate your imagination. When you enter your special place, your consciousness immediately shifts gears and enables you to focus on creative pursuits.

Establish a ritual to prepare yourself for self-expression. Brew a cup of coffee. Light incense. Take a bath. Play an inspirational CD. The routine becomes a stepping-stone to creativity. Like Pavlov's dogs, which salivated when they heard a bell ring, your subconscious will soon connect the ritual with your objective and start producing ideas.

Remove distractions—television, radio, telephone, reminders of daily tasks—so you can concentrate. Set a goal for yourself. You might opt to write two pages of prose or draw for twenty minutes, even if you end up throwing away what you've done. Through repetition and dedication, you develop the habit of creating. After a while, it becomes second nature. And, as is true with everything, you'll improve with practice.

Creativity and Dreams

Dream books are filled with stories about how a dream provided the missing piece of an invention, vital scenes in a novel, the finishing touches of a movie, or some unique image in a painting. Dreams are so intimately connected to the creative process that you'll cheat yourself if you ignore them.

Dreams provide fodder in ways that are unique to each individual. Some dreams are symbolic, while others are literal. Some are ordinary, others bizarre. Some are fun, and some are terrifying. Regardless of how a dream presents itself, it is *your* dream, intimately connected to the source of your own creativity, a process that operates inside you around the clock, seven days a week.

In *Writers Dreaming,* Naomi Epel quotes Stephen King, who writes movingly of the roles that dreams have played in his creative life. In some instances, he has taken a scene from a dream and written it as it happened, right into a book. "Creative imaging and dreaming are just so similar that they've got to be related," he says.

Dreams provide a conduit through which you connect to other people and to the deeper, oceanic parts of yourself. Within that vast inner ocean lie creative seeds that may never sprout unless you bring them into the light of day. Dreams, by their fundamental nature, are magic. They take you into other realms of existence, other levels of time, and offer answers that your waking intellect can't comprehend. Here are some guidelines for working with dreams to enhance your creativity:

- **Ask for what you need or want.** Before you fall asleep at night, say aloud that you would like to remember the most important dreams of the night. If you're trying to find a particular solution to a problem, request that an answer come to you in a dream and that you'll remember the dream in detail.

- **Record your dreams.** Put a tape recorder by your bed or slide a notebook under your pillow so that you can immediately record what you remember when you wake up. You might even jot your request on a page in your journal. Date it.
- **Pay attention.** Any dream fragment that you remember may relate to your request, even if it doesn't appear to do so. Don't judge it. Just write down the fragment.
- **If you don't succeed at first, keep trying.** Yes, it's a cliché. It also happens to be true. If you've spent thirty or forty years forgetting the bulk of what goes on while you sleep, it may take a while before you start recalling your dreams again. Don't give up.

When you dream with purpose, you bring your intent, will, emotions, and anything else you can muster to get a creative solution to your request. It's visualization in another form. It's magic.

Timing Spells for Creativity

The spells you do to enhance your creativity will be more powerful if you do them at the right time. In most cases, you'll get better results if you do spells for creativity while the moon is waxing. However, if your goal is to eliminate an obstacle or condition that's blocking your imagination, do a spell during the waning moon. Spells to inspire a new project should be performed on the new moon; spells to bring a project to fruition should be done at the full moon.

FACT

Leo is the zodiac sign of self-expression and creativity. Therefore, an ideal time to do spells for creativity is while the moon and/or the sun is in Leo. Astrologers connect Pisces with imagination and Libra with artistic pursuits. If your intention involves these things, do a spell when the sun and/or moon is in one of these signs.

The best days of the week for doing spells for creativity are Friday and Sunday, the days ruled by Venus and the sun, respectively. These heavenly bodies govern the arts, beauty, creativity, self-expression, confidence, and identity. The best times for doing each of the spells in this chapter are indicated at the end of each spell.

If you know astrology or can consult with an astrologer, look for periods when transiting or progressed Venus or Neptune influences your birth chart in a positive way. Transiting or progressed Jupiter can expand your creativity, especially when it makes connections with Venus, Neptune, or the sun in your birth chart.

Spell to Release Outmoded Patterns

Tools:
- 2 candles in a color that corresponds to your intentions
- 1 piece of string
- Scissors

When:
- During the waning moon

Identify the patterns you want to change that are holding you back or limiting your ability to express yourself. Choose candles of a color that relates to your objective. If you want to be more creative with your financial investments, use green candles. If you want to be more creative in your professional life, use gold candles.

Set the candles on your altar and tie them together with the string. Imagine the string is a limiting force that binds your creativity and keeps you from expressing it as fully as you could. Feel the energy of that self-limiting bond. Let your emotions come to the surface until they reach a peak and you experience a strong desire to remove the fetters.

Then cut the string and burn it. Say aloud, "All beliefs, emotions, and attachments that once limited my creativity are now removed. I am free to express myself as I choose and desire." Sense the relief that accompanies this symbolic release.

Feng Shui Spell to Enhance Creativity

Tools:

- An affirmation written on a slip of paper
- 3 coins
- 1 bowl
- Yellow rose petals

When:

- When the moon is waxing, in Leo or Libra

To locate the area of your home that corresponds to creativity, stand at the doorway that you use most often to enter or exit your home, facing in. Halfway between the furthest right-hand corner and the nearest right-hand corner is the sector known as the creativity gua.

Write an affirmation on a slip of paper, describing your intention. Remember to state it in the present tense. For example, you might write, "A major publishing company now buys my novel and I am content with all aspects of the contract." Or you could state, "I now land a role in the upcoming community play" or, "My tulips win an award in the spring gardening show."

"Keep knocking, and the joy inside will eventually open a window and look to see who's there."—Jelaluddin Rumi

Place your written affirmation in the creativity sector of your home, then position the three coins on top of it. The coins symbolize receiving money (or other rewards) for your creativity. Next, set the bowl on top of the coins and the affirmation. The bowl, a variation of the chalice (discussed in Chapter 9), represents receptivity and your willingness to attract and hold onto creative ideas. Fill the bowl with the rose petals. Yellow, the color associated with creativity and self-esteem, suggests that your creative ideas are blossoming and taking shape in the material world. Leave this spell in place until the full moon or until your wish materializes.

Gemstone Talisman

Tools:
- Almond oil
- 1 piece of amethyst
- 1 piece of carnelian
- 1 piece of jade
- 1 piece of coral
- 1 quartz crystal
- A small wooden box with a lid
- 1 red ribbon

When:
- During the waxing moon

Place a little almond oil in your palms, then gently rub each of the gemstones with the oil, coating them completely. As you do this, feel a connection with the stones. Allow their vibrations and yours to commingle while you infuse them with your intentions. Set the stones in the wooden box and close the lid. Tie the red ribbon around the box to seal it with good luck. Dab a little more almond oil on the box, and then bury it beneath a tree (preferably an apple or cedar tree) near your home.

Spell to Bring about Vivid Dreams

Tools:
- 1 spray bottle
- Water
- Lavender essential oil
- 1 piece of amethyst

When:
- Before going to bed

This spell helps your mind relax so you can receive insights and inspiration from the dream world. Fill the bottle with water, and then add a few drops of the lavender essential oil. Shake the bottle three times to charge the water. Mist your pillow and bed linens with the scented water. Focus on your intention as you inhale the fragrant scent, allowing your mind to grow calm, open, and receptive. Hold the amethyst in your left hand and feel its vibrations. Then place the gemstone under your pillow or on your nightstand.

Repeat this ritual nightly in order to continue the flow of inspirational dreams. Place a notepad nearby so you can jot down impressions as soon as you wake up. Keep a dream log and date the entries. By demonstrating your desire to have vivid dreams, you'll encourage your subconscious to continue sending them to you.

Spell to Sell Your Creative Work

Tools:
- Pen and paper
- Something that represents what you want to sell
- Cinnamon or clove essential oil
- 3 candles: 1 red, 1 gold, and 1 violet

When:
- Three consecutive nights, beginning with the new moon

The item you choose to represent what you want to sell is especially important in this spell. If, for instance, you're a realtor trying to sell a particular house or property, you might choose a little house from a Monopoly game to represent the property. If you want to sell a manuscript or screenplay, then perhaps a book or a video can serve as a symbol. On a piece of paper, write your intention in the form of an affirmation, in the present tense: "My screenplay sells for a large sum of money" or "The Smith house is now sold." Slip this affirmation under the item that symbolizes your desire.

On the first night, dress the red candle with oil. As you light the candle, say your wish out loud three times. Red is the color of action and energy. Leave the candle on your altar (or another safe place) and allow it to burn out naturally. On the second night, repeat this ritual with the gold candle. Gold represents your intention to make money. Again, let the candle burn out—don't blow it out. On the third night, light the purple candle. Purple symbolizes spiritual power, wisdom, and your highest good. When the purple candle finishes burning, burn the piece of paper on which you've written your affirmation to release your wish into the cosmos.

Chapter 17

Health Spells

Long before the advent of modern medicine, surgery, and pharmaceuticals, healers practiced magic—mind over matter—to remedy diseases. Medicine men and wise women were entrusted with the care and well being of their people. Their knowledge of the spirit world and the healing energies in plants made them respected members of their communities. Today, healing remains a primary focus for many magicians. Miraculous cures that baffle conventional doctors can be achieved through the same magical practices that are used to attract wealth or love.

The Human Energy Field

The human energy field surrounds the physical body and permeates it. Sometimes called *chi* or *prana* or *orgone,* this vital life force animates the physical body; at death, the energy field disperses. In most people, the field extends a few inches to as much as several feet out from the physical body and looks like a halo or cocoon of light. This sphere of light is often referred to as an *aura.* With practice, you can train yourself to detect the aura. Some people see it, others feel it, and some do both.

FACT

All living things have energy fields. You can train yourself to see the auras of animals, plants, and even crystals and other stones. Wilhelm Reich talked about seeing orgone energy radiating from bodies of water. Practice observing the vital life force emanating from all things in the same way you see auras in people.

In a healthy person, the colors in the aura are brilliant, clear, and smooth. When the aura contains dark or white splotches, has tiny rips or tears, or is discolored in some way, physical illness or emotional imbalances may be indicated. According to holistic healers, disease exists in the energy field before it materializes in the physical body. By healing a disturbance in the energy field, physical problems can be corrected or averted.

Sensing Auras

Sensing auras isn't difficult; it just takes a little observation and practice. Try this technique with a partner. Ask your partner to stand against a white, blank wall. Dim the lights in the room. Stand about six feet away from your partner and ask her to think of something that makes her happy and to hold on to that feeling. Stare at a point slightly above her head or to one side of it. Don't strain—just relax your gaze.

After a few moments, you should be able to see a pale nimbus of light around her head. At first, it may resemble a heat wave, the kind you see radiating from pavement on a hot summer day. The wave may grow as your partner experiences her joyful feelings.

If you don't see any colors, ask your partner to turn up her emotions. You may see sparks of colored light now: yellow, gold, brilliant blues, and violets. Next, ask your partner to think of something that enraged her. Ask her to hold that emotion for a few minutes. Do you see any perceptible change in her aura? Does the wave shrink or get larger? Do the colors change?

If you would rather work alone, you can do the same exercise in front of a mirror. Stand with a pale, blank wall behind you. Observe the changes in your own aura as you recall a variety of emotions.

Reading the Energy Field

When a medical intuitive looks at a person's energy field, he perceives a number of details. As Caroline Myss writes in *Anatomy of the Spirit,* "In addition to reading specific dramatic childhood experiences, sometimes an intuitive can pick up on superstitions, personal habits, behavior patterns, moral beliefs, and preferences in music and literature. At other times the energy impressions are more symbolic." To a medical intuitive, your aura reveals every aspect of you.

Medical intuitive Donna Eden explains, "If I know your chakras, I know your history, the obstacles to your growth, your vulnerabilities to illness, and your soul's longings."

Intuitives usually agree that illness and disease are signals that indicate a need to address certain issues in your life. "Your body is designed to heal itself," writes Donna Eden in *Energy Medicine.* Holistic healing operates on the principle that well-being results from balancing the energy patterns in the body. Ultimately, healing doesn't come from something outside you, such as a medical procedure or drug; instead, it resides within your own mind.

The Chakras

You already possess all the tools you need to heal yourself. The first step is developing an awareness of the subtle energies that enliven your physical body. This vital force runs through meridians in your body and the seven major energy centers, or chakras, that align from the base of the spine to the crown of the head.

Chakra literally means wheel, disk, or vortex. Imagine a swirling disk of colored light, and you'll have a pretty good idea of what a chakra looks like. When your energy is balanced, you enjoy good health. When your energy centers become unbalanced or blocked, you get sick. Each energy center has a particular function and governs certain organs and physical systems within its domain. When a chakra isn't functioning properly, the organs and systems it governs suffer, and disease occurs.

Donna Eden claims that each energy center has seven distinct layers. The deeper she intuitively penetrates into an individual chakra, the more information she accesses. Barbara Brennan, a renowned healer and author of *Hands of Light,* also sees layers, but not in the same way. She connects the chakras with several distinct functions. The front of the throat chakra, she says, "is associated with taking responsibility for one's personal needs." But the back of the throat chakra "is associated

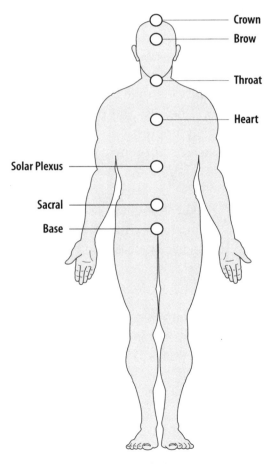

The Chakras

with the person's sense of self within the society, his profession, and with his peers."

The energy centers are said to contain everything you've ever felt, thought, and experienced. They are your body's data bank. The information imprinted on your chakras includes not only your experiences in this lifetime but also your soul's history throughout many incarnations.

The Seven Major Chakras

The first energy center, at the base of the spine, is what Caroline Myss calls "tribal power." It relates to your family, your framework in life, and how your basic needs were met as a child. It reveals your ability to trust and to help yourself. When this center isn't working the way it should, you may experience chronic lower back pain, sciatica, rectal problems, depression, and immune-related disorders.

Myss calls the second center "power and relationships." The issues governed by this chakra have to do with individuating yourself from your tribe or family. It's your locus of autonomy, money and sex, blame and guilt, and creativity. When this chakra doesn't function correctly, troubles arise with the reproductive organs, bladder, urinary tract, hips, and pelvis.

The third energy center represents, in Myss's terminology, "personal power." It is dominant during puberty when young people are attempting to establish themselves. Issues involving confidence, identity, responsibility for making decisions, and self-esteem correspond to this chakra. Dr. Mona Lisa Schulz, author of *Awakening Intuition*, describes this energy center as "me against the world." When the center is off-balance, problems such as ulcers, Crohn's disease, anorexia or bulimia, addictions, liver trouble, obesity, and adrenal dysfunction may result.

The fourth center, or heart chakra, governs the emotions: how you feel or block them, how and to whom you express them. Once you can identify what you feel, you can change what needs to be changed in order to remedy health problems. When this chakra isn't functioning correctly, asthma and allergies, lung cancer, heart attack, bronchial pneumonia, and breast cancer can result.

The fifth or throat chakra is the center of personal will and expression. Issues such as speaking your own truth, living your dreams, and asking for what you want, as well as your capacity for making decisions, reside in this center. When this chakra isn't functioning the way it should, you may experience problems with your throat, gums, or mouth, such as swollen glands, tonsillitis, or thyroid imbalances.

"Most illnesses result from a loss of energy from [the lower] three chakras," writes Caroline Myss. "Emotions such as rage and anger hit us physically below the belt, while an emotion like unexpressed sadness is associated with diseases above the belt."

The sixth energy center corresponds to thought and perception. Its issues involve your intellectual abilities, openness to new ideas, and your ability to learn from experience. When this chakra doesn't function correctly, brain tumors, stroke, neurological problems such as Parkinson's, seizures, spinal difficulties, and problems with the ears, eyes, and nose can result.

The seventh energy center involves your spirituality and your ability to integrate it into your daily life. As Schulz notes, this chakra is concerned with the fundamental question: "Why am I here?" Disorders connected with this chakra include the muscular system, connective tissues, and genetic problems.

Testing Your Chakras

Intuitive and healer Barbara Brennan recommends using a pendulum to diagnose the chakras. You'll need a partner and a pendulum on a chain about six inches long for this exercise.

Lie flat on your back on the floor. Ask your partner to hold the pendulum as close to your body as possible without touching it. The pendulum must be allowed to swing of its own accord, without your friend's moving it.

If the chakra is healthy, the pendulum will circle in a clockwise direction. The larger the circle, the more open the chakra is. If the pendulum doesn't move when it's held over a particular chakra, that chakra is blocked, unbalanced, or so overused that it has shut down.

If the pendulum swings more toward one side of the body, that side is stronger. The right side symbolizes the male, yang, and active side; the left represents the female, yin, or receptive side. If the pendulum's swing toward the right is stronger, you may be too active or aggressive in situations where receptivity would be the better response. A strong swing to the left indicates you might be too passive in situations where assertiveness or decisive action would be more appropriate.

Check all seven chakras this way, and then switch places. Now it's your turn to hold the pendulum and examine your partner's chakras.

Emotional Patterns and Health

Holistic medicine doesn't separate the physical body from the emotions or thoughts. From the perspective of a holistic healer, the body's symptoms indicate psychological issues and emotions that aren't being handled properly. Physical pain alerts you to a deeper problem, a sickness in the soul, and gives you an opportunity to address it.

According to Thorwald Dethlefsen and Rudiger Dahlke, authors of *The Healing Power of Illness,* no ill person is an innocent victim. Every disease originates in an unhealthy emotional or psychological state, and its cure depends on correcting those thoughts, feelings, and resistances. The reason cancer so often returns, even after surgery, chemotherapy, and radiation, is that the underlying cause—the precipitating emotion or attitude—has not been removed.

Body Language

Medical intuitive and author Louise Hay rarely mentions chakras or energy centers. Instead, she associates the various parts of the body with emotions. Each part of the body and each ailment has a distinct meaning.

In Hay's system, the throat "represents our ability to 'speak' up for ourselves, to 'ask for what we want,' to say 'I am' etc. When we have throat problems, it usually means we do not feel we have the right to do these things. We feel inadequate to stand up for ourselves." Even so-called accidents provide insights into emotional conditions. "If you cut your index finger, there is probably anger and fear that has to do with your ego in some current situation," Hay writes in *You Can Heal Your Life*.

ALERT!

Pay attention to the words you use to describe conditions—they reveal the link between body, mind, and spirit. Is a situation at work giving you a "pain in the neck"? Are you having trouble "digesting" an idea? Eye problems may indicate you don't want to see something. Arthritis suggests you are emotionally or mentally inflexible. "Body talk" provides the clues to an ailment's cause.

For example, a few years ago, Meredith's thumb suddenly became very painful, swollen, and stiff, a condition that lasted for several weeks. It felt like her thumb was broken, although she hadn't actually injured it. At the time, she was holding on to a lot of anger toward her ex-husband. One afternoon they were arguing, and a bruise began spreading rapidly across her thumb and hand, even though she was sitting with her hands loosely folded in her lap. When a medical intuitive pointed out that humans need thumbs to "hold on," she realized the connection. Instantly, the pain and stiffness subsided and she could bend her thumb again.

Magical Healing

Many common health problems, especially chronic ones, get better without any outside medical intervention when the person changes his way of perceiving or responding to circumstances. Asthma, for instance, is connected with unexpressed anger. Lower back pain often goes along with relationship difficulties.

The nasal passages, says Louise Hay, often pinch-hit for tears. Nosebleeds indicate sadness at not being loved and recognized. A runny nose substitutes for inner crying. Joel had a painful argument with a woman he loved. They didn't speak or see each other for nearly a week. Being a tough guy, he couldn't express his sadness, but during that week, his nose ran constantly. Once they made peace, his "allergy" magically disappeared.

In the healing modality known as homeopathy, the practitioner treats the patient's emotional body to relieve a physical complaint. The patient ingests a miniscule amount of a substance—usually derived from plants or minerals—whose vibrational quality is similar to the nature of the ailment. Symbolism plays a key role in homeopathic diagnosis and treatment. This like-cures-like method of healing baffles conventional, allopathic physicians because the dosages are so small they contain no measurable substance. Only the essence or vibration of the healing material is present, which is all that's necessary to treat the subtle energy body.

In *Awakening Intuition,* Dr. Mona Lisa Schulz cites studies that show "When someone with lower back pain and marital problems undertakes marriage counseling with his or her partner, the lower back pain often improves significantly, without benefit of surgery or medication, as the relationship improves."

Acupuncture, massage therapy, yoga, and other forms of energetic healing achieve results by enabling the body's vital force to flow smoothly through the system; the body heals itself. Laying on of hands and spiritual healing inspire a shift in thinking that breaks down blockages related to old beliefs and patterns. New thought forms can then create healthier physical conditions.

As you work with your own energy centers, using healing spells or some other method, listen to what your body tells you. Learn to recognize the meanings behind your own symptoms. Pain is always a cry for help. Visualization, affirmations, and other magical techniques can relieve all sorts of ailments and enable you to manifest the physical well being you desire. The more you understand about yourself and your own body language, the better equipped you'll be to maintain your health.

Health Spell Caveats and Cautions

You know someone who's suffering, and you know a little magic could help that person. Shouldn't you do a healing spell for her? Well, *maybe*. Physical pain is a red flag that something needs attention—not just the obvious symptom, but the underlying root of the problem. Perhaps the discomfort your friend feels is actually helping her get in touch with the deeper issues involved. If so, it may be a necessary and beneficial part of her healing process.

Respecting another person's free will is also important when you're doing magic. You can't change anyone else unless he wants to change. And you may not fully understand the issues involved with another person's disease. Perhaps an injury is forcing an overachiever to slow down, work less, and spend more time with his family. Perhaps an illness is giving someone's partner a chance to practice patience and compassion. Unless someone asks for your help, proceed with caution and reserve.

ALERT!

Before you perform a healing spell for someone, ask that person if it's okay. If circumstances prevent you from communicating directly with the person, meditate on the situation and ask his or her spirit for permission. Close the spell with: "This is done in harmony with Divine Will and for [person's name]'s highest good."

Finally, it's important to acknowledge that magic spells, no matter how powerful and well intentioned, aren't a substitute for professional medical care. Although you've perhaps heard of shamans who can cure broken bones by tying sticks carved with affirmations to the damaged limb, in most cases it's wise to have the bone set by a qualified doctor. You may have personally witnessed miraculous healings or undergone instantaneous cures for long-term conditions that orthodox medicine couldn't alleviate. But if you break a tooth, you'll probably be grateful for the skills of a competent dentist. Combine humility, patience, and common sense with magical belief, for both your own good and everyone else's.

Timing Health Spells

Healing spells will be more powerful if you do them at the right time. It's usually best to do spells to increase vitality or repair damage to bone or tissue while the moon is waxing. But if your goal is to eliminate or reduce something, do a spell during the waning moon. Spells to lose weight, for example, should be done while the moon wanes. If your goal is to build your strength and overcome the flu, perform a spell during the waxing period.

The full moon is a high-energy day, and many people experience peak vitality at this time. However, the full moon can also exacerbate stress and bring emotional or psychological issues out into the open. The three days prior to and including the new moon tend to be low-energy days. It may take longer to recover from an illness or injury incurred during this period—don't push yourself at this time.

FACT

Virgo is the zodiac sign of health. Therefore, you may wish to do healing spells while the moon and/or the sun is in Virgo. The sun is connected with vitality, and Mars rules physical strength as well as energy. Consequently, you may wish do a healing spell when the sun and/or moon is in Leo or Aries, depending on your intention.

Spells to limit the spread of disease or to reduce problems associated with a condition should be done on Saturday. Spells to bolster strength and vitality are best done on Tuesday, Thursday, or Sunday. Don't opt for elective surgery or other medical procedures while Mercury is retrograde, as mental errors are more common at this time. If you have tests done while Mercury is retrograde and the results are unfavorable or inconclusive, consider having the tests redone.

Medical astrology is a complex and centuries-old field. You may wish to consult with a qualified medical astrologer before undergoing medical procedures or doing healing spells.

Spell to Strengthen the First Chakra

Tools:
- An object that represents your "tribe"
- Pen and paper
- 1 red candle
- Essential oil of clove

When:
- During the waxing moon, preferably when the sun or moon is in Aries

This spell helps to strengthen your sense of security, stability, and inner power. The tribe symbol should be an object that represents your support system—a family photo, a figurine of a totem animal, or a treasured heirloom or item from your past. Set the power object on your altar. Next, write an affirmation that describes your intention. For example, you might write: "I am safe and secure" or "I am capable of caring for myself and my loved ones." Fold the paper three times and slip it under the power object.

Dress the candle with clove oil. If you wish, dab some oil on your power object, too, and at the base of your spine. As you light the candle, inhale the scent of clove and say your affirmation aloud. Focus on the spot at the base of your spine and imagine you are directing energy into it. Imagine a glowing ball of red light there. Allow the candle to finish burning down on its own, and then burn the paper, releasing your affirmation into the universe.

Spell to Heal an Injury

Tools:
- 1 green ribbon
- 1 pen or marker that will write on fabric
- 1 green light bulb

When:
- As needed

Green is the color of growth, healthy plants, and comfort. On the ribbon, write your affirmation, making sure to state the end result you desire. For instance, say "My arm is whole and healthy." Then tie the ribbon loosely around the injured body part (but not directly over the wound).

Screw the green light bulb into a lamp or fixture. Position yourself so the green light shines on the injured body part. Visualize the injury being completely healed. If you have a broken bone, see the pieces knitting together again perfectly. Imagine a cut mending and the skin healing without a scar. Envision swelling and bruises fading away. Make sure to focus on the end result you desire, not the injury, and repeat your affirmation frequently.

Shine the light on the injury several times per day. Leave the ribbon in place until the injury is healed.

Spell to Relieve Digestive Complaints

Tools:
- 1 glass cup
- Chamomile tea
- 1 piece of paper
- 1 pen with green ink
- Tape

When:
- Any time

On the paper, write the words *balance, harmony, peace, love,* and *acceptance.* Tape the paper to a clear glass cup, so the words face in. Then brew some chamomile tea and pour it into the glass cup. Let the tea sit for a few minutes to allow the words to imprint their message into the liquid.

Sip the tea slowly, focusing on its soothing warmth in your stomach. Envision healing green light entering your stomach and abdomen, calming the upsets in your digestive tract. Feel yourself relaxing and becoming more receptive to nourishment. Repeat this ritual daily, until your problem improves.

Spell to Get Rid of a Headache

Tools:
- 1 smoky quartz crystal
- 1 piece of rose quartz
- Lavender-scented incense

When:
- Any time

Wash the stones in running water, then charge them by letting them sit in the sunlight for several minutes. Light the incense. Sit quietly in a comfortable spot and begin breathing slowly and deeply. Hold the rose quartz in your left hand and feel it gently emitting loving, peaceful vibrations. Hold the smoky quartz crystal to your forehead and imagine the quartz absorbing the pain. When you're finished, cleanse and charge the stones again.

Ritual to Increase Vitality

Tools:
- 4 bayberry candles
- 4 clear quartz crystals

When:
- As needed

Perform this ritual outside. Place the candles at the four compass directions. Set the crystals between the candles to form a circle. Step inside the circle and light the candles, beginning in the east and working in a clockwise direction. Stand facing east, with your arms outstretched at your sides, parallel to the ground, palms up.

The candles represent the fire element and the masculine force. The crystals symbolize the earth element and the feminine force. Feel the balanced energy around you flowing into your body from every direction. Receive it in your open hands and allow it to fill you up, energizing you.

Draw Mother Earth's nurturing energy upward through your feet, into your legs, torso, arms, and head. Feel the sun's vitalizing energy flowing into the top of your head and down through your body, all the way to your feet. Envision the two forces—yin and yang, heaven and earth—blending and balancing one another in your heart center.

Stand in the center of the circle as long as you choose. When you feel invigorated, extinguish the candles in a counterclockwise direction and leave the circle. Repeat this ritual as often as needed. If you wish, you can invite other people to join you in the healing circle.

Chapter 18

Travel Spells

Every day the world grows smaller. Faster cars, planes, and trains ferry people around the globe for work, pleasure, personal growth, adventure, study, healing, and a host of other reasons. At best, travel expands your horizons and opens doors to rewarding experiences. Too often, however, traveling involves stress, annoyances, and even potential danger. Although you may not be able to climb on a broom and fly to your destination or to dematerialize and rematerialize someplace else at will, you can use magic to make traveling safer and smoother.

Your Perceptions and Expectations about Traveling

If you fly commercially, you're no doubt familiar with this scenario. You arrive at the airport an hour or more before your flight is scheduled to depart, stand in line to check your bags, and go through the security check only to find out that your flight will be delayed two hours. Maybe you're fortunate and your flight leaves on time, but every seat is filled and you're crammed in a center seat between someone who sneezes constantly and a crying baby. To make things worse, the guy in front of you lowers the back of his seat all the way down, almost in your lap. By the time you reach your destination, you're tired, cranky, and wondering if it's worth the trouble. Is there a way to mitigate the aggravation?

"A pessimist sees the difficulty in every opportunity; an optimist sees the opportunity in every difficulty."—Winston Churchill

As you already know, your attitude and expectations influence what happens to you. Your ideas create the circumstances you encounter while traveling, just as they sow the seeds for outcomes in other areas of your life. If you expect a trip to go smoothly, look forward to meeting interesting people, and anticipate enjoying pleasant experiences, that's exactly what will transpire. If, on the other hand, you focus on prospective problems, that's what you'll draw to you.

Writer George Sand expressed it this way: "Since it always happens that one gives form and substance to the dangers upon which one broods to excess, the dread of the possibility [becomes] an accurate forecast of the future."

Fear and Control

Alcoholics Anonymous considers the word *fear* as an acronym for "false evidence appearing real." Often, the things people fear are simply ideas that may never come to pass. You may worry for days, weeks, or longer, only to find that your fears never materialize. Although you may be relieved that the worst didn't occur, you suffered needlessly over something that wasn't real.

"Many of our fears are tissue-paper thin, and a single courageous step would carry us clear through them."—Brendan Francis

What scares you about traveling? Are you uncomfortable being in a strange place, away from your familiar surroundings? Do you feel anxious when you're not in control? Does being in a crowd of people make you edgy? Do you experience claustrophobia or motion sickness?

According to author Louise Hay, the probable emotional cause of motion sickness is fear of being trapped, of not being in control. (Most people don't get carsick when they're driving, only when they're passengers.) If you feel trapped or anxious in a car, plane, boat, or train, and start to feel sick, repeat the affirmation "I am in control." If possible, sing it aloud until the motion sickness passes.

Loss of control is at the root of most travel-related fears. If you're flying in an airplane, you have to trust the pilot will get you to your destination safely—you don't have control. If you visit a foreign country, you'll be confronted with strange food, unfamiliar customs, and a language you don't understand—you don't have control. When you travel, you can't control things like the weather, other cars on the road, how your baggage gets handled, or the people you encounter along the way.

Changing Your Perspective

Chelsea decided to go on a hiking trip around Europe. She had no agenda, no timetable, and no fixed destinations. She saw each day as a new adventure, with no preconceptions or fears. Occasionally, she hit a snag, but overall she met wonderful people and enjoyed a plethora of positive experiences—including many happy accidents—because she approached the journey with an open mind and trusted the universe to guide her. Of course, this sort of trip isn't for everyone. But regardless of where you're going, for what reason, your expectations will color your experiences.

Whether you're the type who organizes every detail or someone who prefers to wing it, it can be helpful to examine your ideas before you head off into the wild blue yonder. Make a list of the things you're anxious about. Address the ones you can control, and consider what options might be available to you.

Are you afraid your luggage might get lost? Maybe you can ship it to your destination ahead of time. Do you fear that your car might break down? Get it serviced before you leave and join AAA. Are you worried that relatives at a family reunion might argue? Make a backup plan—book a motel room, arrange to meet a friend, take a walk—that allows you to get away if things become too stressful.

Next, look at the things you can't control or fix with practical solutions. Here's where magic comes in. This chapter provides spells to help you smooth the bumps in the road, so to speak. Life itself is a journey. You never know what's going to happen tomorrow. But that doesn't prevent you from living. In the words of the great artist Pablo Picasso, "If you know exactly what you're going to do, what's the good of doing it?"

Timing Travel Spells

Like other spells, the ones you do to facilitate travel will be more powerful if you do them at the appropriate time. If you're beginning an adventure, start your journey when the moon is new. If the purpose of your trip is to complete a goal, such as a business trip to land a sale or contract, try to schedule it on or just before the full moon. Plan a vacation to unwind and let go of responsibilities during the waning moon. Arrange a trip for educational purposes or to expand your contacts while the moon is waxing.

FACT

Sagittarius is the zodiac sign of long-distance travel. Therefore, the best time to do most travel spells is while the moon and/or the sun is in Sagittarius. Gemini is connected with short trips, so if you don't plan to go far from home, do a spell when the sun and/or moon is in Gemini.

The best days of the week for doing travel spells are Wednesday and Thursday, the days ruled by Mercury and Jupiter, respectively. Mercury governs short trips, while Jupiter oversees long-distance travel. Consider the purpose of your trip, too. Saturn is associated with work, so you could do a spell for a business trip on Saturday. You might want to do a spell for a happy honeymoon or romantic getaway on Friday, the day ruled by Venus.

If possible, avoid taking a trip while Mercury is retrograde (check an ephemeris for dates). During one of these three-week periods, which happen about four times in a year, you're more likely to encounter travel-related problems. Delays, cancellations, lost luggage, mechanical troubles, crossed signals, communication difficulties, and general confusion occur more frequently when Mercury is retrograde. If you must travel during these periods, use extra care. Plan ahead, confirm reservations, allow plenty of time in your schedule for mishaps, and don't leave anything to chance.

Gemstone Protection Amulet

Tools:
- 1 piece of amber
- 1 piece of quartz crystal
- 1 piece of jade
- 1 piece of turquoise
- 1 piece of topaz
- 1 piece of agate
- Amber essential oil

- 1 white pouch, preferably made of silk
- 1 black ribbon
- Saltwater

When:
- During the new moon, preferably on Wednesday or Thursday

Wash the stones with mild soap and water, then set them in the sun for a few minutes to remove any unwanted energies. Rub a little amber essential oil on each of the stones, and then slip them into the pouch.

Tie the bag closed with the ribbon, making nine knots. Each time you tie a knot, repeat this affirmation: "This amulet keeps me safe and sound at all times and in all situations." When you've finished, sprinkle the amulet with a little saltwater to charge it. Carry the amulet with you whenever you travel.

Quick and Easy Flying Spell

This spell requires no tools—just your imagination—and can be done in a minute or so, right before your plane taxis into position for take-off. Close your eyes and breathe slowly and deeply. Envision a cocoon of pure white light surrounding the entire plane from nose to tail and out to the tips of the wings. See the light swirling around the plane in a clockwise direction, forming a protective barrier against the elements.

"The real voyage of discovery," wrote French author Marcel Proust, "consists not in seeking new landscapes, but in having new eyes."

Mentally repeat the following affirmation three times: "I now enjoy a comfortable trip and land safely at [name of destination airport]." If you wish, visualize the plane traveling through the sky and landing safely on the runway at your final destination.

Spell to Calm a Crying Baby

Infants are sensitive to pressure changes within a plane, and crying may help them clear their ears. If you are seated near a crying infant, the surest way to ease the child's misery—and your own—is to work from your heart energy center. Children are more receptive than adults to telepathic communication and energetic transmissions, so attempt to make a connection between your heart and the baby's.

Imagine pink light pouring from your heart center. Let the light surround the child, cradling it. When you feel the child is encompassed within the light, imagine rocking her gently, as though you were holding the baby in your arms. Mentally whisper comforting words to the child. Project peaceful, loving vibrations in its direction. Keep this up for several moments, even after the child stops crying.

Travel Spell for Cats

Tools:
- Homeopathic remedy Cocculus Indicus 30c
- Bach Flower Rescue Remedy (see E-Fact on page 260)
- 1 piece of amethyst
- 1 spray bottle
- Water
- Lavender essential oil
- 1 blue blanket, towel, or pad
- The largest cage that will fit in your car

When:
- An hour before you start your trip

Most cats hate to travel. They don't like confinement, the motion makes them feel insecure, and they get anxious when taken out of their familiar environments. This spell eases your cat's anxiety and makes the trip more pleasant for both of you.

About an hour before you start your trip, put one tiny Cocculus Indicus pill in your cat's mouth and make sure she swallows it. (If you prefer, you can dissolve the pill in water, then give her the water with an eyedropper.) Then put a drop of Rescue Remedy on her nose (she'll lick it off).

Place the amethyst in the bottle and fill it with water. Add a few drops of essential oil and shake the bottle three times to charge it. Mist the inside of your car with the fragrant water. Repeat this periodically throughout the trip.

Lay the blanket, towel, or pad in the bottom of the cat's cage. Gently place the cat in the cage and, if possible, position the cage so your cat will be able to see you while you're traveling. Send calm, loving vibrations from your heart center to your cat. Talk to her in a quiet, soothing voice. If you wish, play soft music while you're driving. If the trip will take more than one day, repeat the same procedure each morning before you start. (Practical tip: Get a collar for your cat with a name tag that includes your name, address, and phone number on it. Label the cage with the same information.)

Smooth Travel Spell

Tools:
- 1 ballpoint pen
- 1 white candle
- Rosemary essential oil
- 1 piece of rose quartz

When:
- At night, within twenty-four hours prior to your departure

With the ballpoint pen, inscribe the astrological glyph for Jupiter (the planet that rules travel) into the candle's wax. The symbol looks a bit like the number 4. Dress the candle with the rosemary oil and light it. If you wish, you can burn a little dried rosemary herb in a fireproof dish. Set the rose quartz in front of the candle.

Repeat this incantation while you gaze into the candle's flame and inhale the scent of the rosemary.

By the light of Lady Moon,
I reach my destination soon.
The trip shall safe and happy be,
For all concerned, as well as me.

When you're finished, extinguish the candle and pick up the rose quartz. Rub a little rosemary oil on it and carry the stone with you while you're traveling.

Travel Potion

Tools:
- 1 clear glass bottle
- Water
- The Knight of Wands from your favorite tarot deck
- 1 red ribbon

When:
- On a Thursday, before your trip

Fill the bottle with water. Lay the Knight of Wands (the tarot card of travel and adventure) face up on your altar and set the bottle of water on the card. Leave it there overnight. In the morning, write an affirmation that states your intentions for your trip, such as "I enjoy a lovely, relaxing vacation" or "I cinch the business deal with [name of company or person]." Tie the red ribbon around the neck of the bottle, making three knots. As you tie each knot, repeat your affirmation and visualize the end result in your mind's eye.

Carry the bottle of magically imprinted water with you on your trip. Sip the water periodically throughout the journey. As you drink, feel yourself being filled with optimism and envision your intention coming true.

Spell to Manifest a Trip You Desire

Tools:
- 1 large sheet of heavy paper or cardboard
- Colored markers or pens
- Magazine photos of places you want to go
- Maps
- Other symbols that represent travel to you
- Glue
- Sandalwood incense

When:
- During the waxing moon, preferably on a Thursday

Is there someplace you've always wanted to go? Don't worry about how you'll get the money or time for the trip—just do your magic and let the universe handle the arrangements.

Cut out pictures from magazines and travel catalogs of a place you'd like to visit. Gather maps, brochures, and other information about this place. Collect symbols and images that represent travel to you—a toy airplane, a tiny boat, a hotel from a Monopoly game, seashells, and anything that relates to the trip you're planning.

After you've gathered as many images as you feel you need, draw a circle on the piece of paper or cardboard large enough that you can stand within it. Glue all the symbols you've collected inside the circle. Use the colored markers to draw additional pictures and/or write words that describe your intentions, such as the names of the places you plan to visit or affirmations stating your desires.

When your wish board is finished, light the incense. Stand in the middle of the board and envision yourself journeying to the place(s) you've chosen. Make your visualization as clear and vivid as possible. Try to intuit the mood of the place, the sights, sounds, and smells. Enjoy yourself. Remain in the circle, imagining your journey, until the incense finishes burning.

Safety Shield for Your Car

Tools:

- 1 white paper square
- Colored markers
- Amber essential oil
- Tape, glue, or other adhesive

When:

- During the waning moon, preferably when the moon is in Gemini or Sagittarius

The average person drives about 12,000 miles each year. That exposes you to plenty of potential delays, accidents, and other problems. This spell protects you from harm when you're driving your car, whether it's in your own neighborhood or cross-country.

Cut a square of paper four inches wide by four inches high. Within this square draw a circle. Design a sigil using the letters from the word *safe* or from an affirmation of your choice, and draw it in the center of the circle. (See Chapter 3 for instructions on drawing a sigil.) If you wish, add other symbols that represent safety and travel to you. The pattern you've created is your safety shield.

Dot the four corners of the paper with amber essential oil. Then affix the shield to the dashboard of your car. Each time you get into your car, look at the shield and touch it to activate its protective energies. Visualize yourself and your car surrounded by pure white light, and know that you are protected wherever you go.

Traveling Magic Kit

If you're going on a trip, or if your job or lifestyle requires you to travel frequently, you may want to put together a magic kit that you can take along with you. You never know when you might need a little magic on the road. This kit should include some basic magic tools that can be adapted to a variety of spells. Although the choice is completely personal, here are some suggestions as to what you might wish to include in your kit:

- A quartz crystal
- A couple of sticks of your favorite incense
- A favorite essential oil (perhaps peppermint, amber, sandalwood, rose, or almond)
- A box of birthday cake candles
- Tarot cards, runes, or another oracle
- A length of white or red ribbon
- A small container of sea salt
- An image of your totem animal
- A pentagram
- A journal to record dreams and insights

Consider placing all these magic tools in a special bag to protect and contain them. Add to your travel kit as necessary. If most of your traveling is done for a specific purpose, such as business, you might want to include items that relate to your work. The goal is to keep it simple and lightweight. Store your travel kit in your car or suitcase, so it's always handy when you're ready to go.

Chapter 19

Spells for Kids

Children possess an innate under-standing of magic. They follow their intuition, display wonderful imagina-tions, and fully believe that all things are possible. Enchanted castles, wiz-ards, faeries, dragons, trees that talk, and brooms that fly through the air all fit nicely into a kid's view of the world. Because children love make-believe and throw themselves enthusiastically into creating the realities they envision, they're natural magicians. By watching young people immerse themselves in spell-casting, adults can learn a thing or two!

Kids and Imagination

A boy loses a tooth and the Tooth Fairy leaves money under his pillow. A little girl tosses a penny into a fountain and makes a wish, certain her wish will come true. On Christmas Eve, Santa soars through the sky in a magic sleigh drawn by flying reindeer. To children, the adventures of Peter Pan, Cinderella, Harry Potter, and Luke Skywalker are just as real as the daily events in their own lives.

Imagination is a key factor in magic. Although adults often have trouble letting their imaginations run wild, children do it all the time, without effort and without questioning the validity of their fantasies. You don't have to convince a child that he can send energy anywhere he desires, simply by pointing a magic wand at his target. A child doesn't doubt her ability to brew a magic potion.

It's common for young children to communicate with imaginary friends whom they believe are as real as their flesh-and-blood companions. Children also display an uncanny ability at ESP. By the age of seven, however, most kids begin shutting down this sixth sense due to the admonishments of adults.

You can help young children hone their natural magical powers by performing spells and rituals with them. In the beginning, kids need some guidance so they can learn to do spells safely. Working magic with children can be a growth-producing experience for adults, too. A child's energy, curiosity, and passion can be infectious and may inspire you to expand your own magical repertoire. Nurture your children's rich imaginations by encouraging them to believe in themselves. If you're a parent, casting the spells in this chapter with your kids can enhance your closeness. Perhaps that's the real magic.

Spells, Creativity, and Kids

Designing a spell is an endeavor no less creative than sketching a picture or writing a story. As an experiment, ask your child to think of something she really wants. Then work with her to fashion an appropriate spell. Make it fun. Be adventurous. As the adage goes, let your own inner child come out in the process.

FACT

When doing spells with kids, incorporate as many colorful, tactile elements into the ritual as possible. Get out crayons, paints, and construction paper. Concoct potions you can actually drink. Dress up in special clothing. Fashion magic wands and other tools. Work outside under the full moon.

Preteens and teenagers can do these spells alone, if they're so inclined, or with friends. Younger kids can do them with an adult or with older kids, if they're willing. The spells presented here are simple and fun and can be done at any time, on any day, most of them under any phase of the moon.

Sharing Magic with Children

Kids usually enjoy creating their own spells. Here are some simple guidelines that will help them cast safe and effective spells:

- Do no harm. This is the prime directive of all spell-casting. It extends to all life, and that means animals, insects, and plants as well as people.
- Believe that what you're doing is possible. Without this belief, you won't get the results you desire.
- Be clear about your intention and goal. Always ask yourself, "Exactly what do I want?"
- Back your spell with positive emotion. The more strongly you can feel your spell coming true, the quicker you'll get results.
- Keep your request simple. Stick to one wish at a time.

- Always state your wishes in the present tense and in a positive way that describes the end result you desire.
- If you're doing a spell for another person, make sure you have that person's permission. Even if you're trying to help someone else, and even if you have the person's best interests at heart, always ask first.
- Have fun. Spells should always be done in the spirit of happiness and adventure. They're meant to be empowering, and part of empowerment is to enjoy what you're doing while you're doing it.
- Read, read, read. Nonfiction books about magic and spell-casting will bolster your practical skills. Fiction will enable you to experience the magic.
- Don't give up. If your spells don't seem to be working, follow the remedies suggested earlier. Revise your spells, reword them, and develop an inner awareness of what you're doing and why.

The guidelines children should follow when doing magic are the same as those for adults. The rules don't change as you grow up. That's because magic isn't a game (although it can certainly be fun). It's a worldview, a way of being, and a lifelong pursuit.

Some good books for kids to read about magic include the Harry Potter books, J. R. R. Tolkien's *Lord of the Rings*, Marion Zimmer Bradley's *Avalon*, and Warren Murphy and Molly Cochran's *The Forever King*. Fairytales and myths also offer wonderful insights into the world of magic. Adults can enjoy sharing these literary sojourns with children, too.

Charms for Kids

Children of all ages generally enjoy making charms. A child's charm bag should contain only a few objects and be designed to serve a specific purpose.

Allow the child to determine the issue for which he wants to make a charm. Suppose, for instance, that your child is having problems with math and with his math teacher. He must first ask himself what he wants to accomplish. Does he want a better relationship with the teacher? Does he want the teacher to be more helpful? Does he want to develop more interest in the subject?

ALERT!

Remind your child that magic isn't a spectator sport—he must take action to bring about the desired result. A spell alone won't resolve your child's difficulties with math and transform him into a prodigy overnight. He also has to do the required work and study the subject.

Once he's identified the problem and pinpointed his desire, he should decide on the color of the bag. Encourage your child to use his intuition in selecting a color. Then let him choose three objects that symbolize his concern and the outcome he intends to achieve. For help in math, one object might be a string of numbers or a geometric shape. He could include one item that represents the teacher: his or her name written on a piece of paper, the room number of the class, even a picture of the teacher. The third object should describe the end result, such as an A on a test.

Have fun creating the charm bag. The spirit with which the bag is made becomes part of its magic.

Tarot for Kids

With thousands of tarot decks in existence, everyone can find a deck that's right for them. Choosing a deck is a personal matter; none is better than another. Kids are often drawn to tarot decks illustrated with mythological creatures, such as dragons, unicorns, elves and faeries, or those that include animals.

Children usually enjoy the tarot's colorful imagery. They may not be able to comprehend all the occult meanings, but they respond quickly to the symbolism. The immediate impressions a child gets when gazing at a card can be amazingly accurate. Storytelling decks, which depict scenarios that describe the cards' meanings, are easier to use than the antique decks that feature only numbers and suit symbols on the pip cards.

FACT

Some designers have created tarot decks specifically with young people in mind. These decks feature contemporary themes such as action adventure heroes, Goth goddesses, and cat people. Other decks are based on favorite legends and fairytales. There's even a Gummy Bear Tarot!

Many magic spells involve the use of tarot cards. Choosing cards to represent intentions can help young people relate to the meanings of the individual cards. Your child might also like to draw a card each morning to see what the day has in store for him. This practice helps hone the child's divination skills and lets him observe his inner guidance at work.

Birthday Blessings

Tools:
- A birthday cake
- Candles

When:
- The child's birthday

You've done this easy spell before; you just didn't realize you were performing magic. Part of the power behind this spell is the high energy that exists around you on your birthday. This is a time to honor yourself.

Choose candles in a color that represents your wish. Before you light the candles, take a few moments to phrase your wish in the form of an affirmation. Then light the candles while you clearly visualize what you want to happen. As you blow out the candles, imagine the wish being carried into the universe, where it will be energized by cosmic forces and brought into manifestation.

Balloon Magic

Tools:
- 1 balloon
- Helium
- 1 pen that will write on fabric
- Colored ribbon

When:
- Any time

Decide on an intention, and then choose a ribbon in a color that symbolizes your wish. Go to a fabric store and pick out the ribbon. Next, visit a store that sells party supplies and purchase a helium-filled balloon. Select a color that represents your intention.

Take the balloon home or to a place where you'll release it. Write your intention on the ribbon. (If the child is too young to write, an adult or older child can write the wish for her.) Keep the wish simple. Tie the ribbon on the balloon. As you let go of the balloon, say the wish aloud. The higher the balloon goes before you lose sight of it, the greater the chances of the wish coming true.

Your Power Object

Tools:
- A favorite object

When:
- Any time

When Swiss psychologist Carl Jung was a child, he found a smooth stone that he kept in a matchbox. He confided in the stone. He told the stone his deepest secrets. He carried it around with him. Years later, in his autobiography, *Memories, Dreams, Reflections*, Jung movingly described his experiences with this stone, the magic that he associated with it, and the power with which he imbued it.

FACT

A stone, piece of wood, or figurine doesn't possess inherent power: It is powerful only because you make it so. Its magic originates in you, with your intent and your passion. Your power object is a symbol of your own personal power and your magical intentions.

Choose an object that appeals to you. The object should be three-dimensional—a stone, for instance, rather than a picture of a stone—and it should have some sort of personal meaning. It should also be small enough to carry easily in a pocket, purse, or backpack. If you love horses and dream of owning one, a figurine of a horse could be an ideal power object. Crystals, stones, and shells make excellent power objects. So do figures of angels, unicorns, dolphins, and mythical gods and goddesses.

After you've selected an object, wash it with mild soap and water, and then set it in the sun to clear and charge it. Give it a name. Sleep with it under your pillow overnight. In the morning, speak to the object and tell it what you want it to do. It's now imbued with power and will help you in performing magic spells.

Bubble Magic

Tools:
- 1 bottle of bubbles
- A power object

When:
- Any time, but during the full moon is best

On a breezy night when the moon is full, take the power object and bottle of bubbles to a hill, field, or park, someplace wide open. Place the power object on the ground between your feet, then make a wish and blow the bubbles. Project your wishes inside the bubbles. Let your power object direct the bubbles as the breeze carries them high into the air, where the gods and goddesses will hear the wishes and grant them.

As the bubbles, with your wishes inside, rise into the moonlit sky, say the following incantation:

My wishes travel
The whole night through
So that magic's power
Can make them come true.

Spell for a Secret Wish

Tools:
- 1 pen or pencil
- Paper
- Your power object
- 1 gold candle

When:
- Any time

Write a secret wish—something you want but haven't told anyone else about—on a piece of paper. Sign your wish, fold it three times, and place it under your power object. Keep your wish simple and straightforward. Set a gold candle beside your power object. As you light the candle, say:

My wish goes out
Free of doubt,
Lit by the flame
That bears my name.

Let the candle burn down naturally, in a safe place. When it has finished burning, carefully burn the piece of paper to release your wish into the cosmos.

The Magic Box

Tools:
- A box with a lid
- Slips of paper
- Color pens or markers
- Magazine pictures, colored paper, stickers, other decorations
- Glue

When:
- During the waxing moon

Everyone in the family can participate in this spell. You'll need a shoebox or a similar container that's small enough to fit on a shelf but large enough to accommodate lots of wishes. Decorate the box however you like, using positive images that appeal to you. Write words on it. Draw pictures. The point is to personalize the box. On the top, write the words: *The Magic Box.*

ALERT!

Do you have a private wish that you don't want to share with anyone else? Create your own, personal magic box and keep it in a secret place. Write your wishes on slips of paper and date them, then put them in your box. Periodically, go through your magic box and remove wishes that have come true or that are no longer priorities for you.

Put the box in place where everyone in the family has access to it and can see it when they enter the house. When the box is completely decorated, ask each member of the family to write one wish on a slip of paper and read it aloud to the others. Place the wishes in the box.

Sharing your wishes with each other galvanizes the family's collective energy. This builds momentum and attracts what you want more quickly. As each wish comes true, remove it from the box. Then make another wish and slip it into the box.

Designate someone in the family to keep a master record of each wish, the date it was put into the box, and the date it materialized. This gives you a clear idea of how long it takes to manifest what you want. Remember, you have to be willing to back up your intentions with effort in the real world if you want them to come true.

Dream Magic

Before you go to sleep at night, say your wish aloud three times. If you like, you can write your wish on a piece of paper and put it under your pillow. Ask to have a dream that offers insights or guidance about how you can make your wish come true. Make a suggestion to yourself that you will remember the dream and understand its meaning.

You may have to repeat this several nights in a row, but eventually you'll have a dream that guides you toward fulfilling your objective. Pay attention to details. Who was in it? What was going on? What time of the year was it? What were you wearing? These details often hold clues about when the wish will come true and in what form it will appear.

Spell to Attract Friends

Tools:
- Several ribbons

When:
- During the waxing moon

This is a good spell to do when you move into a new neighborhood or enter a new school and don't know anybody. Collect several ribbons in various colors. Each ribbon represents a friend. Tie the ribbons to the branches of a tree. As you tie each ribbon, focus on attracting a new friend into your life. Say aloud: "I now have a friend whom I love, respect, trust, and enjoy."

Spell to Bring a Lost Pet Home

Tools:
- Photo of your pet or an effigy that symbolizes it
- 4 white candles
- A pinch of vervain
- A pinch of myrrh
- A pinch of sage

When:
- As needed

Put the photo of your pet (or its effigy) in a prominent place. Set the four white candles at the four corners of the picture. Sprinkle the herbs around the picture or effigy. As you light the candles, hold your pet's image in your mind. Imagine a sphere of pure white light surrounding your pet, protecting it from harm.

Visualize your pet coming home safely, in good health. See your pet trotting across your yard or sitting on your doorstep. Feel the joy you'll experience when this happens. Put your emotion into the visualization, and then say the following:

(Pet's name) comes home to me,
Together we shall happy be.
Healthy and safe,
no longer a waif.
(Pet's name) comes home to me,
Thank you and so mote it be.

Let the candles burn down in a safe place. Keep your pet's photo or effigy displayed until your animal returns home. Then bury it in the backyard, so that your pet will always remain close to home.

Pet Protection Spell

Tools:
- A collar for your pet
- A marker that will write on fabric or leather
- Amber essential oil

When:
- Any time

Purchase a new collar, made of leather or fabric, for your pet. On the inside of the collar, write: "[Pet's name] is safe and sound at all times." Draw a pentagram—a five-pointed star with a circle around it—at the end of the statement. The pentagram is a symbol of protection. On the outside of the collar, write your name and phone number.

Put four drops of essential oil on the collar, one at each end, on both sides of the collar. Place the collar in the sun for one day to charge it. Then fasten the collar on your pet to keep him safe.

(To be extra safe, get tags made for your pet that include your name, address, phone number, and other pertinent information. Ask your vet about having a computer chip permanently implanted in your pet's skin that will identify him to city pounds, veterinarian's offices, and other agencies with scanners that can read such chips.)

Chapter 20

Where to Go from Here

As you can see from what's been touched upon in this book, the world of magic is vast and complex. Countless books have been written about each individual school of magical thought, and more are published every day. Now that magic has come out of the closet and people around the world are sharing their wisdom openly, the field will continue to grow ever richer. Everyone's experiences contribute to the development of the whole. Each magician is a torch-bearer whose flame, when joined with the others, lights up the world.

Living a Magical Life

As Donald Michael Kraig succinctly puts it in his book *Modern Magick*, "Magick is not something you do, magick is something you are." Once you shift your way of thinking from mundane to magical, you'll never see the world as you did before. Now, when you walk into a building, you'll sense its vibrations. Gemstones won't be just pretty baubles any more; instead, you'll see them as life forms that can help you in your spell work. Dreams will no longer be nightly amusements but messages from your inner wisdom.

As Carol K. Anthony writes in her book *A Guide to the I Ching*, "The light is always there, but we must be open to see it."

Magical awareness brings you into intimate connection with all life on Earth and with the cosmos beyond. You become conscious of how your thoughts produce results. You notice how your emotions and actions influence others and how they create the circumstances you experience. You sense the presence of nonphysical beings in your environment and allow yourself to be guided by your spiritual guardians. You recognize coincidences as meaningful events and learn from them.

Magic exists everywhere, all the time. You are part of the magic.

Magic Isn't a Spectator Sport

According to Aleister Crowley, "Every intentional act is a magical act." Intention, as you already know, is the seed from which outcomes materialize. The more clarity you bring to your spells, the more focused willpower you can use to direct them, and the more passion you put behind them, the better your results are likely to be.

In the beginning, you'll need to read some good books and learn as much as you can about magic. This book is a fairly comprehensive introduction, but you'll want to gain information from a variety of sources. Appendix

B lists several books you may find valuable. Each magician has his or her own ideas and areas of specialty. As you explore the world of magic, you'll find that some concepts, styles, and practices interest you more than others. If you have a theatrical side, you might be drawn to ritual magic. If you love gardening, herbal magic could be your thing.

ALERT!

At some point in your magical process, you'll have to decide why you've chosen this path. Many people, especially teens and young adults, initially get interested in magic because they feel weak and seek to gain power over others. If you stick with it, however, you'll soon discover that magic is about gaining power over yourself and your ego.

When people ask me to do magic spells for them, I usually encourage them to get involved themselves. Spells you do for yourself can be more effective than those performed by someone else because the outcome is more important to you than to another person. You're able to pour your own emotions into the spell. You feel a strong connection to other people involved in the spell. You know the outcome you desire.

Everyone possesses magical ability. But magic isn't for couch potatoes. It's for people who genuinely want to take charge of their lives and their realities. Magic involves study, discipline, and practice. It necessitates building your mental muscles. It requires you to shift your old habit patterns and beliefs, which is easier said than done. It demands that you "clean up your act" and examine your motives. Most importantly, magic forces you to delve deep within yourself to discover who you truly are.

A Lifelong Pursuit

No matter how long you study and practice magic, you'll never know it all. You could be at it your entire adult life and still barely scratch the surface. It's like any other subject: The deeper you dig, the more you discover.

Some people begin studying one type of magic and then move on to learn about another. In the course of your studies, you'll undoubtedly find yourself drawn to certain schools of thought and not others. Your heritage, temperament, natural proclivities, locale, companions, and many other factors will influence your decisions about which path to follow.

"Belief consists in accepting the affirmations of the soul; unbelief, in denying them."—Ralph Waldo Emerson

As you explore different types of magic, you'll discover that despite their outer forms of expression, they contain many common denominators. Gaining knowledge about one school of thought can increase your facility in another. Although some purists might disagree, many people think it's fine to combine features from different magical traditions and schools of thought.

Magic transforms you. It becomes an integral part of your life and your worldview. You might study intensely at one period and then ease off temporarily; you may do lots of rituals for a time, then not perform any for a while. But once you assume the magician's mantle, you wear it forever.

Practice Makes Perfect

Like all skills, magic requires practice to perfect. The more you do it, the better you'll become. The more attention you pay to developing your talents—your intuition, your awareness of the world around you, your knowledge of symbols, and so on—the more skill and power you'll be able to bring to your rituals.

Don't think of magic as a quick fix, or you'll be disappointed. Although magic spells sometimes work very fast, it usually takes time to alter long-standing patterns. Like maneuvering a supertanker, a condition that's been in place for years might take a while to turn around. Especially if other people are involved in the situation and/or outcome, it may be necessary for them to change their attitudes before you see results. In many cases, you must participate on various levels to produce the outcome you desire; doing the spell or ritual is only part of the process.

Record Your Experiences

A grimoire is a journal in which you record your spells. Also known as a Book of Shadows, it's a magician's secret diary and recipe file. Usually, you don't reveal your secrets to anyone else, however, you may choose to share them with a magic partner, members of your coven, or other people you trust.

Some grimoires are handsome, leather-bound volumes, while others are simple spiral notebooks. A loose-leaf binder that allows you to add and remove pages can be a convenient option. Decorate your grimoire in any way you like, with pictures, symbols, and so on. The point is to engage your imagination and personalize your book.

FACT

Many people have trouble focusing their minds. Multitasking isn't a plus when you're doing magic. Because the mind is the most important tool in magical work, you need to discipline your thoughts and learn to concentrate. Focused ideas and clear images generate better outcomes. If your mind keeps jumping about from one thing to another, you'll get mixed results.

Logging your spells in a grimoire enables you to catalog your actions and results. Date your spells and rituals, as well as the outcomes you experience. Note astrological data such as the moon's phase and sign, sun's position, and significant planetary patterns. Describe the situations or conditions in your life that are related to the spell, as they may influence what transpires. You might find it useful to jot down any feelings or thoughts you have while doing the spell, too.

Over time, you'll probably update some spells as you discover which ingredients and procedures work best for you. As you become more proficient at magic, your spells and rituals may become more complex or specialized. Like a cook who's always expanding her culinary repertoire, you'll continue revising, improving, and adding new spells throughout your lifetime.

Creating Your Own Spells

It's fun to design your own unique spells. Personalizing spells makes them more meaningful. You can tailor any spell for specific purposes. If you're doing a love spell that calls for pink candles, but you want to turn up the heat, choose red candles instead. If you don't like the scent of lavender, you could use vanilla to dress a candle for a relaxation ritual. And if you can't find a certain ingredient, it's okay to substitute another. For instance, ash leaves and basil both contain energies that can be used in protection spells. Blending ingredients allows you to fine-tune your magic to produce exactly the result you desire.

Essential oils can be added to water and misted into a room to work their magic. Or you can put a few drops in bathwater. You can also dress candles with them or heat them in an oil diffuser. The objective is to enliven your senses and stimulate your brain's limbic system, in whatever way pleases you.

Become familiar with various botanicals and stones, so you know which ones will serve your purposes best. Chapter 8 includes lists of herbs, oils, gemstones, and other ingredients to choose from when you're concocting your own spells. You might also wish to purchase some more extensive guides, such as those listed in Appendix B. Learn which colors, numbers, and other symbols correspond to which intentions. Chapter 3 provides information about symbolic connections. Again, you can deepen your knowledge by reading books that cover these topics in greater detail, including those in Appendix B.

Setting Up Shop

You don't need to purchase a warehouse full of supplies in the beginning. Start with a few basics: candles, incense, ribbons, and kitchen herbs. As you progress, add some quartz crystals and gemstones. Later on, you may wish to invest in a wand, chalice, athame, and pentagram. Tarot cards, a crystal ball, and pendulum might follow at some point. Allow yourself to be led by your intuition. Build your collection as your need or interest dictates.

ALERT!

Accept the gifts that come your way. Doing so demonstrates your openness to receive the universe's bounty and keeps the circle of abundance operating smoothly. If, for some reason, a particular gift doesn't seem right for you, pass it on to someone else, but don't reject it.

Sometimes magic items find you. People may give you tarot decks. You might find crystals lying on the side of the road. In time, you might decide to set up an extensive apothecary or grow your own magical herbs. Some magicians like to fashion their own candles or even distill their own scents. Others fabricate special ritual clothing or jewelry. Apply your talents however the muse guides you.

Use Your Imagination

When designing rituals and concocting spells, be creative. Use your imagination. The more involved you get in the process, the better. If you want to play a certain kind of music, by all means do so. If donning special garb helps you get into the mood, wear it. If you feel like dancing, singing, chanting, or experimenting with other movements, give it a try. Notice what you experience and record your impressions in your grimoire.

It's fine to follow guidelines—and it's recommended in the beginning— but listen to your intuition, too. Don't be afraid to tweak a spell or vary a particular practice. After a while, you'll learn to connect with the energies of plants, stones, and other substances, and you can incorporate them harmoniously into your spells. Use your knowledge of the elements, correspondences, and symbols to come up with original spells.

Basic Spell-Working Tips

As you go about designing your own spells and rituals, keep these basic guidelines in mind:

- Know what you want and state your intention simply, in the form of an affirmation.
- Refer to lists of ingredients—such as herbs, flowers, stones, oils, and colors—until you memorize them.
- Pay attention to the day of the week, moon phases, and other astrological factors.
- If you cast a circle, abide by the rules of the ritual.
- If you're working with other people, be sure your intentions are in agreement.
- As the old adage goes, be careful what you ask for, because you just might get it.

Beyond these fundamentals, you're pretty much free to put your own personal spin on spells. Like a musician interpreting a composer's song, your unique rendition is as valid as anyone else's and may serve your purposes better than following a prescribed formula to the letter.

Doing Magic with Other People

Many magicians enjoy working with other people. Rituals can be more powerful and beautiful if a number of like-minded people participate in them together. The group dynamic generates an energy field that's much stronger than one individual working alone could produce. When several magicians join forces, the whole is greater than the sum of its parts.

When shamanic healing magic is done in a group, the members of the circle contribute to one another's healing. If you choose to follow the Wiccan path, you might like to join a coven. Some covens have inner circles, which include a limited number of members at a certain level of expertise or of a certain philosophy, and outer circles that are open to others beyond the inner group. If you decide to do sex magic, you'll want to find a partner with whom to share the practice.

At some stage in your development, you may want to work with a teacher. Finding a teacher is a bit like choosing a therapist. Do some research beforehand to determine if the teacher's views, background, and practices are in line with your goals. Magicians don't usually advertise in the Yellow Pages, but some lecture or give workshops publicly. New Age stores and holistic healing centers may be able to put you in touch with a teacher. A recommendation from someone whose opinion you trust is a good start, but ultimately your own feelings about the teacher are what matter most. Again, trust your intuition.

You might also enjoy doing magic with friends and family. Some of the spells in this book are designed to do with other people. Sharing these experiences can bring you closer together and enrich the quality of your personal relationships.

Although magic can certainly be fun, it's not a game. It's serious work and should be undertaken with sincerity and even reverence. Remember, you're connecting with powerful forces beyond yourself and intentionally altering the course of not only your life but perhaps other people's lives as well. That's a big responsibility. As you walk the magical path, do it in the spirit of love, joy, passion, respect, and for the good of all concerned. Blessed be.

Glossary of Magical Terms

Affirmation:
A statement of intent, written or spoken in a positive way and always in the present tense.

Amulet:
A charm used to repel an undesired energy, condition, or entity. Protection amulets are among the most common and ancient magical tokens.

Altar:
A special place you create to hold objects you use in your magic practice.

Athame:
A ritual dagger, usually a double-edged knife about four to six inches long.

Aura:
A halo or cocoon of light that appears to extend a few inches to as much as several feet out from the physical body.

Chakra:
A Sanskrit word that literally means wheel, disk, or vortex. It usually refers to one of seven major energy centers that align from the base of the spine to the crown of the head.

Charm:
A magical incantation or token you create, usually for yourself, for a particular intention.

Chi:
In Eastern philosophy, this is the enlivening force in the universe that animates all life (also spelled qi).

Divination:
The art of predicting the future, it literally means to let the divine realm manifest.

Elementals:
Nonphysical beings that serve as ambassadors for the four elements. Each is a "citizen" of his or her particular realm, and each possesses unique qualities that are characteristic of the element she or he harkens from.

ESP:
An acronym for *extrasensory perception*; an ability to perceive facts outside the range of the usual five senses and independently of any reasoning process.

Feng shui:
Pronounced *fung shway*, this "art of placement" has been practiced in China for more than two millennia. Its objective is to direct the flow of vital energy, known as *chi*, through the environment in order to create balance and harmony.

Gematria:
A practice that attaches a number equivalent to each letter in a word. Gematria was initially connected with the Hebrew language; however, its tenets can be applied to any language.

Grimoire:
A magician's secret journal of spells and rituals.

Incantation:
A rhymed affirmation.

Intention:
A consciously designed wish or objective.

Magick:
A way of spelling "magic" to distinguish it from stage illusion and magic tricks.

Medical intuitive:
Someone who uses intuition to examine a patient and determine disturbances in the physical body, chakras, psyche, and subtle energy fields.

Occult:
Hidden knowledge.

Ogham:
The ancient Celtic tree alphabet consisting of twenty letters, each of which corresponds to a tree. Ogham (pronounced *oh-am*) letters also serve as mystical symbols.

Oracle:
A direct link—either a human being or a tool such as tarot cards or runes—between your conscious self, your subconscious, and Divine Wisdom.

Qabalah:
Sometimes spelled Kabbala, Cabala, and other ways, the Qabalah (pronounced *ka-BA-lah*) is a body of esoteric teachings that underlie Judaism mysticism.

Pentagram:
A five-pointed star with a circle around it. An important symbol of protection, it's often used in magic ceremonies or worn as an amulet.

Runes:
Letters derived from an ancient, usually old Teutonic, alphabet. Each rune is both a letter and a mystical glyph used to convey complex meanings.

Sabbat:
Holy days in the old Celtic and Pagan traditions. Sabbats are based on the sun's position relative to the Earth and are celebrated approximately six weeks apart: on the solstices, the equinoxes, and halfway between these dates.

Scrying:
A form of divination that involves gazing into a reflective surface, such as a crystal ball, to see the future.

Shaman:
Someone who understands both the spirit world and the natural world, and journeys between them to obtain knowledge that can provide healing, guidance, and protection to his or her people.

Sigil:
A uniquely personal symbol created in order to produce a specific result. Although there are various techniques for designing sigils, the easiest one involves fashioning an image from letters.

Synchronicity:
Carl G. Jung's term for meaningful events that defy the usually accepted laws of cause and effect but that occur so often and in such amaz-ing ways that they cannot be discounted as mere coincidences.

Talisman:
A charm designed to attract something its owner desires. Gemstones and jewelry have long been favored as talismans.

Tarot:
Pronounced *tar-OH*, this illustrated deck of cards (usually numbering seventy-eight) dates back to medieval times or earlier. It can be used as a form of divination or as a guide to spiritual/personal growth.

Resources

Alexander, Skye. *The Everything Tarot Book.* Avon, Mass.: Adams Media/F+W Publications, Inc. 2006.

_____. *Nice Spells/Naughty Spells,* Avon, Mass.: Adams Media/F+W Publications, Inc. 2006.

_____. *10-Minute Magic Spells,* Gloucester, Mass.: Fair Winds Press/Rockport Publishers, 2002.

_____. *10-Minute Tarot,* Gloucester, Mass.: Fair Winds Press/Rockport Publishers, 2000.

_____. *10-Minute Crystal Ball,* Gloucester, Mass.: Fair Winds Press/Rockport Publishers, 2000.

_____. *10-Minute Feng Shui,* Gloucester, Mass.: Fair Winds Press/Rockport Publishers, 2000.

_____. *10-Minute Feng Shui Room by Room,* Gloucester, Mass.: Fair Winds Press/Rockport Publishers, 2000.

_____. *Magickal Astrology.* Franklin Lakes, NJ: New Page Books/The Career Press, 2000.

_____. *Planets in Signs*, West Chester, Pa.: Whitford Press/Schiffer Publishing, 1988.

Anthony, Carol K. *A Guide to the I Ching*. Stow, Mass.: Anthony Publishing, 1982.

Astrolabe, Inc. *The Astrolabe World Ephemeris 2001–2050*, West Chester, Pa.: Whitford Press/Schiffer Publishing, 1998.

Beyerl, Paul. *The Master Book of Herbalism*, Custer, Wash.: Phoenix Publishing Co., 1984.

Bunker, Dusty. *Numerology, Astrology, & Dreams*, West Chester, Pa.: Whitford Press/Schiffer Publishing, 1987.

_____. *Numerology and Your Future*, West Chester, Pa.: Whitford Press/Schiffer Publishing, 1988.

Dethlefsen, Thorwald, and Dahlke, Rudiger, M.D. *The Healing Power of Illness*, Shafesbury, Dorset, England: Element Books, 1992.

Dyer, Dr. Wayne W. *The Power of Intention*, Carlsbad, Calif.: Hay House, Inc., 2004.

Hay, Louise L. *You Can Heal Your Life*, Carlsbad, Calif.: Hay House, Inc., 1987.

Kraig, Donald Michael. *Modern Magick, Second Edition*, St. Paul, Minn.: Llewellyn Publications, 1999.

Kraig, Donald Michael. *Modern Sex Magick*, St. Paul, Minn.: Llewellyn Publications, 1999.

Lawless, Julia. *The Encyclopaedia of Essential Oils*, Shafesbury, Dorset, England: Element Books, 1992.

Long, Max Freedom. *The Secret Science at Work*, Marina del Rey, Calif., DeVorss & Co., 1953.

Mella, Dorothee L. *Stone Power*, New York, NY: Warner Books, 1986.

Regardie, Israel. *The Golden Dawn*, 5th edition, St. Paul, Minn.: Llewellyn Publications, 1986.

Schulz, Mona Lisa, M.D., Ph.D., *Awakening Intuition*, New York: Three Rivers Press, 1998.

Starhawk. *The Spiral Dance: A Rebirth of the Ancient Religion of the Great Goddess, 20th Anniversary Edition*, New York: HarperCollins Publishers, 1999.

Sutton, Maya Magee, Ph.D., and Mann, Nicholas R. *Druid Magic*, St. Paul, Minn.: Llewellyn Worldwide, 2000.

Telesco, Patricia. *Exploring Candle Magick*, Franklin Lakes, NJ: New Page Books/The Career Press, 2001.

Wasserman, James. *Art and Symbols of the Occult*, Rochester, Vt.: Destiny Books, 1993.

Watson, Nancy B. *Practical Solitary Magic,* York Beach, Maine: Samuel Weiser, Inc., 1996.

Whitcomb, Bill. *The Magician's Companion,* St. Paul, Minn.: Llewellyn Publications, 1998.

Wilhelm, Richard, and Baynes, Cary F. *The I Ching or Book of Changes,* Princeton, NJ: Princeton University Press, 1950.

Williamson, Marianne. *A Return to Love,* New York: HarperCollins, 1992.

Index

THE EVERYTHING SERIES!

BUSINESS & PERSONAL FINANCE

Everything® Accounting Book
Everything® Budgeting Book
Everything® Business Planning Book
Everything® Coaching and Mentoring Book, 2nd Ed.
Everything® Fundraising Book
Everything® Get Out of Debt Book
Everything® Grant Writing Book
Everything® Guide to Foreclosures
Everything® Guide to Personal Finance for Single Mothers
Everything® Home-Based Business Book, 2nd Ed.
Everything® Homebuying Book, 2nd Ed.
Everything® Homeselling Book, 2nd Ed.
Everything® Improve Your Credit Book
Everything® Investing Book, 2nd Ed.
Everything® Landlording Book
Everything® Leadership Book
Everything® Managing People Book, 2nd Ed.
Everything® Negotiating Book
Everything® Online Auctions Book
Everything® Online Business Book
Everything® Personal Finance Book
Everything® Personal Finance in Your 20s and 30s Book
Everything® Project Management Book
Everything® Real Estate Investing Book
Everything® Retirement Planning Book
Everything® Robert's Rules Book, $7.95
Everything® Selling Book
Everything® Start Your Own Business Book, 2nd Ed.
Everything® Wills & Estate Planning Book

COOKING

Everything® Barbecue Cookbook
Everything® Bartender's Book, 2nd Ed., $9.95
Everything® Calorie Counting Cookbook
Everything® Cheese Book
Everything® Chinese Cookbook
Everything® Classic Recipes Book
Everything® Cocktail Parties & Drinks Book
Everything® College Cookbook
Everything® Cooking for Baby and Toddler Book
Everything® Cooking for Two Cookbook
Everything® Diabetes Cookbook
Everything® Easy Gourmet Cookbook
Everything® Fondue Cookbook
Everything® Fondue Party Book
Everything® Gluten-Free Cookbook
Everything® Glycemic Index Cookbook
Everything® Grilling Cookbook
Everything® Healthy Meals in Minutes Cookbook
Everything® Holiday Cookbook

Everything® Indian Cookbook
Everything® Italian Cookbook
Everything® Low-Carb Cookbook
Everything® Low-Cholesterol Cookbook
Everything® Low-Fat High-Flavor Cookbook
Everything® Low-Salt Cookbook
Everything® Meals for a Month Cookbook
Everything® Mediterranean Cookbook
Everything® Mexican Cookbook
Everything® No Trans Fat Cookbook
Everything® One-Pot Cookbook
Everything® Pizza Cookbook
Everything® Quick and Easy 30-Minute,
     5-Ingredient Cookbook
Everything® Quick Meals Cookbook
Everything® Slow Cooker Cookbook
Everything® Slow Cooking for a Crowd Cookbook
Everything® Soup Cookbook
Everything® Stir-Fry Cookbook
Everything® Sugar-Free Cookbook
Everything® Tapas and Small Plates Cookbook
Everything® Tex-Mex Cookbook
Everything® Thai Cookbook
Everything® Vegetarian Cookbook
Everything® Wild Game Cookbook
Everything® Wine Book, 2nd Ed.

GAMES

Everything® 15-Minute Sudoku Book, $9.95
Everything® 30-Minute Sudoku Book, $9.95
Everything® Bible Crosswords Book, $9.95
Everything® Blackjack Strategy Book
Everything® Brain Strain Book, $9.95
Everything® Bridge Book
Everything® Card Games Book
Everything® Card Tricks Book, $9.95
Everything® Casino Gambling Book, 2nd Ed.
Everything® Chess Basics Book
Everything® Craps Strategy Book
Everything® Crossword and Puzzle Book
Everything® Crossword Challenge Book
Everything® Crosswords for the Beach Book, $9.95
Everything® Cryptic Crosswords Book, $9.95
Everything® Cryptograms Book, $9.95
Everything® Easy Crosswords Book
Everything® Easy Kakuro Book, $9.95
Everything® Easy Large-Print Crosswords Book
Everything® Games Book, 2nd Ed.
Everything® Giant Sudoku Book, $9.95
Everything® Kakuro Challenge Book, $9.95
Everything® Large-Print Crossword Challenge Book
Everything® Large-Print Crosswords Book
Everything® Lateral Thinking Puzzles Book, $9.95

Everything® **Literary Crosswords Book, $9.95**
Everything® Mazes Book
Everything® **Memory Booster Puzzles Book, $9.95**
Everything® Movie Crosswords Book, $9.95
Everything® **Music Crosswords Book, $9.95**
Everything® Online Poker Book, $12.95
Everything® Pencil Puzzles Book, $9.95
Everything® Poker Strategy Book
Everything® Pool & Billiards Book
Everything® **Puzzles for Commuters Book, $9.95**
Everything® Sports Crosswords Book, $9.95
Everything® Test Your IQ Book, $9.95
Everything® Texas Hold 'Em Book, $9.95
Everything® Travel Crosswords Book, $9.95
Everything® **TV Crosswords Book, $9.95**
Everything® Word Games Challenge Book
Everything® Word Scramble Book
Everything® Word Search Book

HEALTH

Everything® Alzheimer's Book
Everything® Diabetes Book
Everything® Health Guide to Adult Bipolar Disorder
Everything® Health Guide to Arthritis
Everything® Health Guide to Controlling Anxiety
Everything® Health Guide to Fibromyalgia
Everything® Health Guide to Menopause
Everything® Health Guide to OCD
Everything® Health Guide to PMS
Everything® Health Guide to Postpartum Care
Everything® Health Guide to Thyroid Disease
Everything® Hypnosis Book
Everything® Low Cholesterol Book
Everything® Nutrition Book
Everything® Reflexology Book
Everything® Stress Management Book

HISTORY

Everything® American Government Book
Everything® American History Book, 2nd Ed.
Everything® Civil War Book
Everything® Freemasons Book
Everything® Irish History & Heritage Book
Everything® Middle East Book
Everything® World War II Book, 2nd Ed.

HOBBIES

Everything® Candlemaking Book
Everything® Cartooning Book
Everything® Coin Collecting Book
Everything® Drawing Book

Everything® Family Tree Book, 2nd Ed.
Everything® Knitting Book
Everything® Knots Book
Everything® Photography Book
Everything® Quilting Book
Everything® Sewing Book
Everything® Soapmaking Book, 2nd Ed.
Everything® Woodworking Book

HOME IMPROVEMENT

Everything® Feng Shui Book
Everything® Feng Shui Decluttering Book, $9.95
Everything® Fix-It Book
Everything® Green Living Book
Everything® Home Decorating Book
Everything® Home Storage Solutions Book
Everything® Homebuilding Book
Everything® Organize Your Home Book, 2nd Ed.

KIDS' BOOKS

All titles are $7.95
Everything® Kids' Animal Puzzle & Activity Book
Everything® Kids' Baseball Book, 4th Ed.
Everything® Kids' Bible Trivia Book
Everything® Kids' Bugs Book
Everything® Kids' Cars and Trucks Puzzle and Activity Book
Everything® Kids' Christmas Puzzle & Activity Book
Everything® Kids' Cookbook
Everything® Kids' Crazy Puzzles Book
Everything® Kids' Dinosaurs Book
Everything® Kids' Environment Book
Everything® Kids' Fairies Puzzle and Activity Book
Everything® Kids' First Spanish Puzzle and Activity Book
Everything® Kids' Gross Cookbook
Everything® Kids' Gross Hidden Pictures Book
Everything® Kids' Gross Jokes Book
Everything® Kids' Gross Mazes Book
Everything® Kids' Gross Puzzle & Activity Book
Everything® Kids' Halloween Puzzle & Activity Book
Everything® Kids' Hidden Pictures Book
Everything® Kids' Horses Book
Everything® Kids' Joke Book
Everything® Kids' Knock Knock Book
Everything® Kids' Learning Spanish Book
Everything® Kids' Magical Science Experiments Book
Everything® Kids' Math Puzzles Book
Everything® Kids' Mazes Book
Everything® Kids' Money Book
Everything® Kids' Nature Book
Everything® Kids' Pirates Puzzle and Activity Book
Everything® Kids' Presidents Book
Everything® Kids' Princess Puzzle and Activity Book
Everything® Kids' Puzzle Book
Everything® Kids' Racecars Puzzle and Activity Book
Everything® Kids' Riddles & Brain Teasers Book
Everything® Kids' Science Experiments Book
Everything® Kids' Sharks Book

Everything® Kids' Soccer Book
Everything® Kids' Spies Puzzle and Activity Book
Everything® Kids' States Book
Everything® Kids' Travel Activity Book

KIDS' STORY BOOKS

Everything® Fairy Tales Book

LANGUAGE

Everything® Conversational Japanese Book with CD, $19.95
Everything® French Grammar Book
Everything® French Phrase Book, $9.95
Everything® French Verb Book, $9.95
Everything® German Practice Book with CD, $19.95
Everything® Inglés Book
Everything® Intermediate Spanish Book with CD, $19.95
Everything® Italian Practice Book with CD, $19.95
Everything® Learning Brazilian Portuguese Book with CD, $19.95
Everything® Learning French Book with CD, 2nd Ed., $19.95
Everything® Learning German Book
Everything® Learning Italian Book
Everything® Learning Latin Book
Everything® Learning Russian Book with CD, $19.95
Everything® Learning Spanish Book with CD, 2nd Ed., $19.95
Everything® Russian Practice Book with CD, $19.95
Everything® Sign Language Book
Everything® Spanish Grammar Book
Everything® Spanish Phrase Book, $9.95
Everything® Spanish Practice Book with CD, $19.95
Everything® Spanish Verb Book, $9.95
Everything® Speaking Mandarin Chinese Book with CD, $19.95

MUSIC

Everything® Drums Book with CD, $19.95
Everything® Guitar Book with CD, 2nd Ed., $19.95
Everything® Guitar Chords Book with CD, $19.95
Everything® Home Recording Book
Everything® Music Theory Book with CD, $19.95
Everything® Reading Music Book with CD, $19.95
Everything® Rock & Blues Guitar Book with CD, $19.95
Everything® Rock and Blues Piano Book with CD, $19.95
Everything® Songwriting Book

NEW AGE

Everything® Astrology Book, 2nd Ed.
Everything® Birthday Personology Book
Everything® Dreams Book, 2nd Ed.
Everything® Love Signs Book, $9.95
Everything® Love Spells Book, $9.95
Everything® Numerology Book
Everything® Paganism Book
Everything® Palmistry Book
Everything® Psychic Book
Everything® Reiki Book
Everything® Sex Signs Book, $9.95

Everything® Spells & Charms Book, 2nd Ed.
Everything® Tarot Book, 2nd Ed.
Everything® Toltec Wisdom Book
Everything® Wicca and Witchcraft Book

PARENTING

Everything® Baby Names Book, 2nd Ed.
Everything® Baby Shower Book, 2nd Ed.
Everything® Baby's First Year Book
Everything® Birthing Book
Everything® Breastfeeding Book
Everything® Father-to-Be Book
Everything® Father's First Year Book
Everything® Get Ready for Baby Book, 2nd Ed.
Everything® Get Your Baby to Sleep Book, $9.95
Everything® Getting Pregnant Book
Everything® Guide to Pregnancy Over 35
Everything® Guide to Raising a One-Year-Old
Everything® Guide to Raising a Two-Year-Old
Everything® Guide to Raising Adolescent Boys
Everything® Guide to Raising Adolescent Girls
Everything® Homeschooling Book
Everything® Mother's First Year Book
Everything® Parent's Guide to Childhood Illnesses
Everything® Parent's Guide to Children and Divorce
Everything® Parent's Guide to Children with ADD/ADHD
Everything® Parent's Guide to Children with Asperger's Syndrome
Everything® Parent's Guide to Children with Autism
Everything® Parent's Guide to Children with Bipolar Disorder
Everything® Parent's Guide to Children with Depression
Everything® Parent's Guide to Children with Dyslexia
Everything® Parent's Guide to Children with Juvenile Diabetes
Everything® Parent's Guide to Positive Discipline
Everything® Parent's Guide to Raising a Successful Child
Everything® Parent's Guide to Raising Boys
Everything® Parent's Guide to Raising Girls
Everything® Parent's Guide to Raising Siblings
Everything® Parent's Guide to Sensory Integration Disorder
Everything® Parent's Guide to Tantrums
Everything® Parent's Guide to the Strong-Willed Child
Everything® Parenting a Teenager Book
Everything® Potty Training Book, $9.95
Everything® Pregnancy Book, 3rd Ed.
Everything® Pregnancy Fitness Book
Everything® Pregnancy Nutrition Book
Everything® Pregnancy Organizer, 2nd Ed., $16.95
Everything® Toddler Activities Book
Everything® Toddler Book
Everything® Tween Book
Everything® Twins, Triplets, and More Book

PETS

Everything® Aquarium Book
Everything® Boxer Book
Everything® Cat Book, 2nd Ed.
Everything® Chihuahua Book

Everything® Cooking for Dogs Book
Everything® Dachshund Book
Everything® Dog Book
Everything® Dog Health Book
Everything® Dog Obedience Book
Everything® Dog Owner's Organizer, $16.95
Everything® Dog Training and Tricks Book
Everything® German Shepherd Book
Everything® Golden Retriever Book
Everything® Horse Book
Everything® Horse Care Book
Everything® Horseback Riding Book
Everything® Labrador Retriever Book
Everything® Poodle Book
Everything® Pug Book
Everything® Puppy Book
Everything® Rottweiler Book
Everything® Small Dogs Book
Everything® Tropical Fish Book
Everything® Yorkshire Terrier Book

REFERENCE

Everything® American Presidents Book
Everything® Blogging Book
Everything® Build Your Vocabulary Book
Everything® Car Care Book
Everything® Classical Mythology Book
Everything® Da Vinci Book
Everything® Divorce Book
Everything® Einstein Book
Everything® Enneagram Book
Everything® Etiquette Book, 2nd Ed.
Everything® Guide to Edgar Allan Poe
Everything® Inventions and Patents Book
Everything® Mafia Book
Everything® Martin Luther King Jr. Book
Everything® Philosophy Book
Everything® Pirates Book
Everything® Psychology Book

RELIGION

Everything® Angels Book
Everything® Bible Book
Everything® Bible Study Book with CD, $19.95
Everything® Buddhism Book
Everything® Catholicism Book
Everything® Christianity Book
Everything® Gnostic Gospels Book
Everything® History of the Bible Book
Everything® Jesus Book
Everything® Jewish History & Heritage Book
Everything® Judaism Book
Everything® Kabbalah Book
Everything® Koran Book

Everything® Mary Book
Everything® Mary Magdalene Book
Everything® Prayer Book
Everything® Saints Book, 2nd Ed.
Everything® Torah Book
Everything® Understanding Islam Book
Everything® Women of the Bible Book
Everything® World's Religions Book
Everything® Zen Book

SCHOOL & CAREERS

Everything® Alternative Careers Book
Everything® Career Tests Book
Everything® College Major Test Book
Everything® College Survival Book, 2nd Ed.
Everything® Cover Letter Book, 2nd Ed.
Everything® Filmmaking Book
Everything® Get-a-Job Book, 2nd Ed.
Everything® Guide to Being a Paralegal
Everything® Guide to Being a Personal Trainer
Everything® Guide to Being a Real Estate Agent
Everything® Guide to Being a Sales Rep
Everything® Guide to Being an Event Planner
Everything® Guide to Careers in Health Care
Everything® Guide to Careers in Law Enforcement
Everything® Guide to Government Jobs
Everything® Guide to Starting and Running a Catering Business
Everything® Guide to Starting and Running a Restaurant
Everything® Job Interview Book
Everything® New Nurse Book
Everything® New Teacher Book
Everything® Paying for College Book
Everything® Practice Interview Book
Everything® Resume Book, 2nd Ed.
Everything® Study Book

SELF-HELP

Everything® Body Language Book
Everything® Dating Book, 2nd Ed.
Everything® Great Sex Book
Everything® Self-Esteem Book
Everything® Tantric Sex Book

SPORTS & FITNESS

Everything® Easy Fitness Book
Everything® Krav Maga for Fitness Book
Everything® Running Book

TRAVEL

Everything® Family Guide to Coastal Florida
Everything® Family Guide to Cruise Vacations
Everything® Family Guide to Hawaii
Everything® Family Guide to Las Vegas, 2nd Ed.
Everything® Family Guide to Mexico
Everything® Family Guide to New York City, 2nd Ed.
Everything® Family Guide to RV Travel & Campgrounds
Everything® Family Guide to the Caribbean
Everything® Family Guide to the Disneyland® Resort, California Adventure®, Universal Studios®, and the Anaheim Area, 2nd Ed.
Everything® Family Guide to the Walt Disney World Resort®, Universal Studios®, and Greater Orlando, 5th Ed.
Everything® Family Guide to Timeshares
Everything® Family Guide to Washington D.C., 2nd Ed.

WEDDINGS

Everything® Bachelorette Party Book, $9.95
Everything® Bridesmaid Book, $9.95
Everything® Destination Wedding Book
Everything® Elopement Book, $9.95
Everything® Father of the Bride Book, $9.95
Everything® Groom Book, $9.95
Everything® Mother of the Bride Book, $9.95
Everything® Outdoor Wedding Book
Everything® Wedding Book, 3rd Ed.
Everything® Wedding Checklist, $9.95
Everything® Wedding Etiquette Book, $9.95
Everything® Wedding Organizer, 2nd Ed., $16.95
Everything® Wedding Shower Book, $9.95
Everything® Wedding Vows Book, $9.95
Everything® Wedding Workout Book
Everything® Weddings on a Budget Book, 2nd Ed., $9.95

WRITING

Everything® Creative Writing Book
Everything® Get Published Book, 2nd Ed.
Everything® Grammar and Style Book
Everything® Guide to Magazine Writing
Everything® Guide to Writing a Book Proposal
Everything® Guide to Writing a Novel
Everything® Guide to Writing Children's Books
Everything® Guide to Writing Copy
Everything® Guide to Writing Graphic Novels
Everything® Guide to Writing Research Papers
Everything® Screenwriting Book
Everything® Writing Poetry Book
Everything® Writing Well Book